COMING OF AGE

VOLUME ONE

Second Edition

To Donald J. Ryan, Colleague and Great Friend

Thanks to the following people for suggestions about and help with this book: Svea Barrett-Tarleton, Anne Bigelow, Zitta Chapman, Faye Conrad, Christopher deVinck, Andy Dunn, Jim Gartenlaub, Pat Riccobene, and Karin Emra. And for the two editions of this book, thanks to five excellent editors: Jane Bachman, Fitzgerald Higgins, John Nolan, Marianne Quinn, and Sue Schumer.

About the Author

Bruce Emra supervises the English Department and teaches English at Northern Highlands Regional High School in Allendale, New Jersey. He is the author of NTC/Contemporary's *Sports in Literature* and *Coming of Age, Volume Two*.

COMING OF AGE

VOLUME ONE

Literature

About Youth and Adolescence

Second Edition

Bruce Emra

National Textbook Company
a division of NTC/CONTEMPORARY PUBLISHING GROUP
Lincolnwood, Illinois USA

Cover Illustration: Diana Ong/Superstock

ISBN (student edition): 0–8442–0360–2 (hardbound); 0361–0 (softbound)
ISBN (teacher's edition): 0–8442–0362–9 (hardbound); 0489–7 (softbound)

Acknowledgments begin on page 309, which is to be considered an extension of this copyright page.

COMING OF AGE

CONTENTS

(An asterisk identifies student writers.)

PART 3   Falling in Love

PART 4   Out in the World

PREFACE

I woke in bits, like all children, piecemeal over the years. I discovered myself and the world, and forgot them, and discovered them again. I woke at intervals until, by that September when Father went down the river, the intervals of waking tipped the scales, and I was more often awake than not. I noticed this process of waking, and predicted with terrifying logic that one of these years not far away I would be awake continuously and never slip back, and never be free of myself again.

—Annie Dillard, from *An American Childhood*

Are *you* now "awake" continuously? Are you taking in the world constantly and reacting to the infinite variety of the world?

This book will help you. You will find yourself in many of these stories, and maybe you will "find yourself" in a larger sense, too. In ancient Greece, "know thyself" was a principal commandment. "Know thyself" should be the personal goal of each of *us*, too.

Every story in this book has been selected because it will help to further awaken you. There are stories about young people with parents, with brothers and sisters, with friends, in love, and out in the world.

In every part of *Coming of Age, Volume One* there is an award-winning story written by a young man or woman. These stories in particular might inspire your own writing. After all, Beth Cassavell, Frederick Pollack, Susie Kretschmer, and Amy Boesky all started with a blank piece of paper.

Start reading. You will find yourself—in more ways than one—in these pages.

Bruce Emra

COMING OF AGE

Do I Fit In?

What adolescent hasn't wondered about his or her place in the classroom, in the grade, in the school—and in the larger world? We are all on a continual search for who we are.

The characters in the eight works of fiction in this section have varying questions about their places in the world. In "The First Day" you will meet a child registering for kindergarten and you will meet an adolescent who has run away from home and who hears a plea on the radio every year, "Louisa, Please Come Home." The narrator in "Two Kinds" and Raymond in "Raymond's Run" may be different ages, different sexes, and from very different backgrounds, but they are both struggling with questions such as, "Am I OK? Do I fit in? What will be my place in this world?"

As you read these stories, you will meet various people facing questions of identity. And you will be given a number of chances to create your own writing that deals with these great questions of who you are.

Edward P. Jones

Edward P. Jones was born in Washington, D.C., in 1950. He graduated from Holy Cross College in Worcester, Massachusetts, and did graduate work in fiction writing at the University of Virginia. "The First Day" appears in Jones's first book, *Lost in the City*, a collection of stories about his original hometown. This book was nominated for the 1992 National Book Award.

What were your first impressions of school?

The First Day

In an otherwise unremarkable September morning, long before I learned to be ashamed of my mother, she takes my hand and we set off down New Jersey Avenue to begin my very first day of school. I am wearing a checkeredlike blue-and-green cotton dress, and scattered about these colors are bits of yellow and white and brown. My mother has uncharacteristically spent nearly an hour on my hair that morning, plaiting and replaiting so that now my scalp tingles. Whenever I turn my head quickly, my nose fills with the faint smell of Dixie Peach hair grease. The smell is somehow a soothing one now and I will reach for it time and time again before the morning ends. All the plaits, each with a blue barrette near the tip and each twisted into an uncommon sturdiness, will last until I go to bed that night, something that has never happened before. My stomach is full of milk and oatmeal sweetened with brown sugar. Like everything else I have on, my pale green slip and underwear are new, the underwear having come three to a plastic package with a little girl on the front who appears to be dancing. Behind my ears, my mother, to stop my whining, has dabbed the stingiest bit of her gardenia perfume, the last present my father gave her before he disappeared into memory. Because I cannot smell it, I have only her word that the perfume is there. I am also wearing yellow socks trimmed with thin lines of black and white around the tops. My shoes are my greatest joy, black patent-leather miracles, and when one is nicked at the toe later that morning in class, my heart will break.

I am carrying a pencil, a pencil sharpener, and a small ten-cent tablet with a black-and-white speckled cover. My mother does not believe that a girl in kindergarten needs such things, so I am taking them only because of my insistent whining and because they are presents from our neighbors, Mary Keith and Blondelle Harris. Miss Mary and Miss Blondelle are watching my two younger sisters until my mother returns. The women are as precious to me as my mother and sisters. Out playing one day, I have overheard an older child, speaking to another child, call Miss Mary and Miss Blondelle a word that is brand new to me. This is my mother: When I say the word in fun to one of my sisters, my mother slaps me across the mouth and the word is lost for years and years.

All the way down New Jersey Avenue, the sidewalks are teeming with children. In my neighborhood, I have many friends, but I see none of them as my mother and I walk. We cross New York Avenue, we cross Pierce Street, and we cross L and K, and still I see no one who knows my name. At I Street, between New Jersey Avenue and Third Street, we enter Seaton Elementary School, a timeworn, sad-faced building across the street from my mother's church, Mt. Carmel Baptist.

Just inside the front door, women out of the advertisements in *Ebony*[1] are greeting other parents and children. The woman who greets us has pearls thick as jumbo marbles that come down almost to her navel, and she acts as if she had known me all my life, touching my shoulder, cupping her hand under my chin. She is enveloped in a perfume that I only know is not gardenia. When, in answer to her question, my mother tells her that we live at 1227 New Jersey Avenue, the woman first seems to be picturing in her head where we live. Then she shakes her head and says that we are at the wrong school, that we should be at Walker-Jones.

My mother shakes her head vigorously. "I want her to go here," my mother says. "If I'da wanted her someplace else, I'da took her there." The

---

1. *Ebony:* a magazine about African American life. Its ads often feature glamorous men and women.

woman continues to act as if she has known me all my life, but she tells my mother that we live beyond the area that Seaton serves. My mother is not convinced and for several more minutes she questions the woman about why I cannot attend Seaton. For as many Sundays as I can remember, perhaps even Sundays when I was in her womb, my mother has pointed across I Street to Seaton as we come and go to Mt. Carmel. "You gonna go there and learn about the whole world." But one of the guardians of that place is saying no, and no again. I am learning this about my mother: The higher up on the scale of respectability a person is—and teachers are rather high up in her eyes—the less she is liable to let them push her around. But finally, I see in her eyes the closing gate, and she takes my hand and we leave the building. On the steps, she stops as people move past us on either side.

"Mama, I can't go to school?"

She says nothing at first, then takes my hand again and we are down the steps quickly and nearing New Jersey Avenue before I can blink. This is my mother: She says "One monkey don't stop no show."

Walker-Jones is a larger, newer school and I immediately like it because of that. But it is not across the street from my mother's church, her rock, one of her connections to God, and I sense her doubts as she absently rubs her thumb over the back of her hand. We find our way to the crowded auditorium where gray metal chairs are set up in the middle of the room. Along the wall to the left are tables and other chairs. Every chair seems occupied by a child or adult. Somewhere in the room a child is crying, a cry that rises above the buzz-talk of so many people. Strewn about the floor are dozens and dozens of pieces of white paper, and people are walking over them without any thought of picking them up. And seeing this lack of concern, I am all of a sudden afraid.

"Is this where they register for school?" my mother asks a woman at one of the tables.

The woman looks up slowly as if she has heard this question once too often. She nods. She is tiny, almost as small as the girl standing beside her. The woman's hair is set in a mass of curlers and all of those curlers are made of paper money, here a dollar bill, there a five-dollar bill. The girl's hair is arrayed in curls, but some of them are beginning to droop and this makes me happy. On the table beside the woman's pocketbook is a large notebook, worthy of someone in high school, and looking at me looking at the notebook, the girl places her hand possessively on it. In her other hand she holds several pencils with thick crowns of additional erasers.

"These the forms you gotta use?" my mother asks the woman, picking up a few pieces of the paper from the table. "Is this what you have to fill out?"

The woman tells her yes, but that she need fill out only one.

"I see," my mother says, looking about the room. Then: "Would you help me with this form? That is, if you don't mind."

The woman asks my mother what she means.

"This form. Would you mind helpin me fill it out?"

The woman still seems not to understand.

"I can't read it. I don't know how to read or write, and I'm askin you to help me." My mother looks at me, then looks away. I know almost all of her looks, but this one is brand new to me. "Would you help me, then?"

The woman says Why sure, and suddenly she appears happier, so much more satisfied with everything. She finishes the form for her daughter and my mother and I step aside to wait for her. We find two chairs nearby and sit. My mother is now diseased, according to the girl's eyes, and until the moment her mother takes her and the form to the front of the auditorium, the girl never stops looking at my mother. I stare back at her. "Don't stare," my mother says to me. "You know better than that."

Another woman out of the *Ebony* ads takes the woman's child away. Now, the woman says upon returning, let's see what we can do for you two.

My mother answers the questions the woman reads off the form. They start with my last name, and then on to the first and middle names. This is school, I think. This is going to school. My mother slowly enunciates each word of my name. This is my mother: As the questions go on, she takes from her pocketbook document after document, as if they will support my right to attend school, as if she has been saving them up for just this moment. Indeed, she takes out more papers than I have ever seen her do in other places: my birth certificate, my baptismal record, a doctor's letter concerning my bout with chicken pox, rent receipts, records of immunization, a letter about our public assistance payments, even her marriage license—every single paper that has anything even remotely to do with my five-year-old life. Few of the papers are needed here, but it does not matter and my mother continues to pull out the documents with the purposefulness of a magician pulling out a long string of scarves. She has learned that money is the beginning and end of everything in this world, and when the woman finishes, my mother offers her fifty cents, and the woman accepts it without hesitation. My mother and I are just about the last parent and child in the room.

My mother presents the form to a woman sitting in front of the stage, and the woman looks at it and writes something on a white card, which she gives to my mother. Before long, the woman who has taken the girl with the drooping curls appears from behind us, speaks to the sitting woman, and introduces herself to my mother and me. She's to be my teacher, she tells my mother. My mother stares.

We go into the hall, where my mother kneels down to me. Her lips are quivering. "I'll be back to pick you up at twelve o'clock. I don't want you to go nowhere. You just wait right here. And listen to every word she say." I touch her lips and press them together. It is an old, old game between us. She puts my hand down at my side, which is not part of the game. She stands and looks a second at the teacher, then she turns and walks away. I see where she has darned one of her socks the night before. Her shoes make loud sounds in the hall. She passes through the doors and I can still hear the loud sounds of her shoes. And even when the teacher turns me toward the classrooms and I hear what must be the singing and talking of all the children in the world, I can still hear my mother's footsteps above it all.

Responding to the Story

1. The narrator hears her mother ask for help because she cannot read or write. Then the narrator tells the reader, "My mother looks at me, then looks away. I know almost all of her looks, but this one is brand new to me." What do you suppose that look is? Explain.
2. What are some differences between the schools where the mother takes her daughter? What reasons might the mother have for preferring Seaton School?

3. Why has the mother brought so many documents to the registration?
4. Reread the final paragraph of the story. What do you think the author is saying in the very last line?

Exploring the Author's Craft

Narrative point of view in a piece of writing involves who is telling the story. "The First Day" is told from first-person point of view: the narrator—the "I" telling the story—is a five-year-old girl registering to attend kindergarten. What kinds of things will the reader learn in a story with a first-person narrator?

Writer's Workshop

Think back to the first school experience you can remember. In two or three paragraphs recount as many details as you can remember of that experience. Be sure to name all the things you see in your recollection.

Alternate Media Response

Draw a scene from this story. Include both the mother and the daughter, and be sure to show the face of each.

Alberto Alvaro Ríos

Alberto Alvaro Ríos is a professor of English at Arizona State University in Tempe and lives in Chandler, Arizona. He was born in 1952 in Nogales, Arizona, of a Mexican father and an English mother. He has degrees in English and psychology and attended law school at the University of Arizona.

He has written both poetry and short fiction. He won the Walt Whitman Award from the Academy of American Poets for *Whispering to Fool the Wind* (1982), and a Western States Book Award for *The Iguana Killer: Twelve Stories of the Heart* (1984). He is also the author of *Pig's Cookies and Other Stories* (1995) and *Teodoro Luna's Two Kisses* (1990), a book of poetry.

In middle school the rug gets pulled out from under you!

The Secret Lion

I was twelve and in junior high school and something happened that we didn't have a name for, but it was there nonetheless like a lion, and roaring, roaring that way the biggest things do. Everything changed. Just like that. Like the rug, the one that gets pulled—or better, like the tablecloth those magicians pull where the stuff on the table stays the same but the gasp! from the audience makes the staying-the-same part not matter. Like that.

What happened was there were teachers now, not just one teacher, teach-erz, and we felt personally abandoned somehow. When a person had all these teachers now, he didn't get taken care of the same way, even though six was more than one. Arithmetic went out the door when we walked in. And we saw girls now, but they weren't the same girls we used to know because we couldn't talk to them anymore, not the same way we used to, certainly not to Sandy, even though she was my neighbor, too. Not even to her. She just played the piano all the time. And there were words, oh there were words in junior high school, and we wanted to know what they were, and how a person did them—that's what school was supposed to be for. Only, in junior high school, school wasn't school, everything was backwardlike. If you went up to a teacher and said the word to try and find out what it meant you got in trouble for saying it. So we didn't. And we figured it must have been that way about other stuff, too, so we never said anything about anything—we weren't stupid.

But my friend Sergio and I, we solved junior high school. We would come home from school on the bus, put our books away, change shoes, and go across the highway to the arroyo.[1] It was the one place we were not supposed to go. So we did. This was, after all, what junior high had at least shown us. It was our river, though, our personal Mississippi, our friend from long back, and it was full of stories and all the branch forts we had built in it when we were still the Vikings of America, with our own symbol, which we had carved everywhere, even in the sand, which let the water take it. That was good, we had decided; whoever was at the end of this river would know about us.

At the very very top of our growing lungs, what we would do down there was shout every dirty word we could think of, in every combination we could come up with, and we would yell about girls, and all the things we wanted to do with them, as loud as we could—we didn't know what we wanted to do with them, just things—and we would yell about teachers, and how we loved some of them, like Miss Crevelone, and how we wanted to dissect some of them, making signs of the cross, like priests, and we would yell this stuff over and over because it felt good, we couldn't explain why, it just felt good and for the first time in our lives there was nobody to tell us we couldn't. So we did.

One Thursday we were walking along shouting this way, and the railroad, the Southern Pacific, which ran above and along the far side of the arroyo, had dropped a grinding ball down there, which was, we found out later, a cannonball thing used in mining. A bunch of them were put in a big vat which turned around and crushed the ore. One had been

---

1. **arroyo:** a small stream or creek. [Spanish]

dropped, or thrown—what do caboose men do when they get bored—but it got down there regardless and as we were walking along yelling about one girl or another, a particular Claudia, we found it, one of these things, looked at it, picked it up, and got very excited, and held it and passed it back and forth, and we were saying, "Guythisis, this is, geeGuythis . . .": we had this perception about nature then, that nature is imperfect and that round things are perfect: we said, "GuyGodthis is perfect, thisisthis is perfect, it's round, round and heavy, it'sit's the best thing we'veeverseen. Whatisit?" We didn't know. We just knew it was great. We just, whatever, we played with it, held it some more.

And then we had to decide what to do with it. We knew, because of a lot of things, that if we were going to take this and show it to anybody, this discovery, this best thing, was going to be taken away from us. That's the way it works with little kids, like all the polished quartz, the tons of it we had collected piece by piece over the years. Junior high kids too. If we took it home, my mother, we knew, was going to look at it and say, "Throw that dirty thing in the, get rid of it." Simple like, like that. "But ma it's the best thing I" "Getridofit." Simple.

So we didn't. Take it home. Instead, we came up with the answer. We dug a hole and we buried it. And we marked it secretly. Lots of secret signs. And came back the next week to dig it up and, we didn't know, pass it around some more or something, but we didn't find it. We dug up that whole bank, and we never found it again. We tried.

Sergio and I talked about that ball or whatever it was when we couldn't find it. All we used were small words, neat, good. Kid words. What we were really saying, but didn't know the words, was how much that ball was like that place, that whole arroyo: couldn't tell anybody about it, didn't understand what it was, didn't have a name for it. It just felt good. It was just perfect in the way it was that place, that whole going to that place, that whole junior high school lion. It was just iron-heavy, it had no name, it felt good or not, we couldn't take it home to show our mothers, and once we buried it, it was gone forever.

The ball was gone, like the first reasons we had come to that arroyo years earlier, like the first time we had seen the arroyo, it was gone like everything else that had been taken away. This was not our first lesson. We stopped going to the arroyo after not finding the thing, the same way we had stopped going there years earlier and headed for the mountains. Nature seemed to keep pushing us around one way or another, teaching us the same thing every place we ended up. Nature's gang was tough that way, teaching us stuff.

When we were young we moved away from town, me and my family. Sergio's was already out there. Out in the wilds. Or at least the new place seemed like the wilds since everything looks bigger the smaller a man is. I was five, I guess, and we had moved three miles north of Nogales,[2] where we had lived, three miles north of the Mexican border. We looked across the highway in one direction and there was the arroyo; hills stood up in the other direction. Mountains, for a small man.

When the first summer came the very first place we went to was of course the one place we weren't supposed to go, the arroyo. We went down in there and found water running, summer rainwater mostly, and we went swimming. But every third or fourth or fifth day, the sewage treatment plant that was, we found out, upstream, would release whatever it was that it released, and we would never know exactly what day that was, and a person couldn't tell right off by looking at the water, not every time, not so a person could get out in time. So, we went swimming that summer and some days we had a lot of fun. Some days we didn't. We found a thousand ways to explain what happened on those other days, constructing elaborate stories about neighborhood dogs, and hadn't she, my mother, miscalculated her step before, too? But she knew something was up because we'd come running into the house those days, wanting to take a shower, even—if this can be imagined—in the middle of the day.

That was the first time we stopped going to the arroyo. It taught us to look the other way. We decided, as the second side of summer came, we wanted to go into the mountains. They were still mountains then. We went running in one summer Thursday morning, my friend Sergio and I, into my mother's kitchen, and said, well, what'zin, whatz'in those hills over there—we used her words so she'd understand us—and she said nothingdon'tworryaboutit. So we went out, and we weren't dumb, we thought with our eyes to each other, ohhoshe'stryingtokeep somethingfromus. We knew adults.

We had read the books, after all; we knew about bridges and castles and wildtreacherousraging alligatormouth rivers. We wanted them. So

---

2. **Nogales:** city in northwest Mexico, across the border from Nogales, Arizona.

we were going to go out and get them. We went back that morning
into that kitchen and we said, "We're going out there, we're going into
the hills, we're going away for three days, don't worry." She said, "All
right."

"You know," I said to Sergio, "if we're going to go away for three days,
well, we ought to at least pack a lunch."

But we were two young boys with no patience for what we thought at
the time was mom-stuff: making sa-and-wiches. My mother didn't offer.
So we got our little kid knapsacks that my mother had sewn for us, and
into them we put the jar of mustard. A loaf of bread. Knivesforksplates,
bottles of Coke, a can opener. This was lunch for the two of us. And we
were weighed down, humped over to be strong enough to carry this
stuff. But we started walking, anyway, into the hills. We were going to eat
berries and stuff otherwise. "Goodbye." My mom said that.

After the first hill we were dead. But we walked. My mother could
still see us. And we kept walking. We walked until we got to where the
sun is straight overhead, noon. That place. Where that is doesn't matter;
it's time to eat. The truth is we weren't anywhere close to that place.
We just agreed that the sun was overhead and that it was time to eat,
and by tilting our heads a little we could make that the truth.

"We really ought to start looking for a place to eat."

"Yeah. Let's look for a good place to eat." We went back and forth
saying that for fifteen minutes, making it lunch time because that's what
we always said back and forth before lunch times at home. "Yeah, I'm
hungry all right." I nodded my head. "Yeah, I'm hungry all right too. I'm
hungry. He nodded his head. I nodded my head back. After a good deal
more nodding, we were ready, just as we came over a little hill. We
hadn't found the mountains yet. This was a little hill.

And on the other side of this hill we found heaven.

It was just what we thought it would be.

Perfect. Heaven was green, like nothing else in Arizona. And it wasn't
a cemetery or like that because we had seen cemeteries and they had
gravestones and stuff and this didn't. This was perfect, had trees, lots of
trees, had birds, like we had never seen before. It was like *The Wizard of
Oz*, like when they got to Oz and everything was so green, so emerald,
they had to wear those glasses, and we ran just like them, laughing,
laughing that way we did that moment, and we went running down to
this clearing in it all, hitting each other that good way we did.

We got down there, we kept laughing, we kept hitting each other, we unpacked our stuff, and we started acting "rich." We knew all about how to do that, like blowing on our nails, then rubbing them on our chests for the shine. We made our sandwiches, opened our Cokes, got out the rest of the stuff, the salt and pepper shakers. I found this particular hole and I put my Coke right into it, a perfect fit, and I called it my Coke-holder. I got down next to it on my back, because everyone knows that rich people eat lying down, and I got my sandwich in one hand and put my other arm around the Coke in its holder. When I wanted a drink, I lifted my neck a little, put out my lips, and tipped my Coke a little with the crook of my elbow. Ah.

We were there, lying down, eating our sandwiches, laughing, throwing bread at each other and out for the birds. This was heaven. We were laughing and we couldn't believe it. My mother *was* keeping something from us, ah ha, but we had found her out. We even found water over at the side of the clearing to wash our plates with—we had brought plates. Sergio started washing his plates when he was done, and I was being rich with my Coke, and this day in summer was right.

When suddenly these two men came, from around a corner of trees and the tallest grass we had ever seen. They had bags on their backs, leather bags, bags and sticks.

We didn't know what clubs were, but I learned later, like I learned about the grinding balls. The two men yelled at us. Most specifically, one wanted me to take my Coke out of my Coke-holder so he could sink his golf ball into it.

Something got taken away from us that moment. Heaven. We grew up a little bit, and couldn't go backward. We learned. No one had ever told us about golf. They had told us about heaven. And it went away. We got golf in exchange.

We went back to the arroyo for the rest of that summer, and tried to have fun the best we could. We learned to be ready for finding the grinding ball. We loved it, and when we buried it we knew what would happen. The truth is, we didn't look so hard for it. We were two boys and twelve summers then, and not stupid. Things get taken away.

We buried it because it was perfect. We didn't tell my mother, but together it was all we talked about, till we forgot. It was the lion.

Responding to the Story

1. Why do the narrator and his friend cross the highway and go to the arroyo?
2. How is the missing ball "like that place, that whole arroyo"?
3. What does the sentence "They were still mountains then" mean?
4. In a paragraph, describe the way you think the narrator looks at the age of twelve.
5. Why do you think the story has the title it does?

Exploring the Author's Craft

Tone is an author's attitude about his or her subject. A tone can be humorous or angry, serious or satirical about a topic. What is the tone of "The Secret Lion"? Give examples from the story to back up your answer.

Writer's Workshop

Imagine that you are one of the boys who has stumbled on the place that was "green, like nothing else in Arizona." What are your feelings at discovering and existing for a while in this place? What makes this place special? List as many nouns and adjectives as you can to describe the place and the emotions it evokes. Then turn this list into a poem.

Alternate Media Response

1. Draw a map that captures the world these boys live in. Give places a size and importance that is relative to the importance those places play in the boys' lives when they are twelve. Be able to justify everything in your drawing.
2. Write a script for a video dramatization of this story. Do not use a narrator to communicate the author's ideas; everything must be communicated through what is seen or spoken by the characters. Produce this video dramatization of "The Secret Lion."

Sandra Cisneros

Poet Gwendolyn Brooks called Sandra Cisneros "one of the most brilliant of today's young writers." Cisneros won an American Book Award from the Before Columbus Foundation in 1985 for *The House on Mango Street*, a collection of sketches and stories, and a Lannan Literary Award in 1991. Her other books include *My Wicked, Wicked Ways* (1987), a book of poetry, and *Women Hollering Creek and Other Stories* (1991), and *Loose Woman* (1994). Cisneros's unique writing style is succinct and minimalist. Her stories often imply and suggest more than they may seem to express.

She was born in 1954 in Chicago to a Mexican father and a Mexican American mother. Cisneros has been a teacher, a poet in the schools, a college recruiter, and an arts administrator. She lives in San Antonio, Texas.

As you grow, your earlier selves stay inside you—like the layers of an onion.

Eleven

What they don't understand about birthdays and what they never tell you is that when you're eleven, you're also ten, and nine, and eight, and seven, and six, and five, and four, and three, and two, and one. and when you wake up on your eleventh birthday you expect to feel eleven, but you don't. You open your eyes and everything's just like yesterday, only it's today. And you don't feel eleven at all. You feel like you're still ten. And you are—underneath the year that makes you eleven.

Like some days you might say something stupid, and that's the part of you that's still ten. Or maybe some days you might need to sit on your mama's lap because you're scared, and that's the part of you that's five. And maybe one day when you're all grown up maybe you will need to cry like if you're three, and that's okay. That's what I tell Mama when she's sad and needs to cry. Maybe she's feeling three.

Because the way you grow old is kind of like an onion or like the rings inside a tree trunk or like my little wooden dolls that fit one inside the other, each year inside the next one. That's how being eleven years old is.

You don't feel eleven. Not right away. It takes a few days, weeks even, sometimes even months before you say Eleven when they ask you. And you don't feel smart eleven, not until you're almost twelve. That's the way it is.

Only today I wish I didn't have only eleven years rattling inside me like pennies in a tin Band-Aid box. Today I wish I was one hundred and two instead of eleven because if I was one hundred and two I'd have known what to say when Mrs. Price put the red sweater on my desk. I would've known how to tell her it wasn't mine instead of just sitting there with that look on my face and nothing coming out of my mouth.

"Whose is this?" Mrs. Price says, and she holds the red sweater up in the air for all the class to see. "Whose? It's been sitting in the coatroom for a month."

"Not mine," says everybody. "Not me."

"It has to belong to somebody," Mrs. Price keeps saying, but nobody can remember. It's an ugly sweater with red plastic buttons and a collar and sleeves all stretched out like you could use it for a jump rope. It's maybe a thousand years old and even if it belonged to me I wouldn't say so.

Maybe because I'm skinny, maybe because she doesn't like me, that stupid Sylvia Saldívar says, "I think it belongs to Rachel." An ugly sweater like that, all raggedy and old, but Mrs. Price believes her. Mrs. Price takes the sweater and puts it right back on my desk, but when I open my mouth nothing comes out.

"That's not, I don't, you're not . . . Not mine," I finally say in a little voice that was maybe me when I was four.

"Of course it's yours," Mrs. Price says. "I remember you wearing it once." Because she's older and the teacher, she's right and I'm not.

Not mine, not mine, not mine, but Mrs. Price is already turning to page thirty-two, and math problem number four. I don't know why but all of a sudden I'm feeling sick inside, like the part of me that's three wants to come out of my eyes, only I squeeze them shut tight and bite down on my teeth real hard and try to remember today I am eleven, eleven. Mama is making a cake for me tonight, and when Papa comes home everybody will sing Happy birthday, happy birthday to you.

But when the sick feeling goes away and I open my eyes, the red sweater's still sitting there like a big red mountain. I move the red sweater to the corner of my desk with my ruler. I move my pencil and books and eraser as far from it as possible. I even move my chair a little to the right. Not mine, not mine, not mine.

In my head I'm thinking how long till lunchtime, how long till I can take the red sweater and throw it over the schoolyard fence, or leave it hanging on a parking meter, or bunch it up into a little ball and toss it in the alley. Except when math period ends Mrs. Price says loud and in front of everybody, "Now, Rachel, that's enough," because she sees I've shoved the red sweater to the tippy-tip corner of my desk and it's hanging all over the edge like a waterfall, but I don't care.

"Rachel," Mrs. Price says. She says it like she's getting mad. "You put that sweater on right now and no more nonsense."

"But it's not—"

"Now!" Mrs. Price says.

This is when I wish I wasn't eleven, because all the years inside of me—ten, nine, eight, seven, six, five, four, three, two, and one—are pushing at the back of my eyes when I put one arm through one sleeve of the sweater that smells like cottage cheese, and then the other arm through the other and stand there with my arms apart like if the sweater hurts me and it does, all itchy and full of germs that aren't even mine.

That's when everything I've been holding in since this morning, since when Mrs. Price put the sweater on my desk, finally lets go, and all of a sudden I'm crying in front of everybody. I wish I was invisible but I'm not. I'm eleven and it's my birthday today and I'm crying like I'm three in front of everybody. I put my head down on the desk and bury my face in my stupid clown-sweater arms. My face all hot and spit coming out of my mouth because I can't stop the little animal noises from coming out of me, until there aren't any more tears left in my eyes, and it's just my body shaking like when you have the hiccups, and my whole head hurts like when you drink milk too fast.

But the worst part is right before the bell rings for lunch. That stupid Phyllis Lopez, who is even dumber than Sylvia Saldívar, says she remembers the red sweater is hers! I take it off right away and give it to her, only Mrs. Price pretends like everything's okay.

Today I'm eleven. There's a cake Mama's making for tonight, and when Papa comes home from work we'll eat it. There'll be candles and presents and everybody will sing Happy birthday, happy birthday to you, Rachel, only it's too late.

I'm eleven today. I'm eleven, ten, nine, eight, seven, six, five, four, three, two, and one, but I wish I was one hundred and two. I wish I was anything but eleven, because I want today to be far away already, far away like a runaway balloon, like a tiny *o* in the sky, so tiny-tiny you have to close your eyes to see it.

Responding to the Story

1. What does the narrator mean when she says, "When you're eleven, you're also ten, and nine, and eight, and seven, and six, and five, and four, and three, and two, and one"? Do you think her reasoning makes sense? Explain.
2. Why does the narrator wish this day—her birthday, a day that should be happy—would be "far away already"?
3. Are the narrator's feelings this day recognizable to you—believable?

Exploring the Author's Craft

This story, like "The First Day," is written from the first-person point of view. A story told by first-person narrator is often very compelling; we can be lured into caring about the narrator's concerns and maybe even identify with the narrator.

1. What is Rachel like? Describe her personality.
2. Is this story an accurate portrait of someone turning eleven? Why or why not?
3. In a story told from a first-person point of view, are we likely to know what the other characters are really thinking or feeling? Explain.

Writer's Workshop

Create a first-person narrator and tell about something that happens to that person. Have the character establish his or her age early in your narration. Have your narrator's voice be appropriate to the age of the character—just as Sandra Cisneros tried to have Rachel sound like an eleven-year-old rather than a teenager.

Toni Cade Bambara

Toni Cade Bambara, who died in 1995, was praised for her ability to capture street talk and for her depiction of the love that exists in African-American families and communities. Born in 1939 in New York City, she was educated at Queens College and studied at the University of Florence and in Paris. Her works include *Gorilla, My Love* (1972), a collection of short stories; *The Sea Birds Are Still Alive* (1977); *The Salt Eaters* (1980), a novel; and *If Blessing Comes* (1987). She also wrote screenplays, among them "Raymond's Run," produced by PBS in 1985; and "The Bombing of Osage," for which she won the Best Documentary of 1986 Award from the Pennsylvania Association of Broadcasters and the Documentary Award from the National Black Programming Consortium.

What would you do to help your brother?

Raymond's Run

I don't have much work to do around the house like some girls. My mother does that. And I don't have to earn my pocket money by hustling; George runs errands for the big boys and sells Christmas cards. And anything else that's got to get done, my father does. All I have to do in life is mind my brother Raymond, which is enough.

Sometimes I slip and say my little brother Raymond. But as any fool can see he's much bigger and he's older too. But a lot of people call him my little brother cause he needs looking after cause he's not quite right. And a lot of smart mouths got lots to say about that too, especially when George was minding him. But now, if anybody has anything to say to Raymond, anything to say about his big head, they have to come by me. And I don't play the dozens[1] or believe in standing around with somebody in my face doing a lot of talking. I much rather just knock you down and take my chances even if I am a little girl with skinny arms and a squeaky voice, which is how I got the name Squeaky. And if things get too rough, I run. And as anybody can tell you, I'm the fastest thing on two feet.

There is no track meet that I don't win the first place medal. I used to win the twenty-yard dash when I was a little kid in kindergarten. Nowadays, it's the fifty-yard dash. And tomorrow I'm subject to run the quarter-meter relay all by myself and come in first, second, and third. The big kids call me Mercury[2] cause I'm the swiftest thing in the neighborhood. Everybody knows that—except two people who know better, my father and me. He can beat me to Amsterdam Avenue with me having a two fire-hydrant headstart and him running with his hands in his pockets and whistling. But that's private information. Cause can you imagine some thirty-five-year-old man stuffing himself into PAL shorts to race little kids? So as far as everyone's concerned, I'm the fastest and that goes for Gretchen, too, who has put out the tale that she is going to win the first-place medal this year. Ridiculous. In the second place, she's got short legs. In the third place, she's got freckles. In the first place, no one can beat me and that's all there is to it.

I'm standing on the corner admiring the weather and about to take a stroll down Broadway so I can practice my breathing exercises, and I've got Raymond walking on the inside close to the buildings, cause he's subject to fits of fantasy and starts thinking he's a circus performer and that the curb is a tightrope strung high in the air. And sometimes after a rain he likes to step down off his tightrope right into the gutter and slosh around getting his shoes and cuffs wet. Then I get hit when I get home. Or sometimes if you don't watch him he'll dash across traffic to the island in the middle of Broadway and give the pigeons a fit. Then I have to go behind him apologizing to all the old people sitting around trying to get some sun and getting all upset with the pigeons fluttering around them, scattering their newspapers and upsetting the waxpaper

---

1. **play the dozens:** a game in which each of two persons tries to outdo the other in insults directed against members of the other's family.
2. **Mercury:** in Roman myth, the messenger of the gods, often pictured with a winged helmet.

lunches in their laps. So I keep Raymond on the inside of me, and he plays like he's driving a stage coach which is O.K. by me so long as he doesn't run me over or interrupt my breathing exercises, which I have to do on account of I'm serious about my running, and I don't care who knows it.

Now some people like to act like things come easy to them, won't let on that they practice. Not me. I'll high-prance down 34th Street like a rodeo pony to keep my knees strong even if it does get my mother uptight so that she walks ahead like she's not with me, don't know me, is all by herself on a shopping trip, and I am somebody else's crazy child. Now you take Cynthia Procter for instance. She's just the opposite. If there's a test tomorrow, she'll say something like, "Oh, I guess I'll play handball this afternoon and watch television tonight," just to let you know she ain't thinking about the test. Or like last week when she won the spelling bee for the millionth time, "A good thing you got 'receive,' Squeaky, cause I would have got it wrong. I completely forgot about the spelling bee." And she'll clutch the lace on her blouse like it was a narrow escape. Oh, brother. But of course when I pass her house on my early morning trots around the block, she is practicing the scales on the piano over and over and over and over. Then in music class she always lets herself get bumped around so she falls accidently on purpose onto the piano stool and is so surprised to find herself sitting there that she decides just for fun to try out the ole keys. And what do you know— Chopin's waltzes[3] just spring out of her fingertips and she's the most surprised thing in the world. A regular prodigy.[4] I could kill people like that. I stay up all night studying the words for the spelling bee. And you can see me any time of day practicing running. I never walk if I can trot, and shame on Raymond if he can't keep up. But of course he does, cause if he hangs back someone's liable to walk up to him and get smart, or take his allowance from him, or ask him where he got that great big pumpkin head. People are so stupid sometimes.

So I'm strolling down Broadway breathing out and breathing in on counts of seven, which is my lucky number, and here comes Gretchen and her sidekicks: Mary Louise, who used to be a friend of mine when

---

3. **Chopin's:** Frédéric Chopin (1810–1849), Polish composer and pianist.
4. **prodigy:** person, especially a child, who is remarkably talented.

she first moved to Harlem from Baltimore and got beat up by everybody till I took up for her on account of her mother and my mother used to sing in the same choir when they were young girls, but people ain't grateful, so now she hangs out with the new girl Gretchen and talks about me like a dog; and Rosie, who is as fat as I am skinny and has a big mouth where Raymond is concerned and is too stupid to know that there is not a big deal of difference between herself and Raymond and that she can't afford to throw stones.[5] So they are steady coming up Broadway and I see right away that it's going to be one of those Dodge City scenes cause the street ain't that big and they're close to the buildings just as we are. First I think I'll step into the candy store and look over the new comics and let them pass. But that's chicken and I've got a reputation to consider. So then I think I'll just walk straight on through them or even over them if necessary. But as they get to me, they slow down. I'm ready to fight, cause like I said I don't feature a whole lot of chitchat, I much prefer to just knock you down right from the jump and save everybody a lotta precious time.

"You signing up for the May Day races?" smiles Mary Louise, only it's not a smile at all. A dumb question like that doesn't deserve an answer. Besides, there's just me and Gretchen standing there really, so no use wasting my breath talking to shadows.

"I don't think you're going to win this time," says Rosie, trying to signify with her hands on her hips all salty, completely forgetting that I have whupped her behind many times for less salt than that.

"I always win cause I'm the best," I say straight at Gretchen who is, as far as I'm concerned, the only one talking in this ventriloquist-dummy routine. Gretchen smiles, but it's not a smile, and I'm thinking that girls never really smile at each other because they don't know how and don't want to know how and there's probably no one to teach us how, cause grown-up girls don't know either. Then they all look at Raymond who has just brought his mule team to a standstill. And they're about to see what trouble they can get into through him.

"What grade you in now, Raymond?"

---

5. **can't afford to throw stones**: An allusion to the expression "People who live in glass houses shouldn't throw stones," meaning that one can't afford to criticize another for a fault that one also has.

"You got anything to say to my brother, you say it to me, Mary Louise Williams of Raggedy Town, Baltimore."

"What are you, his mother?" sasses Rosie.

"That's right, Fatso. And the next word out of anybody and I'll be *their* mother too." So they just stand there and Gretchen shifts from one leg to the other and so do they. Then Gretchen puts her hands on her hips and is about to say something with her freckle-face self but doesn't. Then she walks around me looking me up and down but keeps walking up Broadway, and her sidekicks follow her. So me and Raymond smile at each other and he says, "Gidyap" to his team and I continue with my breathing exercises, strolling down Broadway toward the ice man on 145th with not a care in the world cause I am Miss Quicksilver herself.

I take my time getting to the park on May Day because the track meet is the last thing on the program. The biggest thing on the program is the May Pole dancing, which I can do without, thank you, even if my mother thinks it's a shame I don't take part and act like a girl for a change. You'd think my mother'd be grateful not to have to make me a white organdy dress with a big satin sash and buy me new white baby-doll shoes that can't be taken out of the box till the big day. You'd think she'd be glad her daughter ain't out there prancing around a May Pole getting the new clothes all dirty and sweaty and trying to act like a fairy or a flower or whatever you're supposed to be when you should be trying to be yourself, whatever that is, which is, as far as I am concerned, a poor Black girl who really can't afford to buy shoes and a new dress you only wear once a lifetime cause it won't fit next year.

I was once a strawberry in a Hansel and Gretel pageant when I was in nursery school and didn't have no better sense than to dance on tiptoe with my arms in a circle over my head doing umbrella steps and being a perfect fool just so my mother and father could come dressed up and clap. You'd think they'd know better than to encourage that kind of nonsense. I am not a strawberry. I do not dance on my toes. I run. That is what I am all about. So I always come late to the May Day program, just in time to get my number pinned on and lay in the grass till they announce the fifty-yard dash.

I put Raymond in the little swings, which is a tight squeeze this year and will be impossible next year. Then I look around for Mr. Pearson, who pins the numbers on. I'm really looking for Gretchen if you want to know the truth, but she's not around. The park is jam-packed. Parents in hats and corsages and breast-pocket handkerchiefs peeking up. Kids in white dresses and light-blue suits. The parkees unfolding chairs and chasing the rowdy kids from Lenox as if they had no right to be there. The big guys with their caps on backwards, leaning against the fence swirling the basketballs on the tips of their fingers, waiting for all these crazy people to clear out of the park so they can play. Most of the kids in my class are carrying bass drums and glockenspiels and flutes. You'd think they'd put in a few bongos or something for real like that.

Then here comes Mr. Pearson with his clipboard and his cards and pencils and whistles and safety pins and fifty million other things he's always dropping all over the place with his clumsy self. He sticks out in a crowd because he's on stilts. We used to call him Jack and the Beanstalk to get him mad. But I'm the only one that can outrun him and get away, and I'm too grown for that silliness now.

"Well, Squeaky," he says, checking my name off the list and handing me number seven and two pins. And I'm thinking he's got no right to call me Squeaky, if I can't call him Beanstalk.

"Hazel Elizabeth Deborah Parker," I correct him and tell him to write it down on his board.

"Well, Hazel Elizabeth Deborah Parker, going to give someone else a break this year?" I squint t him real hard to see if he is seriously thinking I should lose the race on purpose just to give someone else a break. "Only six girls running this time," he continues, shaking his head sadly like it's my fault all of New York didn't turn out in sneakers. "That new girl should give you a run for your money." He looks around the park for Gretchen like a periscope in a submarine movie. "Wouldn't it be a nice gesture if you were . . . to ahhh . . ."

I give him such a look he couldn't finish putting that idea into words. Grownups got a lot of nerve sometimes. I pin number seven to myself and stomp away, I'm so burnt. And I go straight for the track and stretch out on the grass while the band winds up with "Oh, the Monkey Wrapped His Tail Around the Flag Pole," which my teacher calls by some other name. The man on the loudspeaker is calling everyone over to the track and I'm on my back looking at the sky, trying to pretend I'm in the country, but I can't, because even grass in the city feels hard as sidewalk, and there's just no pretending you are anywhere but in a "concrete jungle" as my grandfather says.

The twenty-yard dash takes all of two minutes cause most of the little kids don't know better than to run off the track or run the wrong way or run smack into the fence and fall down and cry. One little kid, though, has got the good sense to run straight for the white ribbon up ahead so he wins. Then the second-graders line up for the thirty-yard dash and I don't even bother to turn my head to watch cause Raphael Perez always wins. He wins before he even begins by psyching the runners, telling them they're going to trip on their shoelaces and fall on their faces or lose their shorts or something, which he doesn't really have to do since he is very fast, almost as fast as I am. After that is the forty-yard dash which I use to run when I was in first grade. Raymond is hollering from the swings cause he knows I'm bout to do my thing cause the man on the loudspeaker has just announced the fifty-yard dash, although he might just as well be giving a recipe for angel food cake cause you can hardly make out what he's saying for the static. I get up and slip off my sweat pants and then I see Gretchen standing at the starting line, kicking her legs out like a pro. Then as I get into place I see that ole Raymond is on line on the other side of the fence, bending down with his fingers on the ground just like he knew what he was doing. I was going to yell at him but then I didn't. It burns up your energy to holler.

Every time, just before I take off in a race, I always feel like I'm in a dream, the kind of dream you have when you're sick with fever and feel all hot and weightless. I dream I'm flying over a sandy beach in the early morning sun, kissing the leaves of the trees as I fly by. And there's always the smell of apples, just like in the country when I was little and used to think I was a choo-choo train, running through the fields of corn and chugging up the hill to the orchard. And all the time I'm dreaming this, I get lighter and lighter until I'm flying over the beach again, getting blown through the sky like a feather that weighs nothing at all. But once I spread my fingers in the dirt and crouch over the Get on Your Mark, the dream goes and I am solid again and am telling myself, Squeaky you must win, you must win, you are the fastest thing in the world, you can even beat your father up Amsterdam if you really try. And then I feel my weight coming back just behind my knees then down to my feet then into the earth and the pistol shot explodes in my blood and I am off and weightless again, flying past the other runners, my arms pumping up and down and the whole world is quiet except for the crunch as I zoom over the gravel in the track. I glance to my left and there is no one. To the right, a blurred Gretchen, who's got her chin jutting out as if it would win the race all by itself. And on the other side of the fence is Raymond with his arms down to his side and the palms tucked up behind him, running in his very own style, and it's the first time I ever saw that and I almost stop to watch my brother Raymond on his first run. But the white ribbon is bouncing toward me and I tear past it, racing into the distance till my feet with a mind of their own start digging up footfuls of dirt and brake me short. Then all the kids standing on the side pile on me, banging me on the back and slapping my head with their May Day programs, for I have won again and everybody on 151st Street can walk tall for another year.

"In first place . . ." the man on the loudspeaker is clear as a bell now. But then he pauses and the loudspeaker starts to whine. Then static. And I lean down to catch my breath and here comes Gretchen walking back, for she's overshot the finish line too, huffing and puffing with her hands on her hips taking it slow, breathing in steady time like a real pro and I sort of like her a little for the first time. "In the first place . . ." and then three or four voices get all mixed up on the loudspeaker and I dig my sneaker into the grass and stare at Gretchen who's staring back, we both wondering just who did win. I can hear old Beanstalk arguing with the man on the loudspeaker and then a few others running their mouths about what the stopwatches say. Then I hear Raymond, yanking at the fence to call me and I wave to shush him, but he keeps rattling the fence like a gorilla in a cage like in them gorilla movies, but then like a dancer or something he starts climbing up nice and easy but very fast. And it occurs to me, watching how smoothly he climbs hand over hand and remembering how he looked running with his arms down to his side and with the wind pulling his mouth back and his teeth showing and all, it occurred to me that Raymond would make a very fine runner. Doesn't he always keep up with me on my trots? And he surely knows how to breathe in counts of seven cause he's always doing it at the dinner table, which drives my brother George up the wall. And I'm smiling to beat the band cause if I've lost this race, or if me and Gretchen tied, or even if I've won, I can always retire as a runner and begin a whole new career as a coach with Raymond as my champion. After all, with a little more study I can beat Cynthia and her phony self at the spelling bee. And if I bugged my mother, I could get piano lessons and become a star. And I have a big rep as the baddest thing around.

And I've got a roomful of ribbons and medals and awards. But what has Raymond got to call his own?

So I stand there with my new plans, laughing out loud by this time as Raymond jumps down from the fence and runs over with his teeth showing and his arms down to the side, which no one before him has quite mastered as a running style. And by the time he comes over I'm jumping up and down so glad to see him—my brother Raymond, a great runner in the family tradition. But of course everyone thinks I'm jumping up and down because the men on the loudspeaker have finally gotten themselves together and compared notes and are announcing "In first place—Miss Hazel Elizabeth Deborah Parker." (Dig that.) "In second place—Miss Gretchen P. Lewis." And I look over at Gretchen wondering what the "P" stands for. And I smile. Cause she's good, no doubt about it. Maybe she'd like to help me coach Raymond; she obviously is serious about running, as any fool can see. And she nods to congratulate me and then she smiles. And I smile. We stand there with this big smile of respect between us. It's about as real a smile as girls can do for each other, considering we don't practice real smiling every day, you know, cause maybe we too busy being flowers or fairies or strawberries instead of something honest and worthy of respect . . . you know . . . like being people.

Responding to the Story

1. This story could have been placed in the "Families and Friends" unit, but instead we find it in "Do I Fit In?" Does Squeaky fit in her neighborhood? Explain. If she *does* fit in, why does she?
2. Do you think the author was able to create a believable first-person female voice? Explain. Would this story have been different if the main character were a boy? If so, how?
3. Do you agree with Hazel Elizabeth Deborah Parker that "girls never really smile at each other because they don't know how and don't want to know how and there's probably no one to teach us how, cause grown-up girls don't know either"? Do you agree with her explanation—found in the last paragraph—of why this happens? Explain her reasoning and then give your reaction.

Exploring the Author's Craft

Authors use a variety of techniques to define a **character**. In this story, we learn about Squeaky through what she tells us about herself. Therefore, despite its title, this story is not really about Raymond. Nevertheless, Raymond is essential to the story. Explain how his presence helps to characterize Squeaky.

Writer's Workshop

Listen carefully to the way various people around you speak. Notice the words they use, their tone of voice, and whether they speak slowly or quickly. Then create a fictional first-person narrator based on someone you have observed. Tell about a happening the way that person would tell it.

Amy Tan

Amy Tan was born in Oakland in 1952 of Chinese descent. Her first novel, *The Joy Luck Club* (1989), is a series of related stories about four Chinese women and their California-born daughters. Writer Alice Walker observed that "Amy Tan shows us . . . the mystery of the mother-daughter bond in ways that we have not experienced before."

Tan received her B.A. degree from San Jose State in 1973 and her M.A. degree in 1974; she did postgraduate study at the University of California at Berkeley. She worked for several years as a consultant to programs for disabled children. In addition to *The Joy Luck Club*, Amy Tan has produced two novels, *The Kitchen God's Wife* and *The Hundred Secret Senses*, and two books for children, *The Moon Lady* and *The Chinese Siamese Cat*. Her work has been translated into 20 languages. She was married in 1974 and lives in San Francisco.

"Only one kind of daughter can live in this house. Obedient daughter!"

Two Kinds

My mother believed you could be anything you wanted to be in America. You could open a restaurant. You could work for the government and get good retirement. You could buy a house with almost no money down. You could become rich. You could become instantly famous.

"Of course, you can be prodigy, too," my mother told me when I was nine. "You can be best anything. What does Auntie Lindo know? Her daughter, she is only best tricky."

America was where all my mother's hopes lay. She had come to San Francisco in 1949 after losing everything in China: her mother and father, her family home, her first husband, and two daughters, twin baby girls. But she never looked back with regret. There were so many ways for things to get better.

We didn't immediately pick the right kind of prodigy. At first my mother thought I could be a Chinese Shirley Temple.[1] We'd watch Shirley's old movies on TV as though they were training films. My mother would poke my arm and say, "*Ni kan*"—You watch. And I would see Shirley tapping her feet, or singing a sailor song, or pursing her lips into a very round O while saying, "Oh my goodness."

"*Ni kan*," said my mother as Shirley's eyes flooded with tears. "You already know how. Don't need talent for crying!"

Soon after my mother got this idea about Shirley Temple, she took me to a beauty training school in the Mission district and put me in the hands of a student who could barely hold the scissors without shaking. Instead of getting big fat curls, I emerged with an uneven mass of crinkly black fuzz. My mother dragged me off to the bathroom and tried to wet down my hair.

"You look like Negro Chinese," she lamented, as if I had done this on purpose.

The instructor of the beauty training school had to lop off these soggy clumps to make my hair even again. "Peter Pan is very popular these days," the instructor assured my mother. I now had hair the length of a boy's, with straight-across bangs that hung at a slant two inches above my eyebrows. I liked the haircut and it made me actually look forward to my future fame.

In fact, in the beginning, I was just as excited as my mother, maybe even more so. I pictured this prodigy part of me as many different images, trying each one on for size. I was a dainty ballerina girl standing by the curtains, waiting to hear the right music that would send me floating on my tiptoes. I was like the Christ child lifted out of the straw manger, crying with holy indignity. I was Cinderella stepping from her pumpkin carriage with sparkly cartoon music filling the air.

In all of my imaginings, I was filled with a sense that I would soon become *perfect*. My mother and father would adore me. I would be beyond reproach. I would never feel the need to sulk for anything.

---

1. **Shirley Temple:** a child movie star of the 1930s.

But sometimes the prodigy in me became impatient. "If you don't hurry up and get me out of here, I'm disappearing for good," it warned. "And then you'll always be nothing."

Every night after dinner, my mother and I would sit at the Formica kitchen table. She would present new tests, taking her examples from stories of amazing children she had read in *Ripley's Believe It or Not*, or *Good Housekeeping, Reader's Digest*, and a dozen other magazines she kept in a pile in our bathroom. My mother got these magazines from people whose houses she cleaned. And since she cleaned many houses each week, we had a great assortment. She would look through them all, searching for stories about remarkable children.

The first night she brought out a story about a three-year-old boy who knew the capitals of all the states and even most of the European countries. A teacher was quoted as saying the little boy could also pronounce the names of the foreign cities correctly.

"What's the capital of Finland?" my mother asked me, looking at the magazine story.

All I knew was the capital of California, because Sacramento was the name of the street we lived on in Chinatown. "Nairobi!" I guessed, saying the most foreign word I could think of. She checked to see if that was possibly one way to pronounce "Helsinki" before showing me the answer.

The tests got harder—multiplying numbers in my head, finding the queen of hearts in a deck of cards, trying to stand on my head without using my hands, predicting the daily temperatures in Los Angeles, New York, and London.

One night I had to look at a page from the Bible for three minutes and then report everything I could remember. "Now Jehoshaphat had riches and honor in abundance and . . . that's all I remember, Ma," I said.

After seeing my mother's disappointed face once again, something inside of me began to die. I hated the tests, the raised hopes and failed expectations. Before going to bed that night, I looked in the mirror above the bathroom sink and when I saw only my face staring back— and that it would always be this ordinary face—I began to cry. Such a sad, ugly girl! I made high-pitched noises like a crazed animal, trying to scratch out the face in the mirror.

And then I saw what seemed to be the prodigy side of me—because I had never seen that face before I looked at my reflection, blinking so I could see more clearly. The girl staring back at me was angry, powerful.

This girl and I were the same. I had new thoughts, willful thoughts, or rather thoughts filled with lots of won'ts. I won't let her change me, I promised myself. I won't be what I'm not.

So now on nights when my mother presented her tests, I performed listlessly, my head propped on one arm. I pretended to be bored. And I was. I got so bored I started counting the bellows of the foghorns out on the bay while my mother drilled me in other areas. The sound was comforting and reminded me of the cow jumping over the moon. And the next day, I played a game with myself, seeing if my mother would give up on me before eight bellows. After a while I usually counted only one, maybe two bellows at most. At last she was beginning to give up hope.

Two or three months had gone by without any mention of my being a prodigy again. And then one day my mother was watching *The Ed Sullivan Show*[2] on TV. The TV was old and the sound kept shorting out. Every time my mother got halfway up from the sofa to adjust the set, the sound would go back on and Ed would be talking. As soon as she sat down, Ed would go silent again. She got up, the TV broke into loud piano music. She sat down. Silence. Up and down, back and forth, quiet and loud. It was like a stiff embraceless dance between her and the TV set. Finally she stood by the set with her hand on the sound dial.

She seemed entranced by the music, a little frenzied piano piece with this mesmerizing quality, sort of quick passages and then teasing lilting ones before it returned to the quick playful parts.

"*Ni kan*," my mother said, calling me over with hurried hand gestures, "Look here."

I could see why my mother was fascinated by the music. It was being pounded out by a little Chinese girl, about nine years old, with a Peter Pan haircut. The girl had the sauciness of a Shirley Temple. She was proudly modest like a proper Chinese child. And she also did this fancy sweep of a curtsy, so that the fluffy skirt of her white dress cascaded slowly to the floor like the petals of a large carnation.

In spite of these warning signs, I wasn't worried. Our family had no piano and we couldn't afford to buy one, let alone reams of sheet music and piano lessons. So I could be generous in my comments when my mother badmouthed the little girl on TV.

---

2. *The Ed Sullivan Show:* a weekly television show of the 1950s and 1960s that featured various kinds of performers.

"Play note right, but doesn't sound good! No singing sound," complained my mother.

"What are you picking on her for?" I said carelessly. "She's pretty good. Maybe she's not the best, but she's trying hard." I knew almost immediately I would be sorry I said that.

"Just like you," she said. "Not the best. Because you not trying." She gave a little huff as she let go of the sound dial and sat down on the sofa.

The little Chinese girl sat down also to play an encore of "Anitra's Dance" by Grieg.[3] I remember the song, because later on I had to learn how to play it.

Three days after watching *The Ed Sullivan Show*, my mother told me what my schedule would be for piano lessons and piano practice. She had talked to Mr. Chong, who lived on the first floor of our apartment building. Mr. Chong was a retired piano teacher and my mother had traded housecleaning services for weekly lessons and a piano for me to practice on every day, two hours a day, from four until six.

When my mother told me this, I felt as though I had been sent to hell. I whined and then kicked my foot a little when I couldn't stand it anymore.

"Why don't you like me the way I am? I'm *not* a genius! I can't play the piano. And even if I could, I wouldn't go on TV if you paid me a million dollars!" I cried.

My mother slapped me. "Who ask you to be genius?" she shouted. "Only ask you be your best. For your sake. You think I want you to be genius? Hnnh! What for! Who ask you!"

"So ungrateful," I heard her mutter in Chinese. "If she had as much talent as she has temper, she would be famous now."

Mr. Chong, whom I secretly nicknamed Old Chong, was very strange, always tapping his fingers to the silent music of an invisible orchestra. He looked ancient in my eyes. He had lost most of the hair on top of his head and he wore thick glasses and had eyes that always looked tired and sleepy. But he must have been younger than I thought, since he lived with his mother and was not yet married.

I met Old Lady Chong once and that was enough. She had this peculiar smell like a baby that had done something in its pants. And her

---

3. **Grieg:** Edvard Grieg (1843–1907), Norwegian composer.

fingers felt like a dead person's, like an old peach I once found in the back of the refrigerator; the skin just slid off the meat when I picked it up.

I soon found out why Old Chong had retired from teaching piano. He was deaf. "Like Beethoven!"[4] he shouted to me. "We're both listening only in our head!" And he would start to conduct his frantic silent sonatas.

Our lessons went like this. He would open the book and point to different things, explaining their purpose. "Key! Treble! Bass! No sharps or flats! So this is C major! Listen now and play after me."

And then he would play the C scale a few times, a simple chord, and then, as if inspired by an old, unreachable itch, he gradually added more notes and running trills and a pounding bass until the music was really something quite grand.

I would play after him, the simple scale, the simple chord, and then I just played some nonsense that sounded like a cat running up and down on top of garbage cans. Old Chong smiled and applauded and then said, "Very good! But now you must learn to keep time!"

So that's how I discovered that Old Chong's eyes were too slow to keep up with the wrong notes I was playing. He went through the motions in half-time. To help me keep rhythm, he stood behind me, pushing down on my right shoulder for every beat. He balanced pennies on top of my wrists so I would keep them still as I slowly played scales and arpeggios. He had me curve my hand around an apple and keep that shape when playing chords. He marched stiffly to show me how to make each finger dance up and down, staccato like an obedient little soldier.

He taught me all these things, and that was how I also learned I could be lazy and get away with mistakes, lots of mistakes. If I hit the wrong notes because I hadn't practiced enough, I never corrected myself. I just kept playing in rhythm. And Old Chong kept conducting his own private reverie.

So maybe I never really gave myself a fair chance. I did pick up the basics pretty quickly, and I might have become a good pianist at that young age. But I was so determined not to try, not to be anybody

---

4. **Beethoven:** Ludwig von Beethoven (1770–1827), German composer who became deaf and unable to hear his own compositions.

different that I learned to play only the most ear-splitting preludes, the most discordant[5] hymns.

Over the next year, I practiced like this, dutifully in my own way. And then one day I heard my mother and her friend Lindo Jong both talking in a loud bragging tone of voice so others could hear. It was after church, and I was leaning against the brick wall wearing a dress with stiff white petticoats. Auntie Lindo's daughter, Waverly, who was about my age, was standing farther down the wall about five feet away. We had grown up together and shared all the closeness of two sisters squabbling over crayons and dolls. In other words, for the most part, we hated each other. I thought she was snotty. Waverly Jong had gained a certain amount of fame as "Chinatown's Littlest Chinese Chess Champion."

"She bring home too many trophy," lamented Auntie Lindo that Sunday. "All day she play chess. All day I have no time to do nothing but dust off her winnings." She threw a scolding look at Waverly, who pretended not to see her.

"You lucky you don't have this problem" said Auntie Lindo with a sigh to my mother

And my mother squared her shoulders and bragged: "Our problem worser than yours. If we ask Jing-mei wash dish, she hear nothing but music. It's like you can't stop this natural talent."

And right then, I was determined to put a stop to her foolish pride.

A few weeks later, Old Chong and my mother conspired to have me play in a talent show which would be held in the church hall. By then, my parents had saved up enough to buy me a secondhand piano, a black Wurlitzer spinet with a scarred bench. It was the showpiece of our living room.

For the talent show, I was to play a piece called "Pleading Child" from Shumann's[6] *Scenes from Childhood*. It was a simple, moody piece that sounded more difficult than it was. I was supposed to memorize the whole thing, playing the repeat parts twice to make the piece sound longer. But I dawdled over it, playing a few bars and then cheating,

---

5. **discordant:** not in harmony, harsh.
6. **Schumann:** Robert Schumann (1810–1856), German composer.

looking up to see what notes followed. I never really listened to what I was playing. I daydreamed about being somewhere else, about being someone else.

The part I liked to practice best was the fancy curtsy: right foot out, touch the rose on the carpet with a pointed foot, sweep to the side, left leg bends, look up and smile.

My parents invited all the couples from the Joy Luck Club[7] to witness my debut. Auntie Lindo and Uncle Tin were there. Waverly and her two older brothers had also come. The first two rows were filled with children both younger and older than I was. The littlest ones got to go first. They recited simple nursery rhymes, squawked out tunes on miniature violins, twirled Hula Hoops, pranced in pink ballet tutus, and when they bowed or curtsied, the audience would sigh in unison, "Awww," and then clap enthusiastically.

When my turn came, I was very confident. I remember my childish excitement. It was as if I knew, without a doubt, that the prodigy side of me really did exist. I had no fear whatsoever, no nervousness. I remember thinking to myself, This is it! This is it! I looked out over the audience, at my mother's blank face, my father's yawn, Auntie Lindo's stiff-lipped smile, Waverly's sulky expression. I had on a white dress layered with sheets of lace, and a pink bow in my Peter Pan haircut. As I sat down I envisioned people jumping to their feet and Ed Sullivan rushing up to introduce me to everyone on TV.

And so I started to play. It was so beautiful. I was so caught up in how lovely I looked that at first I didn't worry how I would sound. So it was a surprise to me when I hit the first wrong note and realized something didn't sound quite right. And then I hit another and another followed that. A chill started at the top of my head and began to trickle down. Yet I couldn't stop playing, as though my hands were bewitched. I kept thinking my fingers would adjust themselves back, like a train switching to the right track. I played this strange jumble through two repeats, the sour notes staying with me all the way to the end.

When I stood up, I discovered my legs were shaking. Maybe I had just been nervous and the audience, like Old Chong, had seen me go through the right motions and had not heard anything wrong at all.

---

7. **Joy Luck Club:** social group to which the family belongs.

I swept my right foot out, went down on my knee, looked up and smiled. The room was quiet, except for Old Chong, who was beaming and shouting, "Bravo! Bravo! Well done!" But then I saw my mother's face, her stricken face. The audience clapped weakly, and as I walked back to my chair, with my whole face quivering as I tried not to cry, I heard a little boy whisper loudly to his mother. "That was awful," and the mother whispered back, "Well, she certainly tried."

And now I realized how many people were in the audience, the whole world it seemed. I was aware of eyes burning into my back. I felt the shame of my mother and father as they sat stiffly throughout the rest of the show.

We could have escaped during intermission. Pride and some strange sense of honor must have anchored my parents to their chairs. And so we watched it all: the eighteen-year-old boy with a fake mustache who did a magic show and juggled flaming hoops while riding a unicycle. The girl with white makeup who sang from *Madama Butterfly* and got honorable mention. And the eleven-year-old boy who won first prize playing a tricky violin song that sounded like a busy bee.

After the show, the Hsus, the Jongs, and the St. Clairs from the Joy Luck Club came up to my mother and father.

"Lots of talented kids," Auntie Lindo said vaguely, smiling broadly.

"That was somethin' else," said my father, and I wondered if he was referring to me in humorous way, or whether he even remembered what I had done.

Waverly looked at me and shrugged her shoulders. "You aren't a genius like me," she said matter-of-factly. And if I hadn't felt so bad, I would have pulled her braids and punched her stomach.

But my mother's expression was what devastated me: a quiet, blank look that said she had lost everything. I felt the same way, and it seemed as if everybody were now coming up, like gawkers at the scene of an accident, to see what parts were actually missing. When we got on the bus to go home, my father was humming the busy-bee tune and my mother was silent. I kept thinking she wanted to wait until we got home before shouting at me. But when my father unlocked the door to our apartment, my mother walked in and then went to the back, into the bedroom. No accusations. No blame. And in a way, I felt disappointed. I had been waiting for her to start shouting, so I could shout back and cry and blame her for all my misery.

I assumed my talent show fiasco[8] meant I never had to play the piano again. But two days later, after school, my mother came out of the kitchen and saw me watching TV.

"Four clock," she reminded me as if it were any other day. I was stunned, as though she were asking me to go through the talent-show torture again. I wedged myself more tightly in front of the TV.

"Turn off the TV," she called from the kitchen five minutes later.

I didn't budge. And then I decided. I didn't have to do what my mother said anymore. I wasn't her slave. This wasn't China. I had listened to her before and look what happened. She was the stupid one.

She came out from the kitchen and stood in the arched entryway of the living room. "Four clock," she said once again, louder.

"I'm not going to play anymore," I said nonchalantly. "Why should I? I'm not a genius."

She walked over and stood in front of the TV. I saw her chest was heaving up and down in an angry way.

"No!" I said, and I now felt stronger, as if my true self had finally emerged. So this was what had been inside me all along.

"No! I won't!" I screamed.

She yanked me by the arm, pulled me off the floor, snapped off the TV. She was frighteningly strong, half pulling, half carrying me toward the piano as I kicked the throw rugs under my feet. She lifted me up and onto the hard bench. I was sobbing by now, looking at her bitterly. Her chest was heaving even more and her mouth was open, smiling crazily as if she were pleased. I was crying.

"You want me to be someone that I'm not!" I sobbed. "I'll never be the kind of daughter you want me to be!"

"Only two kinds of daughters," she shouted in Chinese. "Those who are obedient and those who follow their own mind! Only one kind of daughter can live in this house. Obedient daughter!"

"Then I wish I wasn't your daughter. I wish you weren't my mother," I shouted. As I said these things I got scared. It felt like worms and toads and slimy things were crawling out of my chest, but it also felt good, as if this awful side of me had surfaced at last.

"Too late change this," said my mother shrilly.

---

8. **fiasco:** complete failure.

And I could sense her anger rising to its breaking point. I wanted to see it spill over. And that's when I remembered the babies she had lost in China, the ones we never talked about. "Then I wish I'd never been born!" I shouted. "I wish I were dead! Like them."

It was as if I had said the magic words. Alakazam!—and her face went blank, her mouth closed, her arms went slack, and she backed out of the room, stunned, as if she were blowing away like a small brown leaf, thin, brittle, lifeless.

It was not the only disappointment my mother felt in me. In the years that followed, I failed her so many times, each time asserting my own will, my right to fall short of expectations. I didn't get straight As. I didn't become class president. I didn't get into Stanford.[9] I dropped out of college.

For unlike my mother, I did not believe I could be anything I wanted to be. I could only be me.

And for all those years, we never talked about the disaster at the recital or my terrible accusations afterward at the piano bench. All that remained unchecked, like a betrayal that was now unspeakable. So I never found a way to ask her why she had hoped for something so large that failure was inevitable.

And even worse, I never asked her what frightened me the most: Why had she given up hope?

For after our struggle at the piano, she never mentioned my playing again. The lessons stopped. The lid to the piano was closed, shutting out the dust, my misery, and her dreams.

So she surprised me. A few years ago, she offered to give me the piano, for my thirtieth birthday. I had not played in all those years. I saw the offer as a sign of forgiveness, a tremendous burden removed.

"Are you sure?" I asked shyly. "I mean, won't you and Dad miss it?"

"No, this is your piano," she said firmly. "Always your piano. You only one can play."

"Well, I probably can't play anymore,' I said. 'It's been years."

"You pick up fast," said my mother, as if she knew this was certain. "You have natural talent. You could been genius if you want to."

"No. I couldn't."

---

9. **Stanford:** university in California.

"You just not trying," said my mother. And she was neither angry nor sad. She said as if to announce a fact that could never be disproved. 'Take it," she said.

But I didn't at first. It was enough that she had offered it to me. And after that, every time I saw it in my parents' living room, standing in front of the bay windows, it made me feel proud, as if it were a shiny trophy I had won back.

Last week I sent a tuner over to my parents' apartment and had the piano reconditioned, for purely sentimental reasons. My mother had died a few months before and I had been getting things in order for my father, a little bit at a time. I put the jewelry in special silk pouches. The sweaters she had knitted in yellow, pink, bright orange—all the colors I hated—I put those in moth-proof boxes. I found some old Chinese silk dresses, the kind with little slits up the sides. I rubbed the old silk against my skin, then wrapped them in tissue and decided to take them home with me.

After I had the piano tuned, I opened the lid and touched the keys. It sounded even richer than I remembered. Really, it was a very good piano. Inside the bench were the same exercise notes with handwritten scales, the same secondhand music books with their covers held together with yellow tape.

I opened up the Schumann book to the dark little piece I had played at the recital. It was on the left-hand side of the page. "Pleading Child." It looked more difficult than I remembered. I played a few bars, surprised at how easily the notes came back to me.

And for the first time, or so it seemed, I noticed the piece on the right-hand side. It was called "Perfectly Contented." I tried to ply this one as well. It had a lighter melody but the same flowing rhythm and turned out to be quite easy. "Pleading Child" was shorter but slower; "Perfectly Contented" was longer, but faster. And after I played them both few times, I realized they were two halves of the same song.

Responding to the Story

1. Why do you think the narrator started performing "listlessly" and decided "I won't let her [the girl's mother] change me"?
2. What does the mother say is her reason for pushing her daughter to take piano lessons? Do you think the mother is right to do this? Explain your answer in at least one paragraph.
3. Why does the mother say to Auntie Lindo, "Our problem worser than yours. If we ask Jing-mei wash dish, she hear nothing but music. It's like you can't stop this natural talent"?
4. What are the final outrageous "magic" words the narrator says to her mother? Why does she choose these words?
5. How do "Pleading Child" and "Perfectly Contented" have a double meaning in the story? What does the last sentence of the story mean?

Exploring the Author's Craft

A **simile** compares two things that have common characteristics but are essentially unlike each other. The words *like* or *as* are usually used in similes. When Amy Tan describes Old Lady Chong, she writes, ". . .her fingers felt like a dead person's, like an old peach I once found in the back of the refrigerator; the skin just slid off the meat when I picked it up." What are the similarities when the two dissimilar things are compared?

Later the narrator describes playing "some nonsense that sounded like a cat running up and down on top of garbage cans." Recognizing that similes can make characters and events more vivid, try writing several.

1. Write a word portrait of a person you know. Limit yourself to two paragraphs, and in your description, create an appropriate simile.
2. Describe an action. Include a simile for comic effect as the narrator of "Two Kinds" did when she described her piano playing.

Writer's Workshop

Tell about an incident of your own growing up that deals with parental expectations and your reactions. Did you rise to your parents' hopes and perform beautifully, or did you resist? Use dialogue to create scenes that show the incident; don't just sum up the event.

Alternate Media Response

1. Write and perform a piece of music that captures the tension between mother and daughter in this story. There my be several sections to your creation, sections that parallel parts of the story.
2. Create and perform a dance that tells the story of mother and daughter in "Two Kinds."
3. With others in your class, dramatize a segment of this story and record it on videotape. Your scene should stand on its own without a need for viewers to read the short story.

Judith Ortiz Cofer

Judith Ortiz Cofer was born in Puerto Rico in 1952. She moved to Paterson, New Jersey, as a child, and traveled back and forth between Puerto Rico and Paterson while she was growing up. Cofer has published several collections of stories for young adult readers, including *An Island Like You* and *Help Wanted*. Her book *Silent Dancing: A Partial Remembrance of a Puerto Rican Childhood* was included in the New York Public Library's list of Best Books for the Teenager in 1991. Cofer teaches English and creative writing at the University of Georgia.

When Rita's parents send her to Puerto Rico for the summer to escape "bad influences," she encounters mala influencia *of another sort.*

Bad Influence

When I was sent to spend the summer at my grandparents' house in Puerto Rico, I knew it was going to be strange, I just didn't know how strange. My parents insisted that I was going to go either to a Catholic girls' retreat or to my mother's folks on the island. Some choice. It was either breakfast, lunch, and dinner with the Sisters of Charity in a convent somewhere in the woods—far from beautiful downtown Paterson, New Jersey, where I really wanted to spend my summer— or *arroz y habichuelas*[1] with the old people in the countryside of my parents' Island.

My whole life, I had seen my grandparents only once a year when we went down for a two-week vacation, and frankly, I spent all my time at

---

1. *arroz y habichuelas:* rice and beans. [Spanish]

the beach with my cousins and let the adults sit around drinking their hot *café con leche*[2] and sweating, gossiping about people I didn't know. This time there would be no cousins to hang around with—vacation time for the rest of the family was almost three months away. It was going to be a long hot summer.

Did I say hot? When I stepped off that airplane in San Juan, it was like I had opened an oven door. I was immediately drenched in sweat, and felt like I was breathing water. To make matters worse, there were Papá Juan, Mamá Ana, and about a dozen other people waiting to hug me and ask me a million questions in Spanish—not my best language. The others were *vecinos*, neighbors who had nothing better to do than come to the airport to pick me up in a caravan of cars. My friends from Central High would have died laughing if they had seen the women with their fans going back and forth across their shiny faces fighting over who was going to take my bags, and who was going to sit next to whom in the cars for the fifteen-minute drive home. Someone put a chubby brown baby on my lap, and even though I tried to ignore her, she curled up around me like a koala bear and went to sleep. I felt her little chest going up and down and I made my breath match hers. I sat in the back of Papá Juan's *un*-air-conditioned *sub*compact in between Doña This and Doña That, practicing Zen. I had been reading about it in a magazine on the airplane, about how to lower your blood pressure by concentrating on your breathing, so I decided to give it a try. My grandmother turned around with a worried look on her face and said, "Rita, do you have asthma? Your mother didn't tell me."

Before I could say anything, everybody in the car started talking at once, telling asthma stories. I continued to take deep breaths, but it didn't help. By the time we got to Mamá Ana's house, I had a pounding headache. I excused myself from my welcoming committee, handed the damp baby (she was really cute) over to her grandmother, and went to lie down in the room where Papá Juan had put my bags.

Of course, there was no AC. The window was thrown wide open, and right outside, perched on a fence separating our house from the neighbors' by about six inches, there was a red rooster. When I looked at him, he started screeching at the top of his lungs. I closed the window,

---

2. *café con leche:* coffee with milk. [Spanish]

but I could still hear him crowing; then someone turned on a radio, *loud*. I put a pillow over my head and decided to commit suicide by sweating to death. I must have dozed off, because when I opened my eyes, I saw my grandfather sitting on a chair outside my window, which had been opened again. He was stroking the rooster's feathers and seemed to be whispering something in his ear. He finally noticed me sitting in a daze on the edge of my four-poster bed, which was about ten feet off the ground.

"You were dreaming about your boyfriend," he said to me. "It was not a pleasant dream. No, I don't think it was *muy bueno.*"[3]

Great. My mother hadn't told me that her father had gone senile. But I *had* been dreaming about Johnny Ruiz, one of the reasons I had been sent away for the summer. Just a coincidence, I decided. But what about privacy? Had I or had I not closed the window in my room?

"Papá," I said assertively, "I think we need to talk."

"There is no need to talk when you can see into people's hearts," he said, setting the rooster on my window ledge. "This is Ramón. He is a good rooster and makes the hens happy and productive, but Ramón has a little problem that you will soon notice. He cannot tell time very accurately. To him, day is night and night is day. It is all the same to him, and when the spirit moves him, he sings. This is not a bad thing in itself, *entiendes?*[4] But it sometimes annoys people. *Entonces,*[5] I have to come and calm him down."

I could not believe what I was hearing. It was like I was in a *Star Trek* rerun where reality is being controlled by an alien, and you don't know why weird things are happening all around you until the end of the show.

Ramón jumped into my room and up on my bed, where he spread his wings and crowed like a madman.

"He is welcoming you to Puerto Rico," my grandfather said. I decided to go sit in the living room.

"I have prepared you a special tea for your asthma." Mamá Ana came in carrying a cup of some foul-smelling green stuff.

---

3. *muy bueno:* very good. [Spanish]
4. *entiendes:* you understand? [Spanish]
5. *Entonces:* then. [Spanish]

"I don't have asthma," I tried to explain. But she had already set the cup in my hands and was on her way to the TV.

"My *telenovela*[6] comes on at this hour," she announced.

Mamá Ana turned the volume way up as the theme music came on, with violins wailing like cats mating. I had always suspected that all my Puerto Rican relatives were a little bit deaf. She sat in a rocking chair right next to the sofa where I was lying down. I was still feeling like a wet noodle from the heat.

"Drink your *guarapo*[7] while it's still hot," she insisted, her eyes glued to the TV screen, where a girl was crying about something.

"*Pobrecita,*"[8] my grandmother said sadly, "her miserable husband left her without a penny, and she's got three little children and one on the way."

"Oh, God," I groaned. It was really going to be *The Twilight Zone* around here. Neither one of the old guys could tell the difference between fantasy and reality—Papá with his dream-reading and Mamá with her telenovelas. I had to call my mother and tell her that I had changed my mind about the convent.

I was going to have to locate a telephone first, though—AT&T had not yet sold my grandparents on the concept of high-tech communications. Letters were still good enough for them, and a telegram when someone died. The nearest phone was at the house of a neighbor, a nice fat woman who watched you while you talked. I had tried calling a friend last summer from her house. There had been a conversation going on in the same room where I was using the phone, a running commentary on what I was saying in English as understood by her granddaughter. They had both thought that eavesdropping on me was a good way to practice their English. My mother had explained that it was not malicious. It was just that people on the Island did not see as much need for privacy as people who lived on the mainland. "Puerto Ricans are friendlier. Keeping secrets among friends is considered offensive," she had told me.

My grandmother explained the suffering woman's problems in the telenovela. She'd had to get married because the man she loved was a

---

6. *telenovela:* soap opera. [Spanish]
7. *guarapo:* drink made of fermented sugar cane. [Spanish]
8. *Pobrecita:* poor little thing. [Spanish]

villain who had forced her to prove her love for him. *"Tú sabes como.*
You know how."* Then he had kept her practically a prisoner, isolated
from her own *familia. Ay, bendito,*[9] my grandmother exclaimed as the
evil husband came home and started demanding food on the table and a
fresh suit of clothes. He was going out, he said, with *los muchachos. Pero
no.*[10] My grandmother knew better than that. He had another woman.
She was sure of it. She spoke to the crying woman on the TV: *"Mira,"*[11]
she advised her, "open your eyes and see what is going on. For the sake
of your children. Leave this man. Go back home to your *mamá.* She's a
good woman, although you have hurt her, and she is ill. Perhaps with
cancer. But she will take you and the children back."

"Ohhh," I moaned.

"Sit up and drink your tea, Rita. If you're not better by tomorrow, I'll
have to take you to my *comadre.*[12] She makes the best herbal laxatives
on the island. People come from all over to buy them—because what
ails most people is a clogged system. You clean it out like a pipe,
entiendes? You flush it out and then you feel good again."

"I'm going to bed," I announced, even though it was only nine—hours
before my usual bedtime. I could hear Ramón crowing from the
direction of my bedroom.

"It's a good idea to get some rest tonight, *hija.*[13] Tomorrow Juan has
to do a job out by the beach, a woman whose daughter won't eat or get
out of bed. They think it is a spiritual matter. You and I will go with
him. I have a craving for crab meat, and we can pick some up."

"Pick some up?"

"*Sí,* when the crabs crawl out of their holes and into our traps.
We'll take some pots and boil them on the beach. They'll be
sabrosos."[14]

"I'm going to bed now," I repeated like a zombie. I took a running
start from the door and jumped on the bed with all my clothes on.
Outside my window, Ramón crowed; the neighbor woman called out,

---

9. **bendito:** foolish person. [Spanish]
10. **los muchachos. Pero no:** the boys. But no. [Spanish]
11. **Mira:** look. [Spanish]
12. **comadre:** a close friend, like a godmother, who has your best interests at heart. [Spanish]
13. **hija:** daughter. [Spanish]
14. **sabrosos:** tasty. [Spanish]

"Ana, Ana, do you think she'll leave him?" while my grandmother yelled back, "No. *Pienso que no.*[15] She's a fool for love, that one is."

I shut my eyes and tried to fly back to my room at home. When I had my own telephone, I could sometimes sneak a call to Johnny late at night. He had basketball practice every afternoon, so we couldn't talk earlier. I was desperate to be with him. He was on the varsity team at Eastside High and a very popular guy. That's how we met: at a game. I had gone with my friend Meli from Central because her boyfriend played for Eastside, too. He was an Anglo, though. Actually, he was Italian but looked Puerto Rican. Neither of the guys was exactly into meeting parents, and our folks didn't let us go out with anybody whose total ancestry they didn't know, so Meli and I had to sneak out and meet them after games.

Dating is not a concept adults in our barrio really "get." It's supposed to be that a girl meets a guy from the neighborhood, and their parents went to school together, and everybody knows everybody's business. But Meli and I were doing all right until Joey and Johnny asked us to spend the night in Joey's house. The Molieris had gone out of town and we would have the place to ourselves. Meli and I talked about it constantly for days, until we came up with a plan. It was risky, but we thought we could get away with it. We each said we were spending the night at the other's house. We'd done it a lot of times before, and our mothers never checked on us. They just told us to call if anything went wrong. Well, it turned out Meli's mom got a case of heartburn that she thought was a heart attack, and her husband called our house. She almost did have one for real when she found out Meli wasn't there. They called the cops, and woke up everybody they thought we knew. When Meli's little sister cracked under pressure and mentioned Joey Molieri, all four of them drove over to West Paterson at 2:00 A.M. and pounded on the door like crazy people. The guys thought it was a drug bust. But I knew, and when I looked at Meli and saw the look of terror on her face, I knew she knew what we were in for.

We were put under house arrest after that, not even allowed to make phone calls, which I think is against the law. Anyway, it was a mess. That's when I was given the two choices for my summer. And naturally

---

15. *Pienso que no:* I don't think so. [Spanish]

I picked the winner—spending three months with two batty old people and one demented rooster.

The worst part is that I didn't deserve it. My mother interrogated me about what had happened between me and *that boy*, as she called him. Nothing. I admit that I was thinking about it. Johnny had told me that he liked me and wanted to take me out, but he usually dated older girls and he expected them to have sex with him. Apparently, he and Joey had practiced their speeches together, because Meli and I compared notes in the bathroom at one point, and she had heard the same thing from him.

But our parents had descended on us while we were still discussing it. Would I do it? To have a boyfriend like Johnny Ruiz? He can go out with any girl, white, black, or Puerto Rican. But he says I'm mature for almost fifteen. After the mess, I snuck a call to him one night when my mother had forgotten to unplug the phone and lock it up like she'd been doing whenever she had to leave me alone in the apartment. Johnny said he thinks my parents are nuts, but he's willing to give me another chance when I come back in the fall.

"We'll be getting up real early tomorrow." My grandmother was at my door. Barged in without knocking, of course. "We'll be up with the chickens, so we can catch the crabs when the sun brings them out. *Está bien?*"[16] Then she came to sit on my bed, which took some doing, since it was almost as tall as she.

"I am glad that you are here, *mi niña.*"[17] She grabbed my head and kissed me hard on my cheek. She smelled like coffee with boiled milk and sugar, which the natives drink by the gallon in spite of the heat. I was thinking that my grandmother didn't remember that I was almost fifteen years old and I would have to remind her.

But then she got serious and said to me, "I was your age when I met Juan. I married him a year later and started having babies. They're scattered all over *los Estados Unidos*[18] now. Did I ever tell you that I wanted to be a professional dancer? At your age I was winning contests

---

16. *Está bien:* all right? [Spanish]
17. *mi niña:* my little girl. [Spanish]
18. *los Estados Unidos:* the United States. [Spanish]

and traveling with a mambo band. Do you dance, Rita? You should, *sabes?*[19] It's hard to be unhappy when your feet are moving to music."

I was more than a little surprised by what Mamá Ana said about wanting to be a dancer and marrying at fifteen, and wouldn't have minded hearing more, but then Papá Juan came into my room too. I guessed it was going to be a party, so I sat up and turned on the light.

"Where is my bottle of holy water, Ana?" he asked.

"On the altar in our room, *señor,*" she replied, "where it always is."

Of course, I thought, the holy water was on the altar, where everybody keeps their holy water. I must have made a funny noise, because both of them turned their eyes to me, looking very concerned.

"Is it that asthma again, Rita?" My grandmother felt my forehead. "I noticed you didn't finish your tea. I'll go make you some more as soon as I help your *abuelo*[20] find his things for tomorrow."

"I'm not sick. Please. Just a little tired," I said firmly, hoping to get my message across. But I had to know. "What is it he's going to do tomorrow, exorcise[21] demons out of somebody, or what?"

They looked at each other then as if I was crazy.

"You explain it to her, Ana," he said. "I have to prepare myself for this *trabajo.*"[22]

My grandmother came back to the bed, climbed up on it, and began telling me how Papá was a medium, a spiritist. He had special gifts, *facultades,* which he had discovered as a young man, that allowed him to see into people's hearts and minds through prayers and in dreams.

"Does he sacrifice chickens and goats?" I had heard about these voodoo priests who went into trances and poured blood and feathers all over everybody in secret ceremonies. There was a black man from Haiti in our neighborhood who people said could even call back the dead and make them his zombie slaves. There was always a dare on to go to his door on some excuse and try to see what was in his basement apartment, but nobody I knew had ever done it. What had my own mother sent me into? I would probably be sent back to Paterson as one of the walking dead.

---

19. *sabes:* you know? [Spanish]
20. *abuelo:* grandfather. [Spanish]
21. **exorcise:** hold a solemn religious ceremony to drive evil spirits out of a person.
22. *trabajo:* work. [Spanish]

"No, *Dios mío*, no!" Mamá Ana shouted, and crossed herself and kissed the cross on her neck chain. "Your grandfather works with God and His saints, not with Satan!"

"Excuse *me*," I said, thinking that I really should have been given an instruction manual before being sent here on my own.

"Tomorrow you will see how Juan helps people. This *muchacha*[23] that he has been summoned to work on has stopped eating. She does not want to speak to her mother, who is the one who called us. Your grandfather will see what is making her spirit sick."

"Why don't they take her to a . . ." I didn't know the word for shrink in Spanish, so I just said, "to a doctor for crazy people."

"Because not everyone who is sad or troubled is crazy. If it is their brain that is sick, that is one thing, but if it is their soul that is in pain— then Juan can sometimes help. He can contact the guides, that is, spirits who are concerned about the ailing person, and they can sometimes show him what needs to be done. *¿Entiendes?*"

"Uh-huh," I said.

She planted another smack on my face and left to help her husband pack his Ghostbuster equipment. I finally fell asleep thinking about Johnny and what it would be like to be his girlfriend.

"Getting up with the chickens" meant that both my grandparents were up and talking at the top of their lungs by about four in the morning. I put my head under the sheet and hoped that my presence in their house had slipped their minds. No luck. Mamá Ana came into my room, turned on the overhead light, and pulled down the sheet. It had been years since my own parents had dared to barge into my bedroom. I would have been furious, except I was so sleepy I couldn't build up to it, so I just curled up and decided it was time to use certain things to my advantage.

"Ohhh . . ." I moaned and gasped for air.

"Hija, what is wrong?" Mamá sounded so worried that I almost gave up my little plan.

"It's my asthma, Mamá," I said in a weak voice. "I guess all the excitement is making it act up. I'll just take my medicine and stay in bed today."

---

23. *muchacha:* girl. [Spanish]

"*Positivamente no!*"[24] she said, putting a hand that smelled of mint from her garden on my forehead. "I will stay with you and have my comadre come over. She will prepare you a tea that will clear your system like—"

"Like a dogged sewer pipe." I completed the sentence for her. "No, I'll go with you. I'm feeling better now."

"Are you sure, Rita? You are more important to me than any poor girl sick in her soul. And I don't need to eat crab, either. Once in a while I get these *antojos*, you know, whims, like a pregnant woman, ha, ha. But they pass."

Somehow we got out of the house before the sun came up and sandwiched ourselves into the subcompact, whose muffler must have woken up half the island. Why doesn't anyone ever mention noise pollution around here? was my last thought before I fell asleep crunched up in the backseat.

When I opened my eyes, I was blinded by the glare of the sun coming through the car windows; and when my eyeballs came back into their sockets, I saw that we had pulled up at the side of a house right on the beach. This was no ordinary house. It looked like a huge pink-and-white birthday cake. No joke—it was painted baby pink with white trim and a white roof. It had a terrace that went all the way around it, so that it really did look like a layer cake. If I could afford a house like that, I would paint it a more serious color. Like purple. But around here, everyone is crazy about pastels: lime green, baby pink and blue— nursery school colors.

The ocean was incredible, though. It was just a few yards away and it looked unreal. The water was turquoise in some places and dark blue, almost black, in others—I guessed those were the deep spots. I had been left alone in the car, so I looked around to see if the old people were anywhere in sight. I saw my grandmother first, off on the far left side of the beach where it started to curve, up to her knees in water, dragging something by a rope. Catching crabs, I guessed. I needed to stretch, so I walked over to where she was. Although the sun was a little white ball in the sky, it wasn't unbearably hot yet. In fact, with the breeze blowing, it was almost perfect. I wondered if I could get them to leave me here.

---

24. *Positivamente no:* Absolutely not! [Spanish]

Then I remembered the "job" my grandfather had come to do. I glanced up at the top layer of the cake, where I thought the bedroom would be—to see if anything was flying out of the windows. Morning was a strange time for weird stuff, but no matter how hard I tried, I couldn't feel down about anything right then. It was so sunny, and the whole beach was empty except for one old lady out there violating the civil rights of sea creatures, and me.

"Mira, mira!" Mamá Ana yelled, pulling a cagelike box out of the water. Claws stuck through the slats, snapping like scissors. She looked very proud, so even though I didn't approve of what was going to happen to her prisoners, I said, "Wow, I'm impressed," or something stupid like that.

"They'll have to boil for a long time before we can sink our teeth into them," she said, a cold-blooded killer look in her eye, "but then we'll have a banquet, right here on the beach."

"I can't wait," I said, moving toward the nearest palm tree. The trees grow right next to the water here. It looked wild, like it must have when Columbus dropped in. If you didn't look at the pink house, you could imagine yourself on a deserted tropical island. I lay down on one of the big towels she had spread out, and soon she came over and sat down real close to me. She got her thermos out of a sack and two plastic cups. She poured us some café con leche, which I usually hate because it's like ultra-sweet milk with a little coffee added for color or something. Nobody here asks you if you want cream or sugar in your coffee: the coffee *is* 99 percent cream and sugar. Take it or leave it. But at that hour on that beach, it tasted just right.

"Where is Papá?" I was getting curious about what he was doing in the pink house, and about who lived there.

"He is having a session with the *señora* and her daughter. That poor niña is not doing very well. Pobrecita. Poor little thing. I saw her when I helped him bring his things in this morning. She is a skeleton. Only sixteen, and she has packed her bags for the other world."

"She's that sick? Maybe they ought to take her to the hospital."

"How is your asthma, *mi amor?*"[25] she said, apparently reminded of my own serious illness.

---

25. *mi amor:* my love. [Spanish]

"Great. My asthma is great." I poured myself another cup of coffee. "So why don't they get a doctor for this girl?" I was getting pretty good at keeping conversations more or less on track with at least one person. "What exactly are her symptoms?"

"There was a man there," she said, totally ignoring my question, "not her *papá*, a man with a look that said *mala influencia* all over it." She shook her head and made a *tsk, tsk* sound. This real-life telenovela was beginning to get interesting.

"You mean he's a bad influence on the girl?"

"It is hard to explain, hija. A mala influencia is something that some people who are sensitive to spiritual matters can feel when they go into a house. Juan and I both felt chilled in there." She nodded toward the pink house.

"Maybe they have air conditioning," I said.

"And the feeling of evil got stronger when *ese hombre*, that strange man, came into the room," she added.

"Who is he?"

"The mother's boyfriend."

"So what's going to happen now?"

"It depends on what Juan decides is wrong with this *casa*.[26] The mother is not very stable. She has money from a former husband, so it is not from physical need that these women suffer. La señora is fortunately a believer and that is good for her daughter."

"Why?"

"Because she may do what needs to be done, if not for herself, then for her child—when a mala influencia takes over a house, *pues,*[27] it affects everyone in it."

"Tell me some things that may happen, Mamá."

It was so strange that this rich woman had asked my grandfather to come solve her problems. I mean if things were going this crazy-wrong, someone should call a shrink, right? Here they got the local medicine man to make a house call.

"Well, Juan will interview each of the people under the mala influencia. Separately. So they don't get their stories tangled up, sabes? Then he will decide which spirits need to be contacted for help."

---

26. *casa:* house. [Spanish]
27. *pues:* well. [Spanish]

"Oh," I said, like it all sounded logical to me. Actually, I thought all Mamá had said was not too exciting for a supernatural event. Until she got to the part about contacting the spirits, that is.

"In most of these cases where a restless or bad spirit has settled over a house, it's just a matter of figuring out what it wants or needs. Then you have to help it to find its way to God by giving it a way out—giving it light. The home is purified of the bad influence, and peace returns."

We had a few minutes of quiet then, since she apparently thought she had made it all crystal clear to me, and I was trying to absorb some of the mumbo-jumbo I had just heard. But I got distracted looking at how the sunlight was sparkling off the water. I was feeling pretty good. Must be the caffeine kicking in, I thought.

"*Ven*"[28]—my grandmother pulled me up by the hand; for a pudgy old lady she was pretty strong—"we have to bring dinner in."

So for a while we dragged the crab traps out. She wouldn't let me touch the crabs, since I didn't know how to handle them. "Might bite your fingers off," she explained calmly. So I went for a long walk down the beach. It turned out to be part of an inlet, which was why the water was so still, almost no waves. And I actually found some shells. This was new to me, since the public beach my cousins and I went to was swept clean of trash and everything else, every morning. Sand was all that was left until it was covered by empty cans, bags, disposable diapers, and all the other things people bring for a day at the beach and leave behind as a little gift to Mother Nature. But this was different. How could that girl in the pink house be so unhappy when she could wake up to this every morning?

I sat down on a sea-washed rock that was so smooth and comfortable I could just lounge on it all day. I stared out as far as I could see, and I thought I saw something jump out of the water. Not just one, but two or three—dolphins! Just like at Sea World. They jumped out, made a sort of half circle in the air, then went back under. I couldn't believe it. I ran back to my grandmother, who was stirring a big black pot over a fire, looking like the witch cooking something tasty for Hansel and Gretel. Gasping for air, which made her frown—that old asthma again—I told her what I had seen. I didn't know the Spanish word for dolphin, so I said "Flipper."

---

28. *Ven:* come. [Spanish]

"Ah, *sí*, Fleeperr," she said, rolling that *r* forever like they do here, *"delfines."* She knew what I was talking about. "They like these waters, no fishermen, except for me, ha, ha." I avoided looking into the pot— strange sounds were coming from it.

"Wow," I said to myself. Dolphins. I couldn't wait to tell Meli. I had seen real wild dolphins.

Mamá Ana handed me a sandwich, and after I ate it, I fell asleep on the towel. I woke up when I heard Papá Juan's voice. I pretended to be still sleeping so I could listen in on an uncensored version of the weird stuff happening in the pink house. Mamá Ana had made a tent over our spot on the beach with four sticks and a blanket. She was working over the campfire, pouring things into the pot. I was getting hungry. Whatever she was cooking smelled great. Papá Juan was writing things in a notebook with a pencil that he kept wetting by putting it into his mouth. I was watching them from the corner of my eyes, not moving. It was Mamá who spoke first.

"It's that man, *verdad?*"[29] She spoke very softly. I guess she didn't want to wake me up. I had to really strain to hear.

"I have told the mother that her house needs a spiritual cleansing. The mala influencia has settled over the young girl, but the evil has spread over everything. It is a very cold house."

"I felt it too," Mamá said, making the sign of the cross over her face and chest.

"It is the man who is the agent. He has brought bad ways with him. He has frightened the girl. She will not tell me how."

"I saw a bruise on her arm."

"*Sí.*" My grandfather put his notebook down and seemed to go into a trance or something. He closed his eyes and let his head drop. His lips were moving. I watched Mamá to see what she would do, but she continued cooking like nothing unusual was happening. Then he sort of shook his head like he was just trying to wake up, and went back to writing in his notebook.

"Have you decided what to do?" Mamá came to sit next to him and peeked over his shoulder at the notebook. She nodded, agreeing with whatever it was.

---

29. *verdad:* isn't that true? [Spanish]

"I will tell the mother that she must not allow this man into the house anymore. Then I will prepare the herbs for her so that next Tuesday and Friday she can clean the house and fumigate."[30]

"What about the niña?" Mamá asked. They had their heads together like two doctors discussing a patient.

"I will treat her with some of our comadre's tea. I will also tell her that the only way for us to get rid of the evil in the house is with her help. She will have to work with her mother."

"The woman will not want to throw the man out."

"You will have to help me convince her of the consequences if she doesn't, Ana. She is a believer. And although she is misguided, she loves her daughter."

"We have to bring light into this home, Juan."

"The girl saw Rita from her window. She asked who she was," my grandfather said. "Let us send our niña to invite Angela for dinner."

"Good idea," said Mamá.

Great, I thought, great idea. Send me over to get the girl from *The Exorcist*—good way to ruin my day at the beach.

"Rita! Hija!" Mamá called out loudly. "Time to wake up!"

The house was pale pink on the inside too. The woman who answered my knock was a surprise. She looked elegant in a white sundress. She also looked familiar to me. I guess I must have stared because she said, "I'm Maribel Hernández Jones," like I should recognize the name. Seeing that I didn't, she added, "You may know me from TV. I do toothpaste commercials." That was it. Her commercial had come on about five times during the telenovela.

"I'm Rita. My grandmother wants to know if Angela would like to eat with us." The smile faded into a sad look, but she pointed to a closed door at the other end of the room. The place was like a dollhouse. All the furniture was white and looked like no one ever sat on it.

The girl must have heard me or else been spying from her window, because I'd barely gotten to her door when she flew out, grabbing my hand. We were out of the house before I ever got a good look at her. Shorter than I was by about four inches, she was very thin. She had long

---

30. **fumigate:** disinfect or purify, often with smoke or fumes.

black hair and beautiful, sort of bronze skin. Still, she looked kind of pale too, like you do when you've been sick for a while.

"I'm sorry," she said in English, which surprised me, "I just had to get out of there. I'm Angela." We shook hands.

"You speak English," I said, noticing the huge ring on her thin finger. She was also wearing a gold bracelet. This was a rich girl.

"My stepfather was an American," she said. "We spent a lot of time with him in New York before he died."

"Oh," I said, thinking, I see where the money came from now.

My grandmother had already set out plates and bowls for the crab stew she had made. I ate like a fiend. I was starved. The beach always makes me extra hungry, even when I don't swim. Angela ate a few spoonfuls and put the bowl down. My grandmother put the bowl back in her hands. "I spent all day catching the crabs and cooking them, *señorita*. Do me the honor of eating a little more." She was outrageous. She actually watched Angela as the poor kid forced it all down—you could tell it was an effort. Here is the secret weapon against anorexia, I thought: my grandmother.

It wasn't long before the mother came out to get her daughter. "We have to talk," she said. Mamá and Papá nodded. It was part of the plan, I could see that. I was a little disappointed; I had really been looking forward to getting a little more information directly from the source. Angela looked at me as if she wanted to stay longer too. Then Mamá Ana spoke up.

"In two weeks we are having a *quinceañera*[31] party for Rita. I would like Angela to come."

Angela smiled and kissed her on both cheeks. Mamá hugged her like she did me, that is, so hard that you can't breathe. It didn't seem to take long for people to get familiar with each other around here.

I had thought that the party had just been something Mamá had made up at the beach, but it turned out that she meant it. Although the next two weeks were mainly the usual routines of eating too much, drinking café, watching telenovelas, and accompanying Papá to two more jobs—neither one as interesting as Angela's case: one turned out to be a simple problem of envy between two sisters, easily handled with

---

31. *quinceañera:* formal party in honor of a girl's fifteenth birthday. [Spanish]

special charms Papá carved for them himself; and the other was a cheating husband who was told that he would be haunted forever by the restless spirit of a man shot by his wife if he did not give up womanizing—Mamá and I spent some time shopping for my dress, with money Mamá had had my mother send us, and for food and decorations for the house. It all seemed pretty childish, but on the island they make a big deal of a girl's turning fifteen. I wondered who she was going to invite besides Angela, since I didn't know anyone except old relatives like her. No problem, parties are for everybody, she explained, old relatives, neighbors, kids. Apparently, I was just the excuse to have a blowout.

I chose a blue satin cocktail dress my mother would never have let me buy. Mamá thought it was *muy bonito*, very pretty, even if we had to stuff a little toilet paper in the bra to fill out the bodice.

The party started at noon on a Saturday. There was a ton of food set out on tables in the backyard under a mango tree, and there were Japanese lanterns hanging from the branches, which we would light when it got dark, and a portable record player—about fifty years old—ready to blast out salsa music. I had a few of my tapes of *good* music with me for my Walkman, but there was no player or stereo anywhere around. People piled into the house and hugged and kissed me. I was starting to get a headache when a long white limousine pulled up to the front of our house. Angela and her mother stepped out of it. I looked to see if the "mala influencia" man was with them, but the car drove away. A chauffeur too. Wow. Everyone had stopped talking when Mamá's big-mouthed neighbor shouted, "Oh, my God, it's Maribel Hernández!" And people crowded around her before she could step inside. I saw Angela trying politely to come through several large sweaty women, and I reached for her hand and led her to my room. I had to shoo Ramón off my bed, where he was getting ready to crow, before we sat down. Angela laughed at the crazy rooster, and I saw that she looked different. She didn't have that pale greenish color under her skin. She was still skinny, but she looked healthier.

She winked at me and said, "It worked."

"What worked?" I had no idea what she was talking about.

Outside my door the noise level was climbing. People were pouring out into the yard, which was right outside my window. I saw Mamá Ana dancing up a storm in the middle of a circle of people. When she had taken her bows, she started making her way through the crowd of short people like a small tank aiming right for my room. Papá Juan was taking Ramón around, apparently introducing him to the guests, or trying to keep him from getting trampled to death. I had to give him credit; he didn't seem to care if he made a fool of himself. But most people in town seemed to think he was pretty great. I watched him looking at each guest with his kind brown eyes, and I asked myself whether he really could see inside their heads and their hearts.

"Your grandfather's cure. *Mami* and I cleaned our house from top to bottom. No more bad influences left in it; the first thing we've done together in months. And best of all, she threw him out."

"Rita, Rita!" It was my grandmother, yelling out for me over the noise of people, scratchy records, and a hysterical rooster. "It's time to sing 'Feliz Cumpleaños'!"[32] She looked great in her bright red party dress and seemed to be having a blast. She had this talent for turning every day into a sort of party. I had to laugh.

"I can't believe this," I said to Angela, falling back on the bed and putting my face under a pillow. She giggled and pulled the pillow away from me.

"You'll get used to it," she said. "I wish I had a grandmother like yours. Both of mine are dead."

"You can borrow mine," I offered.

"Come on," she said, and we both jumped off the bed, with me nearly breaking my neck on my new high heels.

The party was fun with Angela there. Even her mother seemed to be enjoying herself, although people continuously bugged her for autographs. I even saw somebody handing her a magazine with a toothpaste ad for her to sign. She just kept smiling and smiling.

They stayed until after midnight, when the last person went home. Papá was snoring in his rocking chair, and Mamá and Angela's mother were cleaning the kitchen. Angela and I talked in my room. We agreed to get together as much as possible until I had to go back home to Paterson. Even then, she said, she would come visit me. She had money to travel.

I spent a lot of time at the pink house over the next weeks. I even began liking the color. I told Angela about Johnny Ruiz even though I

---

32. **Feliz Cumpleaños:** happy birthday. [Spanish]

had not really thought about him, not as much anyway, in the last month. She said that he sounded like a troubled boy. A mala influencia? I suggested. We both laughed at the thought of Johnny's being followed around by a restless ghost. The whole thing with him and Joey Molieri, and the mess with Meli's and my parents, began to seem like a movie I had seen a long time ago. And one day, while we were walking down the beach after dinner, she told me about how hard her life had been, moving from place to place while her mother was trying to make it on TV. She had spent a lot of time with baby-sitters, especially after her father had left them, when Angela was just five.

"Where is he now?" I asked her.

"He lives in New York with his new family. I plan to go see him when I visit you. My mother only lets him come down once a year. But we've been talking about it, and she thinks I can take care of myself now. See, he's not a bad man, but sometimes he drinks too much. That's what started the trouble between them."

Then she told me about Mr. Jones, a rich guy who owned hotels. He had left them the pink house and a lot of money when he died in a small-plane crash a year ago. Angela said that he had been a nice guy too, although not too interested in her, or in much else besides making money. But the man whom she really hated was the boyfriend who had recently been chased out by an "evil spirit." Angela laughed when she said that, but got serious when she told me it had been a really awful time. That's when her mother had called in Don Juan, as she called Papá, for a consultation.

"Your mother seems like a smart person," I said. "Does she really believe in all this ghost-evil spirit-haunted house stuff?"

"She's not the only one, Rita. Don't you see it took someone with special powers to drive out the bad influence in my house?" She looked at me in a really serious way for a minute; then she started giggling.

"Come on!" She started running back to the house. "It's time for the telenovela and my mother's new commercial!"

My family arrived in early August. We went to pick them up in three cars, with two more following for the welcoming committee. My mother kept looking at me at the airport. She acted like she was a little scared of coming too close. She had heard only from her mother about me—since I had forgotten to write home—and she must have thought

Mamá Ana was probably exaggerating when she wrote that I was having a great time and had not had an asthma attack in weeks. They had never gotten it straight on the asthma, which my mother figured was one of my tricks. She knew me a little. Finally I gave her a break and came over and hugged her.

"You are so tanned, mi amor. Have you been to the beach a lot?"

I didn't want her to think it had all been a vacation, so I said, "A few times. Have you seen Meli?" She looked at me with a kind of sad look on her face, scaring me. I hadn't written to Meli either, so I didn't know whether she was dead, or what.

"You don't know? She went on that retreat with the sisters, you know. It turns out that she liked it. So she won't be at Central High with you next year. I'm sorry, hija. Meli is going to start school at St. Mary's in the fall."

I almost burst out laughing. Our parents had really come up with some awful punishments for Meli and me. I'd had one of the best summers of my life with Angela, and I was even really getting to know my grandparents—the Ghostbusting magnificent duo. I had been taking medium lessons from them lately, and had learned a few tricks, like how to look really closely at people and see whether something was bothering them. I saw in my mother's eyes that she was scared I might hate her for sending me away. And she should have been, so I let her suffer a little. But then I squeezed in next to her in Papá's toy car and held her hand while Mamá Ana told her all the intimate details about me, including the fact that she had cured my asthma with a special tea she had made me drink. I looked at my mother and winked. She gave me a loud kiss on my cheek that made my ears ring. I know now where she picked up that bad habit. Since I already knew everything Mamá Ana was going to tell my mother, being a mind reader myself now, I settled back to try to figure out how Meli and I were going to get together in September. I had heard St. Mary's basketball team had some of the best-looking guys.

Responding to the Story

1. What are the two worlds that are a part of Rita's life as the summer begins? In which one does Rita feel more comfortable? Why?
2. How do Rita's views of her family in Puerto Rico change as the summer progresses? Give specific examples.
3. By the time the story ends, where does Rita best "fit in"—at home in Paterson, New Jersey, or in Puerto Rico? Explain your answer.
4. To whom or what do you think the title of this story applies?

Exploring the Author's Craft

Every writer must use specific, **concrete details** to bring a situation alive. List six details that Judith Ortiz Cofer includes in this story to portray the world that Rita visits in Puerto Rico.

Writer's Workshop

From the biography of author Judith Ortiz Cofer it is clear that she really knows the world of Puerto Rico that she writes about in this story. Think of a world you know very well; it may be the society you live in right now. Write an essay or story that brings that world alive. Include as many concrete details as you can, just as Judith Ortiz Cofer did in "Bad Influence."

Alternate Media Response

Write a script for a video of any one scene of this story. Then videotape it, using students in your class as the performers. Have others in the class evaluate the presentation: do they think that your video accurately captures the story? Why or why not?

Shirley Jackson

Shirley Jackson (1919–1965) is known for her stories and novels that contain bizarre situations and terrifying characters, but she also wrote about life in a family of four children.

When she was fourteen, she moved with her family from San Francisco to New York. After a year at the University of Rochester, she spent a year at home writing. She then attended Syracuse University, where she met the literary critic Stanley Edgar Hyman. They were married in 1940 and moved to New York City. Her amusing story, "My Life with R. H. Macy," was based on a job she held there.

In 1945, they moved to North Bennington, Vermont, and in 1948 *The Road Through the Wall* was published and *The New Yorker* printed "The Lottery," Jackson's most famous story. It provoked shock, outrage, and praise. It was included in the 1949 collection of *The O. Henry Award* stories and remains a classic example of Jackson's' ability to turn seemingly ordinary events into shocking tales.

Her novel *Hangsaman* appeared in 1951, followed by the autobiographical *Life Among the Savages* (1953) and *Raising Demons* (1957). *The Sundial* was published in 1958, *The Haunting of Hill House* in 1959, and *We Have Always Lived in the Castle* in 1962. Three collections of her works appeared after her death: *The Magic of Shirley Jackson* (1966), *Come Along with Me* (1968), and *Just An Ordinary Day* (1997).

"I always knew that I was going to run away sooner or later."

Louisa, Please Come Home

Louisa," my mother's voice came over the radio; it frightened me badly for a minute, "Louisa," she said, "please come home. It's been three long long years since we saw you last; Louisa, I promise you that everything will be all right. We all miss you so. We want you back again. Louisa, please come home."

Once a year. On the anniversary of the day I ran away. Each time I heard it I was frightened again, because between one year and the next I would forget what my mother's voice sounded like, so soft and yet strange with that pleading note. I listened every year. I read the stories in the newspapers—"Louisa Tether vanished one year ago"—or two years ago, or three; I used to wait for the twentieth of June as though it were my birthday. I kept all the clippings at first, but secretly; with my picture on all the front pages I would have looked kind of strange if anyone had seen me cutting it out. Chandler, where I was hiding, was close enough to my old home so that the papers made a big fuss about all of it, but of course the reason I picked Chandler in the first place was because it was a big enough city for me to hide in.

I didn't just up and leave on the spur of the moment, you know. I always knew that I was going to run away sooner or later, and I had made plans ahead of time, for whenever I decided to go. Everything had to go right the first time, because they don't usually give you a second chance on that kind of thing and anyway if it had gone wrong I would have looked like an awful fool, and my sister Carol was never one for letting people forget it when they made fools of themselves. I admit I planned it for the day before Carol's wedding on purpose, and for a long time afterward I used to try and imagine Carol's face when she finally realized that my running away was going to leave her one bridesmaid short. The papers said that the wedding went ahead as scheduled, though, and Carol told one newspaper reporter that her sister Louisa would have wanted it that way; "She would never have meant to spoil my wedding," Carol said, knowing perfectly well that that would be exactly what I'd meant. I'm pretty sure that the first thing Carol did when they knew I was missing was go and count the wedding presents to see what I'd taken with me.

Anyway, Carol's wedding may have been fouled up, but *my* plans went fine—better, as a matter of fact, than I had ever expected.

Everyone was hurrying around the house putting up flowers and asking each other if the wedding gown had been delivered, and opening up cases of champagne and wondering what they were going to do if it rained and they couldn't use the garden, and I just closed the front door behind me and started off. There was only one bad minute when Paul saw me; Paul has always lived next door and Carol hates him worse than she does me. My mother always used to say that every time I did something to make my family ashamed of me Paul was sure to be in it somewhere. For a long time they thought he had something to do with my running away, even though he told over and over again how hard I tried to duck away from him that afternoon when he met me going down the driveway. The papers kept calling him "a close friend of the family," which must have overjoyed my mother, and saying that he was being questioned about possible clues to my whereabouts. Of course he never even knew that I was running away; I told him just what I told my mother before I left—that I was going to get away from all the confusion and excitement for a while; I was going downtown and would probably have a sandwich somewhere for supper and go to a movie. He bothered me for a minute there, because of course he wanted to come too. I hadn't meant to take the bus right there on the corner but with Paul tagging after me and wanting me to wait while he got the car so we could drive out and have dinner at the Inn, I had to get away fast on the first thing that came along, so I just ran for the bus and left Paul standing there; that was the only part of my plan I had to change.

I took the bus all the way downtown, although my first plan had been to walk. It turned out much better, actually, since it didn't matter at all if anyone saw me on the bus going downtown in my own home town, and I managed to get an earlier train out. I bought a round-trip ticket; that was important, because it would make them think I was coming back; that was always the way they thought about things. If you did something you had to have a reason for it, because my mother and my father and Carol never did anything unless *they* had a reason for it, so if I bought a round-trip ticket the only possible reason would be that I was coming back. Besides, if they thought I was coming back they would not be frightened so quickly and I might have more time to hide before they came looking for me. As it happened, Carol found out I was gone that same night when she couldn't sleep and came into my room for some aspirin, so all the time I had less of a head start than I thought.

I knew that they would find out about my buying the ticket; I was not silly enough to suppose that I could steal off and not leave any traces. All my plans were based on the fact that the people who get caught are the ones who attract attention by doing something strange or noticeable, and what I intended all along was to fade into some background where they would never see me. I knew they would find out about the round-trip ticket, because it was an odd thing to do in a town where you've lived all your life, but it was the last unusual thing I did. I thought when I bought it that knowing about that round-trip ticket would be some consolation to my mother and father. They would know that no matter how long I stayed away at least I always had a ticket home. I did keep the return-trip ticket quite a while, as a matter of fact. I used to carry it in my wallet as a kind of lucky charm.

I followed everything in the papers. Mrs. Peacock and I used to read them at the breakfast table over our second cup of coffee before I went off to work.

"What do you think about this girl disappeared over in Rockville?" Mrs. Peacock would say to me, and I'd shake my head sorrowfully and say that a girl must be really crazy to leave a handsome, luxurious home like that, or that I had kind of a notion that maybe she didn't leave at all—maybe the family had her locked up somewhere because she was a homicidal maniac. Mrs. Peacock always loved anything about homicidal maniacs.

Once I picked up the paper and looked hard at the picture. "Do you think she looks something like me?" I asked Mrs. Peacock, and Mrs. Peacock leaned back and looked at me and then at the picture and then at me again and finally she shook her head and said, "No. If you wore your hair longer, and curlier, and your face was maybe a little fuller, there might be a little resemblance, but then if you looked like a homicidal maniac I wouldn't ever of let you in my house."

"I think she kind of looks like me," I said.

"You get along to work and stop being vain," Mrs. Peacock told me.

Of course when I got on the train with my round-trip ticket I had no idea how soon they'd be following me, and I suppose it was just as well, because it might have made me nervous and I might have done something wrong and spoiled everything. I knew that as soon as they gave up the notion that I was coming back to Rockville with my round-trip ticket they would think of Crain, which is the largest city that train went to, so I only stayed in Crain part of one day. I went to a big department store where they were having a store-wide sale; I figured that would land me in a crowd of shoppers and I was right; for a while there was a good chance that I'd never get any farther away from home than the ground floor of that department store in Crain. I had to fight my way through the crowd until I found the counter where they were having a sale of raincoats, and then I had to push and elbow down the counter and finally grab the raincoat I wanted right out of the hands of some old monster who couldn't have used it anyway because she was much too fat. You would have thought she had already paid for it, the way she howled. I was smart enough to have the exact change, all six dollars and eighty-nine cents, right in my hand, and I gave it to the salesgirl, grabbed the raincoat and the bag she wanted to put it in, and fought my way out again before I got crushed to death.

That raincoat was worth every cent of the six dollars and eighty-nine cents; I wore it right through until winter that year and not even a button ever came off. I finally lost it the next spring when I left it somewhere and never got it back. It was tan, and the minute I put it on in the ladies' room of the store I began thinking of it as my "old" raincoat; that was good. I had never before owned a raincoat like that and my mother would have fainted dead away. One thing I did that I thought was kind of clever. I had left home wearing a light short coat; almost a jacket, and when I put on the raincoat of course I took off my light coat. Then all I had to do was empty the pockets of the light coat into the raincoat and carry the light coat casually over to a counter where they were having a sale of jackets and drop it on the counter as though I'd taken it off a little way to look at it and had decided against it. As far as I ever knew no one paid the slightest attention to me, and before I left the counter I saw a woman pick up my jacket and look it over; I could have told her she was getting a bargain for three ninety-eight.

It made me feel good to know that I had gotten rid of the light coat. My mother picked it out for me and even though I liked it and it was expensive it was also recognizable and I had to change it somehow. I was sure that if I put it in a bag and dropped it into a river or into a garbage truck or something like that sooner or later it would be found and even if no one saw me doing it, it would almost certainly be found, and then they would know I had changed my clothes in Crain.

That light coat never turned up. The last they ever found of me was someone in Rockville who caught a glimpse of me in the train station in Crain, and she recognized me by the light coat. They never found out where I went after that; it was partly luck and partly my clever planning. Two or three days later the papers were still reporting that I was in Crain; people thought they saw me on the streets and one girl who went into a store to buy a dress was picked up by the police and held until she could get someone to identify her. They were really looking, but they were looking for Louisa Tether, and I had stopped being Louisa Tether the minute I got rid of that light coat my mother bought me.

One thing I was relying on: there must be thousands of girls in the country on any given day who are nineteen years old, fair-haired, five feet four inches tall, and weighing one hundred and twenty-six pounds. And if there are thousands of girls like that, there must be, among those thousands, a good number who are wearing shapeless tan raincoats; I started counting tan raincoats in Crain after I left the department store and I passed four in one block, so I felt well hidden. After that I made myself even more invisible by doing just what I told my mother I was going to—I stopped in and had a sandwich in a little coffee shop, and then I went to a movie. I wasn't in any hurry at all, and rather than try to find a place to sleep that night I thought I would sleep on the train.

It's funny how no one pays any attention to you at all. There were hundreds of people who saw me that day, and even a sailor who tried to pick me up in the movie, and yet no one really *saw* me. If I had tried to check into a hotel the desk clerk might have noticed me, or if I had tried to get dinner in some fancy restaurant in that cheap raincoat I would have been conspicuous, but I was doing what any other girl looking like me and dressed like me might be doing that day. The only person who might be apt to remember me would be the man selling tickets in the railroad station, because girls looking like me in old raincoats didn't buy train tickets, usually, at eleven at night, but I had thought of that, too, of course; I bought a ticket to Amityville, sixty miles away, and what made Amityville a perfectly reasonable disguise is that at Amityville there is a college, not a little fancy place like the one I had left so recently with nobody's blessing, but a big sprawling friendly affair, where my raincoat would look perfectly at home. I told myself I was a student coming back to the college after a weekend at home. We got to Amityville after midnight, but it still didn't look odd when I left the train and went into the station, because while I was in the station, having a cup of coffee and killing time, seven other girls—I counted—wearing raincoats like mine came in or went out, not seeming to think it the least bit odd to be getting on or off trains at that hour of the night. Some of them had suitcases, and I wished that I had had some way of getting a suitcase in Crain, but it would have made me noticeable in the movie, and college girls going home for weekends often don't bother; they have pajamas and an extra pair of stockings at home, and they drop a toothbrush into one of the pockets of those invaluable raincoats. So I didn't worry about the suitcase then, although I knew I would need one soon. While I was having my coffee I made my own mind change from the idea that I was a college girl coming back after a weekend at home to the idea that I was a college girl who was on her way home for a few days; all the time I tried to think as much as possible like what I was pretending to be, and after all, I *had* been a college girl for a while. I was thinking that even now the letter was in the mail, traveling as fast as the U.S. Government could make it go, right to my father to tell him why I wasn't a college student any more; I suppose that was what finally decided me to run away, the thought of what my father would think and say and do when he got that letter from the college.

That was in the paper, too. They decided that the college business was the reason for my running away, but if that had been all, I don't think I would have left. No, I had been wanting to leave for so long, ever since I can remember, making plans till I was sure they were foolproof, and that's the way they turned out to be.

Sitting there in the station at Amityville, I tried to think myself into a good reason why I was leaving college to go home on a Monday night late, when I would hardly be going home for the weekend. As I say, I always tried to think as hard as I could the way that suited whatever I wanted to be, and I liked to have a good reason for what I was doing. Nobody ever asked me, but it was good to know that I could answer them if they did. I finally decided that my sister was getting married the next day and I was going home at the beginning of the week to be one of her bridesmaids. I thought that was very funny. I didn't want to be going home for any sad or frightening reason, like my mother being sick, or my father being hurt in a car accident, because I would have to look sad, and that might attract attention. So I was going home for my sister's wedding. I wandered around the station as though I had nothing to do, and just happened to pass the door when another girl was going out; she had on a raincoat just like mine and anyone who happened to notice would have thought that it was me who went out. Before I bought my ticket I went into the ladies' room and got another twenty dollars out of my shoe. I had nearly three hundred dollars left of the money I had taken from my father's desk and I had most of it in my shoes because I honestly couldn't think of another safe place to carry it. All I kept in my pocketbook was just enough for whatever I had to spend next. It's uncomfortable waking around all day on a wad of bills in your shoe, but they were good solid shoes, the kind of comfortable old shoes you wear whenever you don't really care how you look, and I had put new shoelaces in them before I left home so I could tie them good and tight. You can see, I planned pretty carefully, and no little detail got left out. If they had let me plan my sister's wedding there would have been a lot less of that running around and screaming and hysterics.

I bought a ticket to Chandler, which is the biggest city in this part of the state, and the place I'd been heading for all along. It was a good place to hide because people from Rockville tended to bypass it unless they had some special reason for going there—if they couldn't find the doctors or orthodontists or psychoanalysts or dress material they wanted in Rockville or Crain, they went directly to one of the really big cities, like the state capital; Chandler was big enough to hide in, but not big enough to look like a metropolis to people from Rockville. The ticket seller in the Amityville station must have seen a good many college girls buying tickets for Chandler at all hours of the day or night because he took my money and shoved the ticket at me without even looking up.

Funny. They must have come looking for me in Chandler at some time or other, because it's not likely they would have neglected any possible place I might be, but maybe Rockville people never seriously believed that anyone would go to Chandler from choice, because I never felt for a minute that anyone was looking for me there. My picture was in the Chandler papers, of course, but as far as I ever knew no one ever looked at me twice, and I got up every morning and went to work and went shopping in the stores and went to movies with Mrs. Peacock and went out to the beach all that summer without ever being afraid of being recognized. I behaved just like everyone else, and even *thought* just like everyone else, and the only person I ever saw from Rockville in three years was a friend of my mother's and I knew *she* only came to Chandler to get her poodle bred at the kennels there. She didn't look as if she was in a state to recognize anybody but another poodle fancier, anyway, and all I had to do was step into a doorway as she went by , and she never looked at me.

Two other college girls got on the train to Chandler when I did; maybe both of them were going home for their sisters' weddings. Neither of them was wearing a tan raincoat, but one of them had on an old blue jacket that gave the same general effect. I fell asleep as soon as the train started, and once I woke up and for a minute I wondered where I was and then I realized that I was doing it, I was actually carrying out my careful plan and had gotten better than halfway with it, and I almost laughed, there in the train with everyone asleep around me. Then I went back to sleep and didn't wake up until we got into Chandler about seven in the morning.

So there I was. I had left home just after lunch the day before, and now at seven in the morning of my sister's wedding day I was so far away, in every sense, that I *knew* they would never find me. I had all day to get myself settled in Chandler, so I started off by having breakfast in a restaurant near the station, and then went off to find a place to live, and a job. The first thing I did was buy a suitcase, and it's funny how people don't really notice you if you're buying a suitcase near a railroad station. Suitcases look *natural* near railroad stations, and I picked out one of those stores that sell a little bit of everything and bought a cheap suitcase and a pair of stockings and some handkerchiefs and a little traveling clock, and I put everything into the suitcase and carried that. Nothing is hard to do unless you get upset or excited about it.

Later on, when Mrs. Peacock and I used to read in the papers about my disappearing, I asked her once if she thought that Louisa Tether had gotten as far as Chandler and she didn't.

"They're saying now that she was kidnapped," Mrs. Peacock told me, "and that's what *I* think happened. Kidnapped, and murdered, and they do *terrible* things to young girls they kidnap."

"But the papers say there wasn't any ransom note."

"That's what they *say*." Mrs. Peacock shook her head at me. "How do we know what the family is keeping secret? Or if she was kidnapped by a homicidal maniac, why should *he* send a ransom note? Young girls like you don't know a lot of the things that go on. *I* can tell you."

"I feel kind of sorry for the girl," I said.

"You can't ever tell," Mrs. Peacock said. "Maybe she went with him willingly."

I didn't know, that first morning in Chandler, that Mrs. Peacock was going to turn up that first day, the luckiest thing that ever happened to me. I decided while I was having breakfast that I was going to be a nineteen-year-old girl from upstate with a nice family and a good background who had been saving money to come to Chandler and take a secretarial course in the business school there. I was going to have to find some kind of a job to keep on earning money while I went to school; courses at the business school wouldn't start until fall, so I would have the summer to work and save money and decide if I really wanted to take secretarial training. If I decided not to stay in Chandler I could easily go somewhere else after the fuss about my running away had died down. The raincoat looked wrong for the kind of conscientious young girl I was going to be, so I took it off and carried it over my arm. I think I did a pretty good job on my clothes, altogether. Before I left home I decided that I would have to wear a suit, as quiet and unobtrusive as I could find, and I picked out a gray suit, with a white blouse, so with just one or two small changes like a different blouse or some kind of a pin on the lapel, I could look like whoever I decided to be. Now the suit looked absolutely right for a young girl planning to take a secretarial course, and I looked like a thousand other people when I walked down the street carrying my suitcase and my raincoat over my arm; people get off trains every minute looking just like that. I bought a morning paper and stopped in a drugstore for a cup of coffee and a look to see the rooms for rent. I was all so usual—suitcase, coat, rooms for rent—that when I asked the soda clerk how to get to Primrose Street he never even looked at me. He certainly didn't care whether I ever got to Primrose Street or not, but he told me very politely where it was and what bus to take. I didn't really need to take the bus for economy, but it would have looked funny for a girl who was saving money to arrive in a taxi.

"I'll never forget how you looked that first morning," Mrs. Peacock told me once, much later. "I knew right away you were the kind of girl I like to rent rooms to—quiet and well-mannered. But you looked almighty scared of the big city."

"I wasn't scared," I said. "I was worried about finding a nice room. My mother told me so many things to be careful about I was afraid I'd never find anything to suit her."

"*Anybody's* mother could come into my house at any time and know that her daughter was in good hands," Mrs. Peacock said, a little huffy.

But it was true. When I walked into Mrs. Peacock's rooming house on Primrose Street, and met Mrs. Peacock, I knew that I couldn't have done this part better if I'd been able to plan it. The house was old, and comfortable, and my room was nice, and Mrs. Peacock and I hit it off right away. She was very pleased with me when she heard that my mother had told me to be sure the room I found was clean and that the neighborhood was good, with no chance of rowdies following a girl if she came home after dark, and she was even more pleased when she heard that I wanted to save money and take a secretarial course so I could get a really good job and earn enough to be able to send a little home every week; Mrs. Peacock believed that children owed it to their parents to pay back some of what had been spent on them while they were growing up. By the time I had been in the house an hour, Mrs. Peacock knew all about my imaginary family upstate: my mother, who was a widow; and my sister, who had just gotten married and still lived at my mother's home with her husband, and my young brother Paul, who worried my mother a good deal because he didn't seem to want to settle down. My name was Lois Taylor, I told her. By that time, I think I could have told her my real name and she would never have connected it with the girl in the paper, because by then she was feeling that she almost knew my family, and she wanted me to be sure and tell my mother when I wrote home that Mrs. Peacock would make herself personally responsible for me while I was in the city and take as good care of me as my own mother would. On top of everything else, she told me that a stationery store in the neighborhood was looking for a girl assistant, and there I was. Before I had been away from home for twenty-four hours I was an entirely new person. I was a girl named Lois Taylor who lived on Primrose Street and worked down at the stationery store.

I read in the papers one day about how a famous fortuneteller wrote to my father offering to find me and said that astral signs had convinced him that I would be found near flowers. That gave me a jolt, because of Primrose Street, but my father and Mrs. Peacock and the rest of the world thought that it meant that my body was buried somewhere. They dug up a vacant lot near the railroad station where I was last seen, and Mrs. Peacock was very disappointed when nothing turned up. Mrs. Peacock and I could not decide whether I had run away with a gangster to be a gun moll, or whether my body had been cut up and sent somewhere in a trunk. After a while they stopped looking for me, except for an occasional false clue that would turn up in a small story on the back pages of the paper, and Mrs. Peacock and I got interested in the stories about a daring daylight bank robbery in Chicago. When the anniversary of my running away came around, and I realized that I had really been gone for a year, I treated myself to a new hat and dinner downtown, and came home just in time for the evening news broadcast and my mother's voice over the radio.

"Louisa," she was saying, "please come home."

"That poor poor woman," Mrs. Peacock said. "Imagine how she must feel. They say she's never given up hope of finding her little girl alive someday."

"Do you like my new hat?" I asked her.

I had given up all idea of the secretarial course because the stationery store had decided to expand and include a lending library and a gift shop, and I was now the manager of the gift shop and if things kept on well would someday be running the whole thing; Mrs. Peacock and I talked it over, just as if she had been my mother, and we decided that I would be foolish to leave a good job to start over somewhere else. The money that I had been saving was in the bank, and Mrs. Peacock and I thought that one of these days we might pool our savings and buy a little car, or go on a trip somewhere, or even a cruise.

What I am saying is that I was free, and getting along fine, with never a thought that I knew about ever going back. It was just plain rotten bad luck that I had to meet Paul. I had gotten so I hardly ever thought about any of them any more, and never wondered what they were doing unless I happened to see some item in the papers, but there must have been something in the back of my mind remembering them all the time because I never even stopped to think; I just stood there on the street with my mouth open, and said, "*Paul!*" He turned around and then of course I realized what I had done, but it was too late. He stared at me for a minute, and then frowned, and then looked puzzled; I could see him first trying to remember, and then trying to believe what he remembered; at last he said, "Is it possible?"

He said I had to go back. He said if I didn't go back he would tell them where to come and get me. He also patted me on the head and told me that there was still a reward waiting there in the bank for anyone who turned up with conclusive news of me, and he said that after he had collected the reward I was perfectly welcome to run away again, as far and as often as I liked.

Maybe I did want to go home. Maybe all that time I had been secretly waiting for a chance to get back; maybe that's why I recognized Paul on the street, in a coincidence that wouldn't have happened once in a million years—he had never even *been* to Chandler before, and was only there for a few minutes between trains; he had stepped out of the station for a minute, and found me. If I had not been passing at that minute, if he had stayed in the station where he belonged, I should never have gone back. I told Mrs. Peacock I was going home to visit my family upstate. I thought that was funny.

Paul sent a telegram to my mother and father, saying that he had found me, and we took a plane back; Paul said he was still afraid that I'd try to get away again and the safest place for me was high up in the air where he knew I couldn't get off and run.

I began to get nervous, looking out the taxi window on the way from the Rockville airport; I would have sworn that for three years I hadn't given a thought to that town, to those streets and stores and houses I used to know so well; but here I found that I remembered it all, as though I hadn't ever seen Chandler and *its* houses and streets; it was almost as though I had never been away at all. When the taxi finally turned the corner into my own street, and I saw the big old white house again, I almost cried.

"Of course I wanted to come back," I said, and Paul laughed. I thought of the return-trip ticket I had kept as a lucky charm for so long, and how I had thrown it away one day when I was emptying my pocketbook; I wondered when I threw it away whether I would ever want to go back and regret throwing away my ticket. "Everything looks just the same," I said. "I caught the bus right there on the corner; I came down the driveway that day and met you."

"If I had managed to stop you that day," Paul said, "you would probably never have tried again."

Then the taxi stopped in front of the house and my knees were shaking when I got out. I grabbed Paul's arm and said, "Paul . . . wait a minute," and he gave me a look I used to know very well, a look that said "If you back out on me now I'll see that you never forget it," and put his arm around me because I was shivering and we went up the walk to the front door.

I wondered if they were watching us from the window. It was hard for me to imagine how my mother and father would behave in a situation like this, because they always made such a point of being quiet and dignified and proper; I thought that Mrs. Peacock would have been halfway down the walk to meet us, but here the front door ahead was still tight shut. I wondered if we would have to ring the doorbell; I never had to ring this doorbell before. I was still wondering when Carol opened the door for us. "Carol!" I said. I was shocked because she looked so old, and then I thought that of course it had been three years since I had seen her and she probably thought that *I* looked older, too. "Carol," I said, "Oh, Carol!" I was honestly glad to see her.

She looked at me hard and then stepped back and my mother and father were standing there, waiting for me to come in. If I had not stopped to think I would have run to them, but I hesitated, not quite sure what to do, or whether they were angry with me, or hurt, or only just happy that I was back, and of course once I stopped to think about it all I could find to do was just stand there and say "Mother?" kind of uncertainly.

She came over to me and put her hands on my shoulders and looked into my face for a long time. There were tears running down her cheeks and I thought that before, when it didn't matter, I had been ready enough to cry, but now, when crying would make me look better, all I wanted to do was giggle. She looked old, and sad, and I felt simply foolish. Then she turned to Paul and said, "Oh, *Paul*—how can you do this to me again?"

Paul was frightened; I could see it. "Mrs. Tether—" he said.

"What is your name, dear?" my mother asked me.

"Louisa Tether," I said stupidly.

"No, dear," she said, very gently, "your *real* name?"

Now I could cry, but now I did not think it was going to help matters any. "Louisa Tether," I said. "That's my name."

"Why don't you people leave us alone?" Carol said; she was white, and shaking, and almost screaming because she was so angry. "We've spent years and years trying to find my lost sister and all people like you see in it is a chance to cheat us out of the reward—doesn't it mean *any*thing to you that *you* may think you have a chance for some easy money, but *we* just get hurt and heartbroken all over again? Why don't you leave us *alone*?"

"Carol," my father said, "you're frightening the poor child. Young lady," he said to me, "I honestly believe that you did not realize the cruelty of what you tried to do. You look like a nice girl: try to imagine your own mother—"

I tried to imagine my own mother; I looked straight at her.

"—If someone took advantage of her like this, I am sure you were not told that twice before, this young man—" I stopped looking at my mother and looked at Paul—"has brought us young girls who pretended to be our lost daughter; each time he protested that he had been genuinely deceived and had not thought of profit, and each time we hoped desperately that it would be the right girl. The first time we were taken in for several days. The girl *looked* like our Louisa, she *acted* like our Louisa, she knew all kinds of small family jokes and happenings it seemed impossible that anyone *but* Louisa could know, and yet she was an imposter. And the girl's mother—my wife—has suffered more each time her hopes have been raised." He put his arm around my mother— his wife—and with Carol they stood all together looking at me.

"Look," Paul said wildly, "give her a *chance*—she *knows* she's Louisa. At least give her a chance to *prove* it."

"How?" Carol asked. "I'm sure if I asked her something like—well— like what was the color of the dress she was supposed to wear at my wedding—"

"It was pink," I said. "I wanted blue but you said it had to be pink."

"I'm sure she'd know the answer," Carol went on as though I hadn't said anything. "The other girls you brought here, Paul—*they* both knew."

It wasn't going to be any good. I ought to have known it. Maybe they were so used to looking for me by now that they would rather keep on looking than have me home; maybe once my mother had looked in my face and seen there nothing of Louisa, but only the long careful concentration I had put into being Lois Taylor, there was never any chance of my looking like Louisa again.

I felt kind of sorry for Paul; he had never understood them as well as I did and he clearly felt there was still some chance of talking them into opening their arms and crying out, "Louisa! Our long-lost daughter!" and then turning around and handing him the reward; after that, we could all live happily ever after. While Paul was still trying to argue with my father I walked over a little way and looked into the living room again; I figured I wasn't going to have much time to look around and I wanted one last glimpse to take away with me; sister Carol kept a good eye on me all the time, too. I wondered what the two girls before me had tried to steal, and I wanted to tell her that if I ever planned to steal anything from that house I was three years too late; I could have taken whatever I wanted when I left the first time. There was nothing there I could take now, any more than there had been before. I realized that all I wanted was to stay—I wanted to stay so much that I felt like hanging onto the stair rail and screaming, but even though a temper tantrum might bring them some fleeting recollection of their dear lost Louisa I hardly thought it would persuade them to invite me to stay. I could just picture myself being dragged kicking and screaming out of my own house.

"Such a lovely old house," I said politely to my sister Carol, who was hovering around me.

"Our family has lived here for generations," she said, just as politely.

"Such beautiful furniture," I said.

"My mother is fond of antiques."

"Fingerprints," Paul was shouting. We were going to get a lawyer, I gathered, or at least Paul thought we were going to get a lawyer and I wondered how he was going to feel when he found out that we weren't. I couldn't imagine any lawyer in the world who could get my mother and my father and my sister Carol to take me back when they had made up their minds that I was not Louisa; could the law make my mother look into my face and recognize me?

I thought that there ought to be some way I could make Paul see that there was nothing we could do, and I came over and stood next to him. "Paul," I said, "can't you see that you're only making Mr. Tether angry?"

"Correct, young woman," my father said, and nodded at me to show that he thought I was being a sensible creature. "He's not doing himself any good by threatening me."

"Paul," I said, "these people don't want us here."

Paul started to say something and then for the first time in his life thought better of it and stamped off toward the door. When I turned to follow him—thinking that we'd never gotten past the front hall in my great homecoming—my father—excuse me, Mr. Tether—came up behind me and took my hand. "My daughter was younger than you are," he said to me very kindly, "but I'm sure you have a family somewhere who love you and want you to be happy. Go back to them, young lady. Let me advise you as though *I* were really your father—stay away from that fellow, he's wicked and he's worthless. Go back home where you belong."

"We know what it's like for a family to worry and wonder about a daughter," my mother said. "Go back to the people who love you."

That meant Mrs. Peacock, I guess.

"Just to make sure you get there," my father said, "let us help toward your fare." I tried to take my hand away, but he put a folded bill into it and I had to take it. "I hope someday," he said, "that someone will do as much for our Louisa."

"Good-bye, my dear," my mother said, and she reached up and patted my cheek. "Very good luck to you."

"I hope your daughter comes back someday," I told them. "Good-bye."

The bill was a twenty, and I gave it to Paul. It seemed little enough for all the trouble he had taken and, after all, I could go back to my job in the stationery store. My mother still talks to me on the radio, once a year, on the anniversary of the day I ran away.

"Louisa," she says, "please come home. We all want our dear girl back, and we need you and miss you so much. Your mother and father love you and will never forget you. Louisa, please come home."

Responding to the Story

1. How did you feel while you were reading this story?
2. Did you like Louisa/Lois? Did you hate her? Did you feel sympathetic when she reveals near the story's end, "I realized that all I wanted was to stay . . . "?
3. Give your reactions to Louisa's parents, her sister, and Paul.
4. Why do you think Carol was at the house when Louisa returned, three years after Louisa's disappearance? Remember that Carol was married the day after Louisa left. Is she just visiting her parents? Is she back home because the marriage didn't work out? Does she frequently stay with her parents because they are upset over Louisa's continuing absence? Justify your answer with evidence from the text, if you can.
5. Does the author provide a *motivation* for Louisa's leaving home? If so, what is it?

Exploring the Author's Craft

1. The **plot** of a piece of fiction is the series of actions and events that move the story forward: a certain incident happens first; a certain incident happens second; and so on. These incidents are the plot elements of the story. How does Shirley Jackson use both plot (especially the story's ending) and characterization to make "Louisa, Please Come Home" a unique story?

2. Sometimes the names of characters in a piece of fiction are revealing. Does Louisa's last name—Tether—contribute to the meaning of the story? (If you need to, look *tether* up in a dictionary.)

Writer's Workshop

Here's your chance for some unconventionality. Working with a small group, create a story with a teenager as its main character. The plot should be believable.

Beth Cassavell

Beth Cassavell graduated from Dartmouth College in 1995 with degrees in Russian Language and Russian Area Studies. She is currently working for Ziff Davis, Inc., as an Advertising and Marketing Analyst for its website, ZDNet.com. She has this to say about her story:

"I wrote 'The Man in the Casket' when I was 16 in a creative writing course I was taking in high school. The events described within it are not completely autobiographical, but the search for truth through legacy, loss, and love certainly is."

How could she mourn for a grandfather she didn't love?

The Man in the Casket

I reached into my mom's pocketbook for a tissue. I wasn't the only one who was teary-eyed and sniffling but for me it was because of the pollinating flowers. They cluttered every corner of the cold and gray room. The threatening walls ugly with ornate trimming and the Corinthian columns added to the inelegance.

That day is engraved into my memory not because of the depression but because of boredom. I stared at a brown stain on the worn carpet hoping somebody would see how bored I was and take me home. I scratched my neck; the black woolen dress my mother had vested me in felt like steel wool. I looked at my gawky knees. The dress used to cover them when it was new but my nine-year-old body was too big for it now.

Not to mention that this rambunctious nine-year-old didn't want to be attired in a Stone Age dress, confined in a room with a hundred little Italian ladies in orthopedic shoes weeping into their hand-embroidered handkerchiefs. Clinging to their Rosary beads as if they were the essence of life itself, they bewailed and bemoaned the contents of the cold marble casket. I sat in the last row of folding chairs and longed to frolic in the freshly fallen February snow.

I had no choice. My grandfather loved to inconvenience me. He had had his first heart attack in the middle of our annual February Florida vacation almost exactly a year before his death. We had to fly home. After his first stroke my mom forced me into teaching him how to read. He had lost most of his memory due to the stroke.

His lips would tremble as he tried to conquer each syllable. He had thin pale lips exactly like my dad has.

"The ra . . . ra . . ."

"Rain."

"Don't tell me what rain is. I've lived through hurricanes and downpours you could only imagine!" he snapped at me. "The rain gently fa . . ."

"Falling," I interjected impatiently. As far as patience goes, well, I have never had any. I watched in frustration as my grandfather ran his hands deliberately through his white hair. He was stalling. He didn't want to be there as much as I didn't want to be there but we both had an obligation. I've never been quite sure what mine was.

"I don't know why I have to read. My eyes are bad anyway."

"Dad, it's your duty as a responsible adult to be able to read." My mother was so good to him. He was only her father-in-law but she treated him as her own father. He was my own grandfather and I treated him like gum on the bottom of my shoe. Then again, I was his own grandchild.

Whenever my parents would leave on vacation my grandfather would babysit for me. I resented every minute of his presence in my house. After all, I was eight years old and knew everything.

"It's eight o'clock," he informed me. I hated go-to-bed inferences. "Shouldn't you be in bed?"

"I don't have to be in bed until nine, after 'The Dukes of Hazard.' I don't have to listen to you anyway." I sure told him.

"I've had just about enough from you. You know, you can be so unpleasant and downright obnoxious sometimes?" my grandfather said. "You're a spoiled brat." Bluntness was always an annoying quality of his. "You never smile. You should try to be more like your cousin, Rebecca.

She doesn't have half as much as you have and she's always smiling and laughing."

The ultimate insult! A comparison to your "perfect" cousin. "I don't want to hear it!" I screamed. I wanted to erupt into a fit of anger—bite, scratch, kick. I could feel the animosity pounding through every artery and vein in my eight-year-old body. My skin was taking on a shade of crimson. "I can't wait 'til Mommy and Daddy come home. I hate it when you watch me."

"Who the hell do you think you are speaking to me like that? Do you think I enjoy babysitting for a brat like you?"

I was running up the stairs as he spoke, hoping he didn't think I was listening to him. I despised it when he got the last word in. He always did.

The memories came flooding back to me. I had blocked them out completely during this wake-funeral ordeal but the emotional dam was breaking. I swore to myself I would not cry. Why should I cry over him?

I looked up from the stained carpet and the first thing that caught my attention was my dad. I never really thought about my dad losing his own father. He seemed to be dealing with the situation calmly. I watched as he talked with anyone and everyone. My dad is a born talker. I suppose talking and socializing helped him to block out his emotions. The only emotions my dad usually displays are anger and happiness. My mother always says he's exactly like his father. She's wrong. Although I hate to admit it, my grandfather did have other emotions.

One day when my grandfather was struggling over a Sunday newspaper, I witnessed something I never thought I ever would. My grandfather was crying. Actually, it was more like a whimpering or sulking. And for that one short moment, as I was diverted from "The Dukes of Hazard," I actually felt something for my grandfather. It wasn't love; I never knew enough of him to love him, but the feeling was still there. It was almost a feeling of curiosity. I never knew anything about the person my grandfather was. I had never bothered to ask him and he never bothered to tell me.

I never told anyone about it. It was the kind of incident that just got lost in the shuffle of events. He died the next day and things got intensely hectic in my house—the funeral, the wake, the relatives living in our house. I resented his death more than anything he ever did to me when he was alive. Not only had I been ignored since his death but he also got the last word in. How could I outdo death? And what about the wondering and regretting this put me through?

"What are you, deaf?" my brother yelled at me. "You have to go up there and pay last respects to grandpa."

"Huh?" For a moment I forgot this whole damn thing was a tribute to him. "What are you supposed to do?" I asked. I had never been to a funeral before.

"I don't know, go pray or something." My brother made things so religious.

"Do I have to?"

My brother glared at me. "Go!"

I had been sitting in one of those folding chairs for so long that my legs had fallen asleep. Shooting pains ran through my calves as I walked up to the marble coffin. That coffin must have cost at least eight hundred dollars. The bike I wanted only cost two hundred dollars. There was actually a line of people waiting to pay last respects to my grandfather. I got in line.

I watched as my great aunt Sophie bent over into the coffin and briskly kissed him again and again, wailing and crying. This was going to take all day! I hoped I wasn't supposed to kiss it. All it was was the vapid flesh and bones of someone I barely knew. I might as well kiss a rock.

After my great aunt Sophie, my famed cousin Rebecca was on line. She cried also and her tears dripped into the casket like there was some kind of drought in there. I watched as her lips mumbled some prerehearsed prayer. She bent over and kissed him. I was next on line. Suddenly I felt the great disadvantage I had in my humanness. I looked down at the man in the casket. I couldn't do it; I couldn't pray.

"Why do you always do this to me? Why? Why did you have to be so stubborn and unfriendly, so impatient and unloving? Why couldn't you love me? Why?" I stopped. I realized. I cried.

Responding to the Story

1. Is this reaction of a granddaughter to her grandfather's death believable? Justify your response with your own observations or experiences.
2. Explain how you interpret the last paragraph of the story.

Exploring the Author's Craft

1. **Diction** is an author's choice of words or phrases. This choice has a direct effect on the tone of a work. Describe the overall tone (the author's attitude toward her subject) of this work. Support your opinion with words and phrases from the story.
2. Many young people write sincerely and frankly, yet the work fails to have emotional power for the reader. Beth Cassavell's story does have the power to move most readers. Is the emotional effect of the story created in spite of the tone or because of the tone?

Writer's Workshop

Write a poem, essay, or story about a grandparent-grandchild relationship.

Making Connections in
PART ONE

As the first section of this book ends, you should see a number of connections among the pieces. Here you will try to pull some of these connections together. Complete one or both of the following assignments as your teacher directs.

1. A good thesis essay consists of a main point the writer wishes to make—the thesis—and then ample material to support the thesis. Take the following statement as your thesis: "As they grow up, most people up strive to 'fit in.' " Use three different characters from Part One as your supporting material, showing how each struggles to fit in. Discuss each character in a separate paragraph. Be sure to use clear transitions to link these paragraphs.
2. A story told from a first-person point of view is compelling when the narrator has either unusual experiences or provides fresh insights into experiences we all have in common. Which stories in Part One did you find most compelling? Why?

COMING OF AGE

Families and Friends

Like it or not, we are born into families and we must,
for the most part, manage with those with whom we find
ourselves. Our friends we can choose. However these
various relationships work out, our interactions with
family members and with friends have profound
influences throughout our lives.

   In this section you will meet brothers, sisters, parents,
and friends. You might have a relationship right now like
one of these. Probably you'll have your own variation.
These stories will help you reflect on your own life and
the people you've been closest to over the years. Use the
questions and activities to help you think about the
stories and about your own life, and also to help you
create literature that is distinctly yours.

Margaret Atwood

Margaret Atwood has written poems, novels, short stories, children's books, and plays. In addition, she is a cartoonist and illustrator. Born in 1939 in Ottawa, Ontario, Atwood spent summers in the north woods with her family, where her father did research on insects. Atwood was very close to her older brother and remembers spending days with him overturning rocks to see what was beneath them; if they found something rare, they would simply stare at it and then put the rock back. In her 1997 acceptance speech for the National Arts Club Medal for Literature, Atwood contrasts these childhood activities with writing fiction: "With fiction," she said, "you poke things with a stick to see what will happen." See what this "poking" leads her to discover in the following selection.

"Hatred would have been easier. With hatred I would have known what to do."

They Are My Friends

The black door opens. I'm sitting in the mouse-dropping and formaldehyde smell of the building, on the window-ledge, with the heat from the radiator going up my legs, watching out the window as the fairies and gnomes and snowballs below me slog through the drizzle to the tune of "Jingle Bells" played by a brass band. The fairies look foreshortened, damaged, streaked by the dust and rain on the window glass; my breath makes a foggy circle. My brother isn't here, he's too old for it. This is what he said. I have the whole window-ledge to myself.

On the window-ledge beside mine, Cordelia and Grace and Carol are sitting, jammed in together, whispering and giggling. I have to sit on a window-ledge by myself because they aren't speaking to me. It's something I said wrong, but I don't know what it is because they won't tell me. Cordelia says it will be better for me to think back over everything I've said today and try to pick out the wrong thing. That way I will learn not to say such a thing again. When I've guessed the right answer, then they will speak to me again. All of this is for my own good, because they are my best friends and they want to help me improve. So this is what I'm thinking about as the pipe band goes past in sodden fur hats, and the drum majorettes with their bare wet legs and red smiles and dripping hair: what did I say wrong? I can't remember having said anything different from what I would ordinarily say.

My father walks into the room, wearing his white lab coat. He's working in another part of the building, but he's come to check on us. "Enjoying the parade, girls?" he says.

"Oh yes, thank you," Carol says, and giggles. Grace says, "Yes, thank you." I say nothing. Cordelia gets down off her windowsill and slides up onto mine, sitting close beside me.

"We're enjoying it extremely, thank you very much," she says in her voice for adults. My parents think she has beautiful manners. She puts an arm around me, gives me a little squeeze, a squeeze of complicity,[1] of instruction. Everything will be all right as long as I sit still, say nothing, reveal nothing. I will be saved then, I will be acceptable once more. I smile, tremulous with relief, with gratitude.

But as soon as my father is out of the room Cordelia turns to face me. Her expression is sad rather than angry. She shakes her head. "How could you?" she says. "How could you be so impolite? You didn't even answer him. You know what this means, don't you? I'm afraid you'll have to be punished. What do you have to say for yourself?" And I have nothing to say.

I'm standing outside the closed door of Cordelia's room. Cordelia, Grace, and Carol are inside. They're having a meeting. The meeting is about me. I am just not measuring up, although they are giving me every chance. I will have to do better. But better at what?

Perdie and Mirrie come up the stairs, along the hall, in their armour of being older. I long to be as old as they are. They're the only people

---

1. **complicity:** partnership in wrongdoing.

who have any real power over Cordelia, that I can see. I think of them as my allies; or I think they would be my allies if they only knew. Knew what? Even to myself I am mute.[2]

"Hello, Elaine," they say. Now they say, "What's the little game today? Hide and Seek?"

"I can't tell," I answer. They smile at me, condescending and kind, and head towards their room, to do their toenails and talk about older things.

I lean against the wall. From behind the door comes the indistinct murmur of voices, of laughter, exclusive and luxurious. Cordelia's Mummie drifts by, humming to herself. She's wearing her painting smock. There's a smudge of apple-green on her cheek. She smiles at me, the smile of an angel, benign but remote. "Hello, dear," she says. "You tell Cordelia there's a cookie for you girls, in the tin."

"You can come in now," says the voice of Cordelia from inside the room. I look at the closed door, at the doorknob, at my own hand moving up, as if it's no longer a part of me. . . .

It turns colder and colder. I lie with my knees up, as close to my body as I can get them. I'm peeling the skin off my feet; I can do it without looking, by touch. I worry about what I've said today, the expression on my face, how I walk, what I wear, because all of these things need improvement. I am not normal, I am not like other girls. Cordelia tells me so, but she will help me. Grace and Carol will help me too. It will take hard work and a long time.

In the mornings I get out of bed, put on my clothes, the stiff cotton waist[3] with the garters, the ribbed stockings, the nubbled wool pullover, the plaid skirt. I remember these clothes as cold. Probably they were cold.

I put my shoes on, over my stockings and my peeled feet.

I go out to the kitchen, where my mother is cooking breakfast. There's a pot with porridge in it, Red River cereal or oatmeal or Cream of Wheat, and a glass coffee percolator. I rest my arms on the edge of the white stove and watch the porridge, simmering and thickening,

---

2. **mute:** unable to speak.
3. **waist:** blouselike undergarment.

the flaccid[4] bubbles coming up out of it one at a time and releasing their small puffs of steam. The porridge is like boiling mud. I know that when it comes time to eat the porridge I will have trouble: my stomach will contract, my hands will get cold, it will be difficult to swallow. Something tight sits under my breastbone. But I will get the porridge down somehow, because it's required.

Or I watch the coffee percolator, which is better because I can see everything, the pinpoint bubbles gathering under the upside-down glass umbrella, then hesitating, then the column of water shooting upwards through the stem, falling down over the coffee in its metal basket, the drops of coffee dripping down into the clear water, inking it brown.

Or I make toast, sitting at the table where the toaster is. Each of our spoons has a dark-yellow halibut liver oil capsule in it, shaped like a small football. There are the plates, gleaming whitely, and the glasses of juice. The toaster is on a silver heat pad. It has two doors, with a knob at the bottom of each, and a grid up the centre that glows red-hot. When the toast is done on one side I turn the knobs and the doors open and the toast slides down and turns over, all by itself. I think about putting my finger in there, onto the red-hot grid.

All of these are ways of delaying time, slowing it down, so I won't have to go out through the kitchen door. But no matter what I do, and despite myself, I am pulling on my snowpants, wadding my skirt in between my legs, tugging thick woollen socks on over my shoes, stuffing my feet into boots. Coat, scarf, mittens, knitted hat, I am encased, I am kissed, the door opens, then closes behind me, frozen air shoots up my nose. I waddle through the orchard of leafless apple trees, the legs of my snowpants whisking against each other, down to the bus stop.

Grace is waiting there and Carol, and especially Cordelia. Once I'm outside the house there is no getting away from them. They are on the school bus, where Cordelia stands close beside me and whispers into my ear: "Stand up straight! People are looking!" Carol is in my classroom, and it's her job to report to Cordelia what I do and say all day. They're there at recess, and in the cellar at lunchtime. They comment on the kind of lunch I have, how I hold my sandwich, how I chew. On the way home from school I have to walk in front of them, or behind. In front is

---

4. **flaccid:** weak; not firm.

worse because they talk about how I'm walking, how I look from behind. "Don't hunch over," says Cordelia. "Don't move your arms like that."

They don't say any of the things they say to me in front of others, even other children: whatever is going on is going on in secret, among the four of us only. Secrecy is important, I know that: to violate it would be the greatest, the irreparable sin. If I tell I will be cast out forever.

But Cordelia doesn't do these things or have this power over me because she's my enemy. Far from it. I know about enemies. There are enemies in the schoolyard, they yell things at one another and if they're boys they fight. In the war there were enemies. Our boys and the boys from Our Lady of Perpetual Help are enemies. You throw snowballs at enemies and rejoice if they get hit. With enemies you can feel hatred, and anger. But Cordelia is my friend. She likes me, she wants to help me, they all do. They are my friends, my girlfriends, my best friends. I have never had any before and I'm terrified of losing them. I want to please.

Hatred would have been easier. With hatred, I would have known what to do. Hatred is clear, metallic, one-handed, unwavering; unlike love.

Responding to the Story

1. The narrator, Elaine, tells us that her relationship with Cordelia, Grace, and Carol isn't one of hatred. "Hatred would have been easier," she says. What does she mean by this?
2. How exactly *would* you define the relationship between Elaine and the other girls? Is it believable? Why or why not?
3. When Cordelia tells Elaine's father that they are enjoying the parade, she speaks "in her voice for adults." What is "a voice for adults"? Give some examples from your own experience.
4. Why is the narrator "terrified" of losing these friends?

alive without any dialogue,
r think or do. Reread the seven
t turns colder and colder."

aine's fear and dread in these

w the ordinariness of the
er fears?

ter's strong emotion is clearly
y feelings through the
your scene details of setting
aracter's emotion.

Alternate Media Response

With three classmates, create and perform a pantomime that shows how Elaine's friends treat her and how she responds. Your pantomime can be based on something that actually happens in the story or can be made up, as long as it fits in with what these characters might actually do. Make your pantomime at least one minute long.

Carson McCullers

Carson McCullers (born Lulu Carson Smith in 1917 in Columbus, Georgia) went to New York City at the age of seventeen where she took courses in creative writing at Columbia and New York universities. She was married in 1937 to Reeves McCullers. They were divorced but remarried in 1945.

Her most notable works include *The Heart Is a Lonely Hunter* (1940), *Reflections in a Golden Eye* (1941), and *A Member of the Wedding* (1946), which was adapted for the stage and won a Drama Critics Circle Award. It ran for over five hundred performances and starred Julie Harris, Ethel Waters, and Brandon de Wilde, all of whom starred in the film version as well. It tells of Frankie, a thirteen-year-old, who wants to accompany her brother and his wife on their honeymoon.

Her later works include *The Ballad of the Sad Café* (1951); *The Square Root of Wonderful* (1958); *Clock Without Hands* (1961), and *The Mortgaged Heart* (1971), a posthumous collection of her work. *The Ballad of the Sad Café*, a novella, was dramatized in 1963 by Edward Albee. McCullers died in 1967.

She is frequently linked with the Southern writers Eudora Welty, Flannery O'Connor, and William Faulkner, whose works also are often about lonely misfits. McCullers wrote "Sucker" when she was 17 years old.

Why are you attracted to someone who doesn't even notice you?

Sucker

It was always like I had a room to myself. Sucker slept in my bed with me but that didn't interfere with anything. The room was mine and I used it as I wanted to. Once I remember sawing a trapdoor in the floor. Last year when I was a sophomore in high school I tacked on my wall some pictures of girls from magazines and one of them was just in her underwear. My mother never bothered me because she had the younger kids to look after. And Sucker thought anything I did was always swell.

Whenever I would bring any of my friends back to my room all I had to do was just glance at Sucker and he would get up from whatever he was busy with and maybe half smile at me, and leave without saying a word. He never brought kids back there. He's twelve, four years younger than I am, and he always knew without me even telling him that I didn't want kids that age meddling with my things.

Half the time I used to forget that Sucker isn't my brother. He's my first cousin but practically ever since I remember he's been in our family. You see his folks were killed in a wreck when he was a baby. To me and my kid sisters he was like our brother.

Sucker used to always remember and believe every word I said. That's how he got his nickname. Once a couple of years ago I told him that if he'd jump off our garage with an umbrella it would act as a parachute and he wouldn't fall hard. He did it and busted his knee. That's just one instance. And the funny thing was that no matter how many times he got fooled he would still believe me. Not that he was dumb in other ways—it was just the way he acted with me. He would look at everything I did and quietly take it in.

There is one thing I have learned, but it makes me feel guilty and is hard to figure out. If a person admires you a lot you despise him and don't care—and it is the person who doesn't notice you that you are apt to admire. This is not easy to realize. Maybelle Watts, this senior at school, acted like she was the Queen of Sheba[1] and even humiliated me. Yet at this same time I would have done anything in the world to get her

---

1. **Queen of Sheba:** queen who visited King Solomon; the account is in the Bible in I Kings.

attention. All I could think about day and night was Maybelle until I was nearly crazy. When Sucker was a little kid and on up until the time he was twelve I guess I treated him as bad as Maybelle did me.

Now that Sucker has changed so much it is a little hard to remember him as he used to be. I never imagined anything would suddenly happen that would make us both very different. I never knew that in order to get what has happened straight in my mind I would want to think back on him as he used to be and compare and try to get things settled. If I could have seen ahead maybe I would have acted different.

I never noticed him much or thought about him and when you consider how long we have had the same room together it is funny the few things I remember. He used to talk to himself a lot when he'd think he was alone—all about him fighting gangsters and being on ranches and that sort of kids' stuff. He'd get in the bathroom and stay as long as an hour and sometimes his voice would go up high and excited and you could her him all over the house. Usually, though, he was very quiet. He didn't have many boys in the neighborhood to buddy with and his face had the look of a kid who is watching a game and waiting to be asked to play. He didn't mind wearing the sweaters and coats that I outgrew, even if the sleeves did flop down too big and make his wrists look as thin and white as a little girl's. That is how I remember him—getting a little bigger every year but still being the same. That was Sucker up until a few months ago when all this trouble came.

Maybelle was somehow mixed up in what happened so I guess I ought to start with her. Until I knew her I hadn't given much time to girls. Last fall she sat next to me in General Science class and that was when I first began to notice her. Her hair is the brightest yellow I ever saw and occasionally she will wear it set into curls with some sort of gluey stuff. Her fingernails are pointed and manicured and painted a shiny red. All during class I used to watch Maybelle, nearly all the time except when I thought she was going to look my way or when the teacher called on me. I couldn't keep my eyes off her hands, for one thing. They are very little and white except for that red stuff, and when she would turn the pages of her book she always licked her thumb and held out her little finger and turned very slowly. It is impossible to describe Maybelle. All the boys are crazy about her but she didn't even notice me. For one thing she's almost two years older than I am. Between periods I used to try and pass very close to her in the halls but she would hardly ever smile at me. All I could do was sit and look at her in class—and sometimes it was like the whole room could hear my heart beating and I wanted to holler or light out and run for hell.

At night, in bed, I would imagine about Maybelle. Often this would keep me from sleeping until as late as one or two o'clock. Sometimes Sucker would wake up and ask me why I couldn't get settled and I'd tell him to hush his mouth. I suppose I was mean to him lots of times. I guess I wanted to ignore somebody like Maybelle did me. You could always tell by Sucker's face when his feelings were hurt. I don't remember all the ugly remarks I must have made because even when I was saying them my mind was on Maybelle.

That went on for nearly three months and then somehow she began to change. In the halls she would speak to me and every morning she copied my homework. At lunch time once I danced with her in the gym. One afternoon I got up nerve and went around to her house with a carton of cigarettes. I knew she smoked in the girls' basement and sometimes outside of school—and I didn't want to take her candy because I think that's been run into the ground. She was very nice and it seemed to me everything was going to change.

It was that night when this trouble really started. I had come into my room late and Sucker was already asleep. I felt too happy and keyed up to get in a comfortable position and was awake thinking about Maybelle a long time. Then I dreamed about her and it seemed I kissed her. It was a surprise to wake up and see the dark. I lay still and a little while passed before I could come to and understand where I was. The house was quiet and it was a very dark night.

"Sucker's voice was a shock to me. "Pete? . . ."

I didn't answer anything or even move.

"You do like me as much as if I was your own brother, don't you, Pete?"

I couldn't get over the surprise of everything and it was like this was the real dream instead of the other.

"You have liked me all the time like I was your own brother, haven't you?"

"Sure," I said.

Then I got up for a few minutes. It was cold and I was glad to come back to bed. Sucker hung on to my back. He felt little and warm and I could feel his warm breathing on my shoulder.

"No matter what you did I always knew you liked me."

I was wide awake and my mind seemed mixed up in a strange way. There was this happiness about Maybelle and all that—but at the same time something about Sucker and his voice when he said these things made me take notice. Anyway I guess you understand people better when you are happy than when something is worrying you. It was like I had never really thought about Sucker until then. I felt I had always been mean to him. One night a few weeks before I had heard him crying in the dark. He said he had lost a boy's beebee gun and was scared to let anybody know. He wanted me to tell him what to do. I was sleepy and tried to make him hush and when he wouldn't I kicked at him. That was just one of the things I remembered. It seemed to me he had always been a lonesome kid. I felt bad.

There is something about a dark cold night that makes you feel close to someone you're sleeping with. When you talk together it is like you are the only people awake in the town.

"You're a swell kid, Sucker," I said.

It seemed to me suddenly that I did like him more than anybody else I knew—more than any other boy, more than my sisters, more in a certain way even than Maybelle. I felt good all over and it was like when they play sad music in the movies. I wanted to show Sucker how much I really thought of him and make up for the way I had always treated him.

We talked for a good while that night. His voice was fast and it was like he had been saving up these things to tell me for a long time. He mentioned that he was going to try to build a canoe and that the kids down the block wouldn't let him in on their football team and I don't know what all. I talked some too and it was a good feeling to think of him taking in everything I said so seriously. I even spoke of Maybelle a little, only I made out like it was her who had been running after me all this time. He asked questions about high school and so forth. His voice was excited and he kept on talking fast like he could never get the words out in time. When I went to sleep he was still talking and I could still feel his breathing on my shoulder, warm and close.

During the next couple of weeks I saw a lot of Maybelle. She acted as though she really cared for me a little. Half the time I felt so good I hardly knew what to do with myself.

But I didn't forget about Sucker. There were a lot of old things in my bureau drawer I'd been saving—boxing gloves and Tom Swift books and second rate fishing tackle. All this I turned over to him. We had some more talks together and it was really like I was knowing him for the first time. When there was a long cut on his cheek I knew he had been monkeying around with this new first razor set of mine, but I didn't say anything. His face seemed different now. He used to look timid and sort of like he was afraid of a whack over the head. That expression was gone. His face, with those wide-open eyes and his ears sticking out and his mouth never quite shut, had the look of a person who is surprised and expecting something swell.

Once I started to point him out to Maybelle and tell her he was my kid brother. It was an afternoon when a murder mystery was on at the movie. I had earned a dollar working for my Dad and I gave Sucker a quarter to go and get candy and so forth. With the rest I took Maybelle. We were sitting near the back and I saw Sucker come in. He began to stare at the screen the minute he stepped past the ticket man and he stumbled down the aisle without noticing where he was going. I started to punch Maybelle but couldn't quite make up my mind. Sucker looked a little silly—walking like a drunk with his eyes glued to the movie. He was wiping his reading glasses on his shirt tail and his knickers flopped down. He went on until he got to the first few rows where the kids usually sit. I never did punch Maybelle. But I got to thinking it was good to have both of them at the movie with the money I earned.

I guess things went on like this for about a month or six weeks. I felt so good I couldn't settle down to study or put my mind on anything. I wanted to be friendly with everybody. There were times when I just had to talk to some person. And usually that would be Sucker. He felt as good as I did. Once he said: "Pete, I am gladder that you are like my brother than anything else in the world."

Then something happened between Maybelle and me. I never have figured out just what it was. Girls like her are hard to understand. She began to act different toward me. At first I wouldn't let myself believe this and tried to think it was just my imagination. She didn't act glad to see me anymore. Often she went out riding with this fellow on the football team who owns this yellow roadster.[2] The car was the color of

---

2. **roadster:** a small automobile with a fabric top that seats two people.

her hair and after school she would ride off with him, laughing and looking into his face. I couldn't think of anything to do about it and she was on my mind all day and night. When I did get a chance to go out with her she was snippy and didn't seem to notice me. This made me feel like something was the matter—I would worry about my shoes clopping too loud on the floor, or the fly of my pants, or the bumps on my chin. Sometimes when Maybelle was around, a devil would get into me and I'd hold my face stiff and call grown men by their last names without the Mister and say rough things. In the night I would wonder what made me do all this until I was too tired for sleep.

At first I was so worried I just forgot about Sucker. Then later he began to get on my nerves. He was always hanging around until I would get back from high school, always looking like he had something to say to me or wanted me to tell him. He made me a magazine rack in his Manual Training class[3] and one week he saved his lunch money and bought me three packs of cigarettes. He couldn't seem to take it in that I had things on my mind and didn't want to fool with him. Every afternoon it would be the same—him in my room with this waiting expression on his face. Then I wouldn't say anything or I'd maybe answer him rough-like and he would finally go on out.

I can't divide that time up and say this happened one day and that the next. For one thing I was so mixed p the weeks just slid along into each other and I felt like hell and didn't care. Nothing definite was said or done. Maybelle still rode around with this fellow in his yellow roadster and sometimes she would smile at me and sometimes not. Every afternoon I went from one place to another where I thought she would be. Either she would act almost nice and I would begin thinking how nice things would finally clear up and she would care for me—or else she'd behave so that if she hadn't been a girl I'd have wanted to grab her by that white little neck and choke her. The more ashamed I felt for making a fool of myself the more I ran after her.

Sucker kept getting on my nerves more and more. He would look at me as though he sort of blamed me for something, but at the same time

---

3. **Manual Training class:** class in which boys were trained in various crafts, such as woodworking.

knew that it wouldn't last long. He was growing fast and for some reason began to stutter when he talked. Sometimes he had nightmares or would throw up his breakfast. Mom got him a bottle of cod liver oil.

Then the finish came between Maybelle and me. I met her going to the drugstore and asked for a date. When she said no I remarked something sarcastic. She told me she was sick and tired of my being around and that she had never cared a rap about me. She said all that. I just stood there and didn't answer anything. I walked home very slowly.

For several afternoons I stayed in my room by myself. I didn't want to go anywhere or talk to anyone. When Sucker would come in and look at me sort of funny I'd yell at him to get out. I didn't want to think of Maybelle and I sat at my desk reading *Popular Mechanics* or whittling at a toothbrush rack I was making. It seemed to me I was putting that girl out of my mind pretty well.

But you can't help what happens to you at night. This is what made things how they are now.

You see a few nights after Maybelle said those words to me I dreamed about her again. It was like that first time and I was squeezing Sucker's arm so tight I woke him up. He reached for my hand.

"Pete, what's the matter with you?"

All of a sudden I felt so mad my throat choked—at myself and the dream of Maybelle and Sucker and every single person I knew. I remembered all the times Maybelle had humiliated me and everything bad that had ever happened. It seemed to me for a second that nobody would ever like me but a sap like Sucker.

"Why is it we aren't buddies like we were before? Why—?"

"Shut your trap!" I threw off the cover and got up and turned on the light. He sat in the middle of the bed, his eyes blinking and scared.

There was something in me and I couldn't help myself. I don't think anybody ever gets that mad but once. Words came without me knowing what they would be. It was only afterward that I could remember each thing I said and see it all in a clear way.

"Why aren't we buddies? Because you're the dumbest slob I ever saw! Nobody cares anything about you! And just because I felt sorry for you sometimes and tried to act decent don't think I give a darn about a dumb-bunny like you!"

If I'd talked loud or hit him it wouldn't have been so bad. But my voice was slow and like I was very calm. Sucker's mouth was part way open and he looked as though he'd knocked his funny bone. His face was white and sweat came out on his forehead. He wiped it away with the back of his hand and for a minute his arm stayed raised that way as though he was holding something away from him.

"Don't you know a single thing? Haven't you ever been around at all? Why don't you get a girl friend instead of me? What kind of sissy do you want to grow up to be anyway?"

I didn't know what was coming next. I couldn't help myself or think.

Sucker didn't move. He had on one of my pajama jackets and his neck stuck out skinny and small. His hair was damp on his forehead.

"Why do you always hang round me? Don't you know when you're not wanted?"

Afterward I could remember the change in Sucker's face. Slowly the blank look went away and he closed his mouth. His eyes got narrow and his fists shut. There had never been such a look on him before. It was like every second he was getting older. There was a hard look to his eyes you don't see usually in a kid. A drop of sweat rolled down his chin and he didn't notice. He just sat there with those eyes on me and he didn't speak and his face was hard and didn't move.

"No you don't know when you're not wanted. You're too dumb. Just like your name—a dumb Sucker."

It was like something had busted inside me. I turned off the light and sat down in the chair by the window. My legs were shaking and I was so tired I could have bawled. The room was cold and dark. I sat there for a long time and smoked a squashed cigarette I had saved. Outside the yard was black and quiet. After a while I heard Sucker lie down.

I wasn't mad anymore, only tired. It seemed awful to me that I had talked like that to a kid only twelve. I couldn't take it all in. I told myself I would go over to him and try to make it up. But I just sat there in the cold until a long time had passed. I planned how I could straighten it out in the morning. Then, trying not to squeak the springs, I got back in bed.

Sucker was gone when I woke up the next day. And later when I wanted to apologize as I had planned he looked at me in this new hard way so that I couldn't say a word.

All of that was two or three months ago. Since then Sucker has grown faster than any boy I ever saw. He's almost as tall as I am and his bones have gotten heavier and bigger. He won't wear any of my old clothes any more and has bought his first pair of long pants[4]—with some leather suspenders to hold them up. Those are just the changes that are easy to see and put into words.

Our room isn't mine at all any more. He's gotten up this gang of kids and they have a club. When they aren't digging trenches in some vacant lot and fighting they are always in my room. On the door there is some foolishness written in Mercurochrome saying: ""Woe to the Outsider who Enters" and signed with crossed bones and their secret initials. They have rigged up a radio and every afternoon it blares out music. Once as I was coming in I heard a boy telling something in a loud voice about what he saw in the back of his brother's automobile. I could guess what I didn't hear. *That's what her and my brother do. It's the truth—parked in the car.* For a minute Sucker looked surprised and his face was almost like it used to be. Then he got hard and tough again. "Sure, dumbbell. We know all that." They didn't notice me. Sucker began telling them how in two years he was planning to be a trapper in Alaska.

But most of the time Sucker stays by himself. It is worse when we are alone together in the room. He sprawls across the bed in those long corduroy pants with the suspenders and just stares at me with that hard, half-sneering look. I fiddle around my desk and can't get settled because of those eyes of his. And the thing is I just have to study because I've gotten three bad cards this term already. If I flunk English I can't graduate next year. I don't want to be a bum and I just have to get my mind on it. I don't care a flip for Maybelle or any particular girl any more and it's only this thing between Sucker and me that is the trouble now. We never speak except when we have to before the family. I don't even want to call him Sucker any more and unless I forget I call him by his real name, Richard. At night I can't study with him in the room and I have to hang around the drug store, smoking and doing nothing, with the fellows who loaf there.

More than anything I want to be easy in my mind again. And I miss the way Sucker and I were for a while in a funny, sad way that before

---

4. **long pants:** At the time this story takes place, boys wore either short pants or knickers (pants that came just below the knee) with long socks until they reached a certain age, usually twelve or thirteen.

this I never would have believed. But everything is so different that there seems to be nothing I can do to get it right. I've sometimes thought if we could have it out in a big fight that would help. But I can't fight him because he's four years younger. And another thing— sometimes this look in his eyes makes me almost believe that if Sucker could he would kill me.

Responding to the Story

1. How did you feel about Sucker when the story ended? In several paragraphs explain why you think you came to feel the way you did. (Think about the ways the author described Sucker throughout the story.)
2. "If a person admires you a lot you despise him and don't care—and it is the person who doesn't notice you that you are apt to admire."
    a. Explain what the narrator means by these words. How are these words relevant to the story?
    b. Write a short paper in which you support or refute the idea in this quotation. Base your paper on your own experiences.

Exploring the Author's Craft

This story is carefully structured. Explain how the stories of the narrator and Maybelle and the narrator and Sucker parallel each other.

Writer's Workshop

In any form you wish—story, essay, poem, or short script—create a written work that explores a relationship between two siblings. If you are writing prose, write about two or three different incidents that show the changing nature of the relationship between the two.

Robert Cormier

Robert Cormier worked as a reporter in Worcester and Fitchburg, Massachusetts, before turning to fiction. He was born in 1925 in Leominster, Massachusetts, where he continues to live. He was married in 1948, and he and his wife have four children.

The Chocolate War (1974), *I Am the Cheese* (1977), and *After the First Death* (1979) all won Outstanding Book of the Year awards from *The New York Times* and Best Book for Young Adults awards from the American Library Association. *The Bumblebee Flies Anyway* (1983) also won the ALA award. Cormier's other works include *Beyond the Chocolate War* (1985), *Fade* (1988), *Take Me Where the Good Times Are* (1991), and *Tunes for Bears to Dance To* (1992). His short stories are collected in *Eight Plus One* (1980).

Cormier has said that he writes books with young adult characters, not young adult books. The many letters he receives from his readers attest to the wide popularity of his books, which deal with serious subjects in a way that appeals to adults and younger readers alike.

A boy sees his father with another woman—and his imagination takes off.

Guess What? I Almost Kissed My Father Goodnight!

I've got to get to the bottom of it all somehow and maybe this is the best way. It's about my father. For instance, I found out recently that my father is actually forty-five years old. I knew that he was forty-something but it never meant anything to me. I mean, trying to imagine someone over forty and what it's like to be that old is the same as trying to imagine what the world would be like in, say 1999. Anyway, he's forty-five, and he has the kind of terrible job that fathers have; in his case, he's office manager for a computer equipment concern. Nine-to-five stuff. Four weeks vacation every year but two weeks must be taken between January and May so he usually ends up painting the house or building a patio or something like that in April, and then we travel the other two weeks in July. See America First. He reads a couple of newspapers every day and never misses the seven o'clock news on television.

Here are some other vital statistics my research turned up: He's five ten, weighs 160 pounds, has a tendency toward high blood pressure, enjoys a glass of beer or two while he's watching the Red Sox on television, sips one martini and never two before dinner, likes his steak medium rare and has a habit of saying that "tonight, by God, I'm going to stay up and watch Johnny Carson," but always gropes his way to bed after the eleven o'clock news, which he watches only to learn the next day's weather forecast. He has a pretty good sense of humor but a weakness for awful puns which he inflicts on us at the dinner table: "Do you carrot all for me? I'm in a stew over you." We humor him. By we, I mean my sisters. Annie, who is nineteen and away at college, and Debbie, who is fourteen and spends her life on the telephone. And me: I'm Mike, almost sixteen and a sophomore in high school. My mother's name is Ellen—Dad calls her Ellie—and she's a standard mother. "Clean up your room! Is your homework done?"

Now that you've gotten the basic details, I'll tell you about that day last month when I walked downtown from school to connect with the North Side bus which deposits me in front of my house. It was one of those terrific days in spring and the air smelled like vacation, and it made you ache with all the things you wanted to do and all the places you wanted to see and all the girls you wanted to meet. Like the girl at the bus stop that I've been trying to summon up the nerve to approach for weeks: so beautiful she turns my knees liquid. Anyway, I barreled through Bryant Park, a shortcut, the turf spring-soft and spongy under my feet and the weeping willows hazy with blossom. Suddenly I screeched to a halt, like Bugs Bunny in one of those crazy television cartoons. There's a car parked near the Civil War cannon. Ours. I recognize the dent in the right front fender Annie put there last month when she was home from college. And there are also those decals on the side window that give the geography of our boring vacation trips, *Windy Chasms*, places like that.

The car is unoccupied. Did somebody steal it and abandon it here ? Wow, great! I walk past the splashing fountain that displays one of those embarrassing naked cherubs and stop short again. There he is: my father. Sitting on a park bench. Gazing out over a small pond that used to have goldfish swimming around until kids started stealing them. My father was deep in thought, like a statue in a museum. I looked at my watch. Two-thirty in the afternoon, for crying out loud. What was he doing there at this time of day? I was about to approach him but hesitated, held back for some reason—I don't know why. Although he looked perfectly normal, I felt as though I had somehow caught him naked, had trespassed on forbidden territory, the way I'm afraid to have my mother come barging into my bedroom at certain moments. I drew back, studying him as if he were a sudden stranger. I saw the familiar thinning short hair, the white of his scalp showing through. The way the flesh in his neck has begun to pucker like turkey skin. Now, he sighed. I saw his shoulders heave, and the rest of his body shudder like the chain reaction of freight cars. He lifted his face to the sun, eyes closed. He seemed to be reveling in the moment, all his pores open. I tiptoed away. People talk about tiptoeing but I don't think I ever really tiptoed before in my life. Anyway, I leave him there, still basking on that park bench, because I've got something more important to do at the bus stop. Today, I have vowed to approach the girl, talk to her, say something, *anything*. After all, I'm not exactly Frankenstein and some girls actually think I'm fun to be with. Anyway, she isn't at the bus stop. I stall around and miss the two-forty-five deliberately. She never shows up. At three-thirty, I thumb home and pick up a ride in a green MG, which kind of compensates for a rotten afternoon.

At dinner that evening, I'm uncommunicative, thinking of the girl and all the science homework waiting in my room. Dinner at our house is a kind of ritual that alternates between bedlam and boredom with no sense of direction whatever. Actually, I don't enjoy table talk. I have this truly tremendous appetite and I eat too fast, like my mother says. The trouble is that I'm always being asked a question or expected to laugh at some corny joke when my mouth is full, which it usually is. But that evening I stopped eating altogether when my mother asked my father about his day at the office.

"Routine," he said.

I thought of that scene in the park.

"Did you have to wait around all day for that Harper contract?" my mother asked.

"Didn't even have time for a coffee break," he said, reaching for more potatoes.

I almost choked on the roast beef. He lied: my father actually lied. I sat there, terrified, caught in some kind of terrible no-man's land. It was as if the lie itself had thrust me into panic. Didn't I fake my way through life most of the time—telling half-truths to keep everybody happy, either my parents or my teachers or even my friends? What would happen if everybody started telling the truth all of a sudden? But I was bothered by his motive. I mean—why did he have to pretend that he *wasn't* in the park that afternoon? And the first question came back to haunt me worse than before—what was he doing there, anyway, in the first place?

I found myself studying him across the table, scrutinizing him with the eyes of a stranger. But it didn't work. He was simply my father. Looked exactly as he always did. He was his usual dull unruffled self, getting ready to take his evening nap prior to the television news. Stifling a yawn after dessert. Forget it, I told myself. There's a simple explanation for everything.

Let's skip some time now until the night of the telephone call. And let me explain about the telephone setup at our house. First of all, my father never answers the phone. He lets it ring nine or ten or eleven times and merely keeps on reading the paper and watching television because he claims—and he's right—that most of the calls are for Debbie or me. Anyway, a few nights after that happening at the park, the phone rang about ten-thirty and I barreled out of my room because he and my mother get positively explosive about calls after nine on school nights.

When I lifted the receiver, I found that my father had already picked up the downstairs extension. There was a pause and then he said: "I've got it, Mike."

"Yes, sir," I said. And hung up.

I stood there in the upstairs hallway, not breathing. His voice was a murmur and even at that distance I detected some kind of intimacy. Or did the distance itself contribute that hushed, secretive quality? I returned to my room and put a Blood, Sweat and Tears on the stereo. I remembered that my mother was out for the evening, a meeting of the Ladies' Auxiliary. I got up and looked in the mirror. Another lousy pimple, on the right side of my nose to balance the one on the left. Who had called him on the telephone at that hour of the night? And why had he answered the call in record time? Was it the same person he'd been waiting for in Bryant Park? Don't be ridiculous, Mike, I told myself; think of real stuff, like pimples. Later, I went downstairs and my father was slumped in his chair, newspaper like a fragile tent covering his face. His snores capsized the tent and it slid to the floor. He needed a shave, his beard like small slivers of ice. His feet were fragile, something I had never noticed before; they were mackerel white, half in and half out of his slippers. I went back upstairs without checking the refrigerator, my hunger suddenly annihilated by guilt. He wasn't mysterious: he was my father. And he snored with his mouth open.

The next day I learned the identity of the girl at the bus stop: like a bomb detonating. Sally Bettencourt. There's a Sally Bettencourt in every high school in the world—the girl friend of football heroes, the queen of the prom, Miss Apple Blossom Time. That's Sally Bettencourt of Monument High. And I'm not a football hero, although I scored three points in the intramural basketball tournament last winter. And she *did* smile at me a few weeks ago while waiting for the bus. Just for the record, let me put down here how I found out her name. She was standing a few feet from me, chatting with some girls and fellows, and I drifted toward her and saw her name written on the cover of one of her books. Detective work.

The same kind of detective work sent me investigating my father's desk the next day. He keeps all his private correspondence and office papers in an old battered roll-top my mother found at an auction and sandpapered and refinished. No one was at home. The desk was unlocked. I opened drawers and checked some diarylike type notebooks. Nothing but business stuff. All kinds of receipts. Stubs of cancelled checks. Dull. But a bottom drawer revealed the kind of box that contains correspondence paper and envelopes. Inside, I found envelops of different shapes and sizes and colors. Father's Day cards he had saved through the years. I found one with a scrawled "Mikey" painstakingly written when I was four or five probably. His secret love letters—from Annie and Debbie and me.

"Looking for something?"

His shadow fell across the desk. I mumbled something, letting irritation show in my voice. I have found that you can fake adults out by muttering and grumbling as if you're using some foreign language that they couldn't possibly understand. And they feel intimidated or confused. Anyway, they decide not to challenge you or make an issue of it. That's what happened at that moment. There I was snooping in my father's desk and because I muttered unintelligibly when he interrupted me, *he* looked embarrassed while I stalked from the room as if I was the injured party, ready to bring suit in court.

Three things happened in the next week and they had nothing to do with my father: First, I called Sally Bettencourt. The reason why I called her is that I could have sworn she smiled again at me at the bus stop one afternoon. I mean, not a polite smile but a smile for *me*, as if she recognized me as a person, an individual. Actually I called her three times in four days. She was *(a)* not at home and the person on the line (her mother? Her sister?) had no idea when she'd arrive; *(b)* she was taking a shower—"Any message?" "No"; *(c)* the line was busy. What would I have said to her, if she'd answered? I've always had the feeling that I'm a real killer on the phone when I don't have to worry about what to do with my hands or how bad my posture is. The second thing that happened was a terrible history test which I almost flunked: a low C that could possibly keep me off the Honor Roll, which would send my mother into hysterics. Number 3: I received my assignment from the Municipal Park Department for my summer job—lifeguard at Pool Number 38. Translation: Pool Number 38 is for children twelve years old and younger, not the most romantic pool in our city.

Bugged by history, I talked Mister Rogers, the teacher, into allowing me some extra work to rescue my mark and I stayed up late one night, my stereo earphones clamped on my head so that I wouldn't disturb anyone as the cool sounds of the Tinted Orange poured into my ears. Suddenly, I awoke—shot out of a cannon. My watch said one-twenty. One-twenty in the morning. I yawned. My mouth felt rotten, as if the French Foreign Legion had marched through it barefoot (one of my father's old jokes that I'd heard about a million times). I went downstairs for a glass of orange juice. A light spilled from the den. I sloshed orange juice on my shirt as I stumbled toward the room. He's there: my father. Slumped in his chair. Like death. And I almost drop dead myself. But his lips flutter and he produces an enormous snore. One arm dangles to the floor, limp as a draped towel. His fingers are almost touching a book that had evidently fallen from his hand. I pick it up. Poetry. A poet I never heard of. Kenneth Fearing. Riffling the pages, I find that the poems are mostly about the Depression. In front of the book there's an inscription. Delicate handwriting, faded lavender ink. "To Jimmy, I'll never forget you. Muriel." Jimmy? My father's name is James and my mother and his friends call him Jim. But Jimmy? I notice a date at the bottom of the page, meticulously recorded in that same fragile handwriting—November 2, 1942—when he was young enough to be called Jimmy. By some girl whose name was Muriel, who gave him a book of poems that he takes out and reads in the dead of night even if they are poems about the Depression. He stirs, grunting, clearing his throat, his hand like a big white spider searching the floor for the book. I replace the book on the floor and glide out of the room and back upstairs.

The next day I began my investigation in earnest and overlooked no details. That's when I found out what size shoes, socks, shirts, etc., that he wears. I looked in closets and bureaus, his workbench in the cellar, not knowing what I was searching for but the search itself important. There was one compensation: at least, it kept my mind off Sally Bettencourt. I had finally managed to talk to her on the telephone. We spoke mostly in monosyllables. It took me about ten minutes to identify myself ("The fellow at *what* bus stop?") because apparently all those smiles sent in my direction had been meaningless and my face was as impersonal as a label on a can of soup. The conversation proceeded downward from that point and reached bottom when she said: "Well, thanks for calling, Mark." I didn't bother to correct her. She was so sweet about it all. All the Sally Bettencourts of the world are that way: that's why you keep on being in love with them when you know it's entirely useless. Even when you hang up and see your face in the hallway mirror—what a terrible place to hang a mirror—your face all crumpled up like a paper bag. And the following day, she wasn't at the bus stop, of course. But then neither was I.

What I mean about the bus stop is this: I stationed myself across the street to get a glimpse of her, to see if she really was as beautiful as I remembered or if the phone call had diminished her loveliness. When she didn't arrive, I wandered through the business district. Fellows and girls lingered in doorways. Couples held hands crossing the street. A record store blared out "Purple Evenings" by the Tinted Orange. I spotted my father. He was crossing the street, dodging traffic, as if he was dribbling an invisible ball down a basketball court. I checked my watch: two fifty-five. Stepping into a doorway, I observed him hurrying past the Merchants Bank and Appleton's Department Store and the Army-Navy Surplus Supply Agency. He paused in front of the Monument Public Library. And disappeared inside. My father—visiting the library? He didn't even have a library card, for crying out loud.

I'm not exactly crazy about libraries, either. Everybody whispers or talks low as if the building has a giant volume knob turned down to practically zero. As I stood here, I saw Laura Kincaid drive up in her new LeMans. A quiet, dark green LeMans. Class. "If I had to describe Laura Kincaid in one word, it would be 'class,'" I'd heard my father say once. The car drew into a parking space, as if the space had been waiting all day for her arrival. She stepped out of the door. She is blond, her hair the color of lemonade as it's being poured on a hot day. I stood there, paralyzed. A scene leaped in my mind: Laura Kincaid at a New Year's Party at our house, blowing a toy horn just before midnight while I watched in awe from the kitchen, amazed at how a few glasses of booze could convert all these bankers and Rotary Club members and Chamber of Commerce officials into the terrible kind of people you see dancing to Guy Lombardo on television while the camera keeps cutting back to Times Square where thousands of other people, most of them closer to my age, were also acting desperately happy. I stood there thinking of that stuff because I was doing some kind of juggling act in my mind—trying to figure out why was she at this moment walking across the street, heading for the library, her hair a lemon halo in the sun, her nylons flashing as she hurried. What was her hurry? There was barely any traffic. Was she on her way to a rendezvous? Stop it, you nut, I told myself, even as I made my way to the side entrance.

The library is three stories high, all the stacks and bookshelves built around an interior courtyard. I halted near the circulation desk with no books in my arms to check out. Feeling ridiculous, I made my way to the bubbler. The spray of water was stronger than I expected: my nostrils were engulfed by water. For some reason, I thought of Sally Bettencourt and how these ridiculous events kept happening to me and I ached with longing for her, a terrible emptiness inside of me that needed to be filled. I climbed the stairs to the third floor, my eyes flying all over the place, trying to spot my father. And Laura Kincaid. And knowing all the time that it was merely a game, impossible, ridiculous.

And then I saw them. Together. Standing at the entrance to the alcove that was marked 818 to 897. Two books were cradled in her arms like babies. My father wasn't looking at the books or the shelves or the walls or the ceilings or the floor or anything. He was looking at her. Then, they laughed. It was like a silent movie. I mean—I saw their eyes light up and their lips moving but didn't hear anything. My father shook his head, slowly, a smile lingering tenderly on his face. I drew back into the alcove labeled 453 to 521, across from them, apprehensive, afraid that suddenly they might see me spying on them. His hand reached up and touched her shoulder. They laughed again, still merrily. She indicated the books in her arms. He nodded, an eagerness in his manner. He didn't look as if he had ever snored in his life or taken a nap after dinner. They looked around. She glanced at her watch. He gestured vaguely.

Pressed against the metal bookshelf, I felt conspicuous, vulnerable, as if they would suddenly whirl and see me, and point accusing fingers. But nothing like that happened. She finally left, simply walked away, the books still in her arm. My father watched her go, his face in shadow. She walked along the balcony, then down the spiral stairs, the nylons still flashing, her hair a lemon waterfall. My father watched until she disappeared from view. I squinted, trying to discern his features, to see whether he was still my father, searching for the familiar landmarks of his face and body, needing some kind of verification. I watched him for a minute or two as he stood there looking down, his eyes tracing the path of her departure as if she were still visible. I studied his face: was this my father? And then this terrible numbness invaded my body, like a Novocain of the spirit, killing all my emotions. And the numbness even pervaded my mind, slowing down my thoughts. For which I was grateful. All the way home on the bus, I stared out the window, looking at the landscapes and the buildings and the people but not really seeing them, as if I was storing them in my mind like film to develop them later when they'd have meaning for me.

At dinner, the food lay unappetizingly on my plate. I had to fake my way through the meal, lifting the fork mechanically. I found it difficult not to look at my father. What I mean is—I didn't want to look at him. And because I didn't, I kept doing it. Like when they tell you not to think of a certain subject and you can't help thinking of it.

"Aren't you feeling well, Mike?" my mother asked.

I leaped about five feet off my chair. I hadn't realized how obvious I must have appeared: the human eating machine suddenly toying with his food—steak, at that, which requires special concentration.

"He's probably in love," Debbie said.

And that word *love*. I found it difficult to keep my eyes away from my father.

"I met Laura Kincaid at the library today," I heard my father say.

"Was she able to get a copy of the play?" my mother asked.

"Two of them," he said, munching. "I still think *Streetcar Named Desire* is pretty ambitious for you girls to put on."

"The Women's Auxiliary knows no fear of Tennessee Williams," my mother said in that exaggerated voice she uses when she's kidding around.

"You know, that's funny, Dad," I heard myself saying. "I saw you in the library this afternoon and was wondering what you were doing there."

"Oh? I didn't see you, Mike."

"He was supposed to pick up the play on my library card. But then Laura Kincaid came by . . ." That was my mother explaining it all, although I barely made out the words.

I won't go into the rest of the scene and I won't say that my appetite suddenly came back and that I devoured the steak. Because I didn't. That was two days ago and I still feel funny about it all. Strange I mean. That's why I'm writing this, putting it all down, all the evidence I gathered. That first time in the park when he was sitting there. The telephone call. That book of poetry he reads late at night, "To Jimmy, I'll never forget you, Muriel." Laura Kincaid in the library. Not much evidence, really. Especially when I look at him and see how he's my father all right.

Last night, I came downstairs after finishing my homework and he had just turned off the television set. "Cloudy tomorrow, possible showers," he said, putting out the lights in the den.

We stood there in the half-darkness.

"Homework done, Mike?"

"Yes."

"Hey, Dad."

"Yes, Mike?" Yawning.

I didn't plan to ask him. But it popped out. "I was looking through a book of yours the other day. Poetry by some guy named Fearing or Nearing or something." I couldn't see his face in the half dark. Keeping my voice light, I said: "Who's this Muriel who gave you the book, anyway?"

His laugh was a playful bark. "Boy, that was a long time ago. Muriel Stanton." He closed the kitchen window. "I asked her to go to the Senior Prom but she went with someone else. We were friends. I mean—I thought we were more than friends until she went to the Prom with someone else. And so she gave me a gift—of friendship—at graduation." We walked into the kitchen together. "That's a lousy swap, Mike. A book instead of a date with a girl you're crazy about." He smiled ruefully. "Hadn't though of good old Muriel for years."

You see? Simple explanations for everything. And if I exposed myself as a madman and asked him about the other stuff, the park and the telephone call, I knew there would be perfectly logical reasons. And yet. And yet. I remember that day in the library, when Laura Kincaid walked away from him. I said that I couldn't see his face, not clearly anyway, but I could see a bit of his expression. And it looked familiar but I couldn't pin it down. And now I realized why it was familiar: it reminded me of my own face when I looked into the mirror the day I hung up the phone after talking to Sally Bettencourt. All kind of crumpled up. Or was that my imagination? Hadn't my father been all the way across the library courtyard, too far away for me to tell what kind of expression was on his face?

Last night, standing in the kitchen, as I poured a glass of milk and he said: "Doesn't your stomach ever get enough?" I asked him: "Hey, Dad. You get lonesome sometimes? I mean: that's a crazy question, maybe. But I figure grownups, like fathers and mothers—you get to feeling *down* sometimes, don't you?"

I could have sworn his eyes narrowed and something leaped in them, some spark, some secret thing that had suddenly come out of hiding.

"Sure, Mike. Everybody gets the blues now and then. Even fathers are people. Sometimes, I can't sleep and get up and sit in the dark in the middle of the night. And it gets lonesome because you think of . . ."

"What do you think of, Dad?"

He yawned. "Oh, a lot of things."

That's all. And here I am sitting up in the middle of the night writing this, feeling lonesome, thinking of Sally Bettencourt, and how I haven't a chance with her and thinking, too, of Muriel Stanton who wouldn't go to the Senior Prom with my father. How he gets lonesome sometimes. And sits up in the night, reading poetry. I think of his anguished face at the library and the afternoon at Bryant Park, and all the mysteries of his life that show he's a person. Human.

Earlier tonight, I saw him in his chair, reading the paper, and I said, "Goodnight, Dad," and he looked up and smiled, but an absent kind of smile, as if he was thinking of something else, long ago and far away, and, for some ridiculous feeling, I felt like kissing him goodnight. But didn't, of course. Who kisses his father at sixteen?

Responding to the Story

1. Why is the narrator surprised at seeing his father sitting on a park bench? Do you understand how Mike felt at that moment? Explain.
2. "Didn't I fake my way through life most of the time—telling half-truths to keep everybody happy, either my parents or my teachers or even my friends?" Do these words ring true to life as you know it? Explain.
3. "Even fathers are people." What does Mikes' father mean by these words? What evidence do you have that these words are or aren't true about all fathers, not just Mike's?

Exploring the Author's Craft

Figurative language is language that makes use of comparisons to bring a picture to the reader's mind. **Similes** make comparisons using *like* or *as*; and **metaphors** simply say one thing is another. Note some of the similes and metaphors in this story:

"His beard like small slivers of ice . . ."

"His feet were mackerel white . . ."

"My face was as impersonal as a label on a can of soup."

"Your face all crumpled up like a paper bag . . ."

"He was crossing the street, dodging traffic, as if he was dribbling an
    invisible ball down a basketball court."

"Her hair the color of lemonade . . ."

"Her hair a lemon waterfall . . ."

Find and list several other examples of figurative language in this story.

Writer's Workshop

Think of someone whom you know well and whose physical characteristics are clear to you. Now describe that person in two or three paragraphs; use at least three *original* similes and/or metaphors.

James Purdy

James Purdy, who was born in 1923, studied at and received a master's degree from the University of Chicago. When no one would publish his early writing, he paid to have a novel and several short stories printed and sent the work to important literary figures, hoping to receive some positive comments. He was given a major compliment by Dame Edith Sitwell, British poet, who called several of his short stories "superb, nothing short of masterpieces" and his novel 63: *Dream Palace* "a masterpiece from every point of view." Purdy 's works, which include collections of short stories, novels, poetry, and plays, frequently focus on the devastating effects parents can have on their children—a good description of what happens in the story that follows.

They were just old photographs—but they gave Paul a vital link with his dead father.

Why Can't They Tell You Why?

Paul knew nearly nothing of his father until he found the box of photographs on the back stairs. From then on he looked at them all day and every evening, and when his mother Ethel talked to Edith Gainesworth on the telephone. He had looked amazed at his father in his different ages and stations of life, first as a boy his age, then as a young man, and finally before his death in his army uniform.

Ethel had always referred to him as *your father,* and now the photographs made him look much different from what this had suggested in Paul's mind.

Ethel never talked with Paul about why he was home sick from school and she pretended at first she did not know he had found the photographs. But she told everything she thought and felt about him to Edith Gainesworth over the telephone, and Paul heard all of the conversations from the back stairs where he sat with the photographs, which he had moved from the old shoe boxes where he had found them to two big clean empty candy boxes.

"Wouldn't you know a sick kid like him would take up with photographs," Ethel said to Edith Gainesworth. "Instead of toys or balls, old photos. And my God, I've hardly mentioned a thing to him about his father."

Edith Gainesworth, who studied psychology at an adult center downtown, often advised Ethel about Paul, but she did not say anything tonight about the photographs.

"All mothers should have pensions," Ethel continued. "If it isn't a terrible feeling being on your feet all day before the public and then having a sick kid under your feet when you're off at night. My evenings are worse than my days."

These telephone conversations always excited Paul because they were the only times he heard himself and the photographs discussed. When the telephone bell would ring he would run to the back stairs and begin looking at the photographs and then as the conversation progressed he often ran into the front room where Ethel was talking, sometimes carrying one of the photographs with him and making sounds like a bird or an airplane.

Two months had gone by like this, with his having attended school hardly at all and his whole life seemingly spent in listening to Ethel talk to Edith Gainesworth and examining the photographs in the candy boxes.

Then in the middle of the night Ethel missed him. She rose feeling a pressure in her scalp and neck. She walked over to his cot and noticed the Indian blanket had been taken away. She called Paul and walked over to the window and looked out. She walked around the upstairs, calling him.

"God, there is always something to bother you," she said. "Where are you, Paul?" she repeated in a mad sleepy voice. She went on down into the kitchen, though it did not seem possible he would be there, he never ate anything.

Then she said *Of course*, remembering how many times he went to the back stairs with those photographs.

"Now what are you doing in here, Paul?" Ethel said, and there was a sweet but threatening sound to her voice that awoke the boy from where he had been sleeping, spread out protectively over the boxes of photographs, his Indian blanket over his back and shoulder.

Paul crouched almost greedily over the boxes when he saw this ugly pale woman in the man's bathrobe looking at him. There was a faint smell from her like that of an uncovered cistern[1] when she put on the robe.

"Just here, Ethel," he answered her question after a while.

"What do you mean, *just here*, Paul?" she said going up closer to him.

She took hold of his hair and jerked him by it gently as though this was a kind of caress she sometimes gave him. This gentle jerking motion made him tremble in short successive starts under her hand, until she let go.

He watched how she kept looking at the boxes of photographs under his guard.

"You sleep here to be near them?" she said.

"I don't know why, Ethel," Paul said, blowing out air from his mouth as though trying to make something disappear before him.

"You don't know, Paul," she said, her sweet fake awful voice and the stale awful smell of the bathrobe stifling as she drew nearer.

"Don't, don't!" Paul cried.

"Don't what?" Ethel answered, pulling him toward her by seizing on his pajama tops.

"Don't do anything to me, Ethel, my eye hurts."

"Your eye hurts," she said with unbelief.

"I'm sick to my stomach."

Then bending over suddenly, in a second she had gathered up the two boxes of photographs in her bathrobed arms.

"Ethel!" he cried out in the strongest, clearest voice she had ever heard come from him. "Ethel, those are my candy boxes!"

She looked down at him as though she was seeing him for the first time, noting with surprise how thin and puny he was, and how disgusting was one small mole that hung from his starved-looking throat. She could not see how this was her son.

---

1. **cistern:** a tank below ground for storing water.

"These boxes of pictures are what makes you sick."

"No, no, Mama Ethel," Paul cried.

"What did I tell you about calling me Mama," she said, going over to him and putting her hand on his forehead.

"I called you Mama Ethel, not Mama," he said.

"I suppose you think I'm a thousand years old." She raised her hand as though she was not sure what she wished to do with it.

"I think I know what to do with these," she said with a pretended calm.

"No, Ethel," Paul said, "give them here back. They are my boxes."

"Tell me why you slept out here on this back stairs where you know you'll make yourself even sicker. I want you to tell me and tell me right away."

"I can't, Ethel, I can't," Paul said.

"Then I'm going to burn the pictures," she replied.

He crawled hurrying over to where she stood and put his arms around her legs.

"Ethel, please don't take them, Ethel. Pretty please."

"Don't touch me," she said to him. Her nerves were so bad she felt that if he touched her again she would start as though a mouse had gotten under her clothes.

"You stand up straight and tell me like a little man why you're here," she said, but she kept her eyes half closed and turned from him.

He moved his lips to answer but then he did not really understand what she meant by *little* man. That phrase worried him whenever he heard it.

"What do you do with the pictures all the time, all day when I'm gone, and now tonight? I never heard of anything like it." Then she moved away from him, so that his hands fell from her legs where he had been grasping her, but she continued to stand near his hands as though puzzled what to do next.

"I look is all, Ethel," he began to explain.

"Don't bawl when you talk," she commanded, looking now at him in the face.

Then: "I want the truth!" she roared.

He sobbed and whined there, thinking over what it was she could want him to tell her, but everything now had begun to go away from his attention, and he had not really ever understood what had been expected of him here, and now everything was too hard to be borne.[2]

"Do you hear me, Paul?" she said between her teeth, very close to him now and staring at him in such an angry way he closed his eyes. "If you don't answer me, do you know what I'm going to do?"

"Punish?" Paul said in his tiniest child voice.

"No, I'm not going to punish this time," Ethel said.

"You're not!" he cried, a new fear and surprise coming now into his tired eyes, and then staring at her eyes, he began to cry with panicky terror, for it seemed to him then that in the whole world there were just the two of them, him and Ethel.

"You remember where they sent Aunt Grace," Ethel said with terrible knowledge.

His crying redoubled in fury, some of his spit flying out onto the cold calcimine of the walls. He kept turning the while to look at the close confines of the staircase as though to find some place where he could see things outside.

"Do you remember where they sent her?" Ethel said in a quiet patient voice like a woman who has endured every unreasonable, disrespectful action from a child whom she still can patiently love.

"Yes, yes, Ethel," Paul cried hysterically.

"Tell Ethel where they sent Aunt Grace," she said with the same patience and kind restraint.

"I didn't know they sent little boys there," Paul said.

"You're more than a little boy now," Ethel replied. "You're old enough. . . . And if you don't tell Ethel why you look at the photographs all the time, we'll have to send you to the mental hospital with the bars."

"I don't know why I look at them, dear Ethel," he said now in a very feeble but wildly tense voice, and he began petting the fur on her houseslippers.

"I think you do, Paul," she said quietly, but he could hear her gentle, patient tone disappearing and he half raised his hands as though to protect him from anything this woman might now do.

"But I don't know why I look at them," he repeated, screaming, and he threw his arms suddenly around her legs.

---

2. **borne:** endured; put up with.

She moved back, but still smiling her patient, knowing, forgiving smile.

"All right for you, Paul." When she said that *all right for you* it always meant the end of any understanding or reasoning with her.

"Where are we going?" he cried, as she ushered him through the door, into the kitchen.

"We're going to the basement, of course," she replied.

They had never gone there together before, and the terror of what might happen to him now gave him a kind of quiet that enabled him to walk steady down the long irregular steps.

"You carry the boxes of pictures, Paul," she said, "since you like them so much."

"No, no," Paul cried.

"Carry them," she commanded, giving them to him.

He held them before him and when they reached the floor of the basement, she opened the furnace and, tightening the cord of her bathrobe, she said coldly, her white face lighted up by the fire, "Throw the pictures into the furnace door, Paul."

He stared at her as though all the nightmares had come true, the complete and final fear of what may happen in living had unfolded itself at last.

"They're Daddy!" he said in a voice neither of them recognized.

"You had your choice," she said coolly. "You prefer a dead man to your own mother. Either you throw his pictures in the fire, for they're what makes you sick, or you will go where they sent Aunt Grace."

He began running around the room now, much like a small bird which has escaped from a pet shop into the confusion of a city street, and making odd little sounds that she did not recognize could come from his own lungs.

"I'm not going to stand for your clowning," she called out, but as though to an empty room.

As he ran round and round the small room with the boxes of photographs pressed against him, some of the pictures fell upon the floor and these he stopped and tried to recapture, at the same time holding the boxes tight against him, and making, as he picked them up, frothing cries of impotence[3] and acute grief.

---

3. impotence: powerlessness; helplessness.

Ethel herself stared at him, incredulous. He not only could not be recognized as her son, he no longer looked like a child, but in his small unmended night shirt like some crippled and dying animal running hopelessly from its pain.

"Give me those pictures!" she shouted, and she seized a few which he held in his fingers, and threw them quickly into the fire.

Then turning back, she moved to take the candy boxes from him.

But the final sight of him made her stop. He had crouched on the floor, and, bending his stomach over the boxes, hissed at her, so that she stopped short, not seeing any way to get at him, seeing no way to bring him back, while from his mouth black thick strings of something slipped out, as though he had spewed out the heart of his grief.

Responding to the Story

1. What do the boxes of photographs mean to Paul? Why do you think he calls them his "candy boxes"?
2. Describe the relationship between Paul and his mother. How does each seem to feel about the other?
3. Consider the title of the story. Who do you think is asking the question in it? Explain your answer.
4. What is the point of the story's ending?

Exploring the Author's Craft

A **third-person narrator** tells *about* the characters in a story but is not a participant in the action. Instead of an "I" telling the story, the characters are referred to as "he" or "she." In some fiction the third-person narrator may know the thoughts of one or more characters; in other narratives no characters' thoughts are revealed. To what extent does the narrator in "Why Can't They Tell You Why?" get into the minds of the characters? Give examples.

Writer's Workshop

Write a story using a third-person narrator. Have the plot center on one or more photographs.

Leslie Norris

Leslie Norris was born in Merthyr Tydfil, Glamorganshire, Wales, in 1921.
He attended Training College in Coventry from 1947–49 and the University
of Southampton Institute of Education from 1955–58. He has been assistant
teacher, deputy head teacher, and head teacher in schools in Yeovil, Bath,
and Chichester. He was a resident poet at Eton College in 1977 and is
currently affiliated with Brigham Young University in Utah.

In addition to poetry, Norris has written stories, collected in *Sliding and
Other Stories* (1976) and *The Girl from Cardigan: Sixteen Stories* (1988), and
short radio plays. He has published in *The New Yorker, Atlantic, Esquire,* and
Audubon magazines.

*The simple act of shaving his bedridden father becomes for Barry a
ritual expression of love.*

Shaving

Earlier, when Barry had left the house to go to the game, an overnight
frost had still been thick on the roads. But the brisk April sun had soon
dispersed it, and now he could feel the spring warmth on his back
through the thick tweed of his coat. His left arm was beginning to stiffen
up where he'd jarred it in a tackle, but it was nothing serious. He flexed
his shoulders against the tightness of his jacket and was surprised again
by the unexpected weight of his muscles, the thickening strength of his
body. A few years back, he thought, he had been a small, unimportant
boy, one of a swarming gang laughing and jostling to school, hardly aware
that he possessed an identity. But time had transformed him. He walked
solidly now, and often alone. He was tall, strongly made, his hands and

feet were adult and heavy, the rooms in which all his life he'd moved had grown too small for him. Sometimes a devouring restlessness drove him from the house to walk long distances in the dark. He hardly understood how it had happened. Amused and quiet, he walked the High Street among the morning shoppers.

He saw Jackie Bevan cross the road and remembered how, when they were both six years old, Jackie had swallowed a pin. The flustered teachers had clucked about Jackie as he stood there, bawling, cheeks awash with tears, his nose wet. But now Jackie was tall and suave, his thick, pale hair sleekly tailored, his gray suit enviable. He was talking to a girl as golden as a daffodil.

"Hey, hey!" called Jackie. "How's the athlete, how's Barry boy?"

He waved a graceful hand at Barry.

"Come and talk to Sue," he said.

Barry shifted his bag to his left hand and walked over, forming in his mind the answers he'd make to Jackie's questions.

"Did we win?" Jackie asked. "Was the old Barry Stanford magic in glittering evidence yet once more this morning? Were the invaders sent hunched and silent back to their hovels in the hills? What was the score? Give us an epic account, Barry, without modesty or delay. This is Sue, by the way."

"I've seen you about," the girl said.

"You could hardly miss him," said Jackie. "Four men, roped together, spent a week climbing him—they thought he was Everest. He ought to carry a warning beacon, he's a danger to aircraft."

"Silly," said the girl, smiling at Jackie. "He's not much taller than you are."

She had a nice voice too.

"We won," Barry said. "Seventeen points to three, and it was a good game. The ground was hard, though."

He could think of nothing else to say.

"Let's all go for a frivolous cup of coffee," Jackie said. "Let's celebrate your safe return from the rough fields of victory. We could pour libations[1] all over the floor for you."

"I don't think so," Barry said. "Thanks. I'll go straight home."

---

1. **libations:** liquid, often wine, poured in celebration of something.

"Okay," said Jackie, rocking on his heels so that the sun could shine on his smile. "How's your father?"

"No better," Barry said. "He's not going to get better."

"Yes, well," said Jackie, serious and uncomfortable, "tell him my mother and father ask about him."

"I will," Barry promised. "He'll be pleased."

Barry dropped the bag in the front hall and moved into the room which had been the dining room until his father's illness. His father lay in the white bed, his long body gaunt, his still head scarcely denting the pillow. He seemed asleep, thin blue lids covering his eyes, but when Barry turned away he spoke.

"Hullo, son," he said. "Did you win?"

His voice was a dry, light rustling, hardly louder than the breath which carried it. Its sound moved Barry to a compassion that almost unmanned him, but he stepped close to the bed and looked down at the dying man.

"Yes," he said. "We won fairly easily. It was a good game."

His father lay with his eyes closed, inert,[2] his breath irregular and shallow.

"Did you score?" he asked.

"Twice," Barry said. "I had a try in each half."

He thought of the easy certainty with which he'd caught the ball before his second try; casually, almost arrogantly he had taken it on the tips of his fingers, on his full burst for the line, breaking the fullback's tackle. Nobody could have stopped him. But watching his father's weakness he felt humble and ashamed, as if the morning's game, its urgency and effort, was not worth talking about. His father's face, fine-skinned and pallid, carried a dark stubble of beard, almost a week's growth, and his obstinate, strong hair stuck out over his brow.

"Good," said his father, after a long pause. "I'm glad it was a good game."

Barry's mother bustled about the kitchen, a tempest of orderly energy.

"Your father's not well," she said. "He's down today, feels depressed. He's a particular man, your father. He feels dirty with all that beard on him."

---

2. **inert:** not moving.

She slammed shut the stove door.

"Mr. Cleaver was supposed to come up and shave him," she said, "and that was three days ago. Little things have always worried your father, every detail must be perfect for him."

Barry filled a glass with milk from the refrigerator. He was very thirsty.

"I'll shave him," he said.

His mother stopped, her head on one side.

"Do you think you can?" she asked. "He'd like it if you can."

"I can do it," Barry said.

He washed his hands as carefully as a surgeon. His father's razor was in a blue leather case, hinged at the broad edge and with one hinge broken. Barry unfastened the clasp and took out the razor. It had not been properly cleaned after its last use and lather had stiffened into hard yellow rectangles between the teeth of the guard. There were water-shaped rust stains, brown as chocolate, on the surface of the blade. Barry removed it, throwing it in the wastebin. He washed the razor until it glistened, and dried it on a soft towel, polishing the thin handle, rubbing its metal head to a glittering shine. He took a new blade from its waxed envelope, the paper clinging to the thin metal. The blade was smooth and flexible to the touch, the little angles of its cutting clearly defined. Barry slotted it into the grip of the razor, making it snug and tight in the head.

The shaving soap, hard, white, richly aromatic, was kept in a wooden bowl. Its scent was immediately evocative and Barry could almost see his father in the days of his health, standing before his mirror, thick white lather on his face and neck. As a little boy Barry had loved the generous perfume of the soap, had waited for his father to lift the razor to his face, for one careful stroke to take away the white suds in a clean revelation of the skin. Then his father would renew the lather with a few sweeps of his brush, one with an ivory handle and the bristles worn, which he still used.

His father's shaving mug was a thick cup, plain and serviceable. A gold line ran outside the rim of the cup, another inside, just below the lip. Its handle was large and sturdy, and the face of the mug carried a portrait of the young Queen Elizabeth II, circled by a wreath of leaves, oak perhaps, or laurel. A lion and unicorn balanced precariously on a scroll above her crowned head, and the Union Jack, the Royal Standard, and other flags were furled each side of the portrait. And beneath it all, in small black letters, ran the legend: "Coronation June 2nd 1953." The cup was much older than Barry. A pattern of faint translucent cracks, fine as a web, had worked itself haphazardly, invisibly almost, through the white glaze. Inside, on the bottom, a few dark bristles were lying, loose and dry. Barry shook them out, then held the cup in his hand, feeling its solidness. Then he washed it ferociously, until it was clinically clean.

Methodically he set everything on a tray, razor, soap, brush, towels. Testing the hot water with a finger, he filled the mug and put that, too, on the tray. His care was absorbed, ritualistic. Satisfied that his preparations were complete, he went downstairs, carrying the tray with one hand.

His father was waiting for him. Barry set the tray on a bedside table and bent over his father, sliding an arm under the man's thin shoulders, lifting him without effort so that he sat against the high pillows.

"You're strong . . ." his father said. He was as breathless as if he'd been running.

"So are you," said Barry.

"I was," his father said. "I used to be strong once."

He sat exhausted against the pillows.

"We'll wait a bit," Barry said.

"You could have used your electric razor," his father said. "I expected that."

"You wouldn't like it," Barry said. "You'll get a closer shave this way."

He placed the large towel about his father's shoulders.

"Now," he said, smiling down.

The water was hot in the thick cup. Barry wet the brush and worked up the lather. Gently he built up a covering of soft foam on the man's chin, on his cheeks and his stark cheekbones.

"You're using a lot of soap," his father said.

"Not too much," Barry said. "You've got a lot of beard."

His father lay there quietly, his wasted arms at his sides.

"It's comforting," he said. "You'd be surprised how comforting it is."

Barry took up the razor, weighing it in his hand, rehearsing the angle at which he'd use it. He felt confident.

"If you have prayers to say, . . ." he said.

"I've said a lot of prayers," his father answered.

Barry leaned over and placed the razor delicately against his father's face, setting the head accurately on the clean line near the ear where the long hair ended. He held the razor in the tips of his fingers and drew the blade sweetly through the lather. The new edge moved light as a touch over the harness of the upper jaw and down to the angle of the chin, sliding away the bristles so easily that Barry could not feel their release. He sighed as he shook the razor in the hot water, washing away the soap.

"How's it going?" his father asked.

"No problem," Barry said. "You needn't worry."

It was as if he had never known what his father really looked like. He was discovering under his hands the clear bones of the face and head; they became sharp and recognizable under his fingers. When he moved his father's face a gentle inch to one side, he touched with his fingers the frail temples, the blue veins of his father's life. With infinite and meticulous care he took away the hair from his father's face.

"Now for your neck," he said. "We might as well do the job properly."

"You've got good hands," his father said. "You can trust those hands, they won't let you down."

Barry cradled his father's head in the crook of his left arm, so that the man could tilt back his head, exposing the throat. He brushed fresh lather under the chin and into the hollows alongside the stretched tendons. His father's throat was fleshless and vulnerable, his head was a hard weight on the boy's arm, Barry was filled with unreasing protective love. He lifted the razor and began to shave.

"You don't have to worry," he said. "Not at all. Not about anything."

He held his father in the bend of his strong arm and they looked at each other. Their heads were very close.

"How old are you?" his father said.

"Seventeen," Barry said. "Near enough seventeen."

"You're young," his father said, "to have this happen."

"Not too young," Barry said. "I'm bigger than most men."

"I think you are," his father said.

He leaned his head tiredly against the boy's shoulder. He was without strength, his face was cold and smooth. He had let go all his authority, handed it over. He lay back on his pillow, knowing his weakness and his mortality, and looked at his son with wonder, with a curious humble pride.

"I won't worry then," he said. "About anything."

"There's no need," Barry said. "Why should you worry?"

He wiped his father's face clean of all soap with a damp towel. The smell of illness was everywhere, overpowering even the perfumed lather. Barry settled his father down and took away the shaving tools, putting them by with the same ceremonial precision with which he'd prepared them: the cleaned and glittering razor in its broken case; the soap, its bowl wiped and dried, on the shelf between the brush and the coronation mug; all free of taint.[3] He washed his hands and scrubbed his nails. His hands were firm and broad, pink after their scrubbing. The fingers were short and strong, the little fingers slightly crooked, and soft dark hair grew on the backs of his hands and his fingers just above the knuckles. Not long ago they had been small bare hands, not very long ago.

Barry opened wide the bathroom window. Already, although it was not yet two o'clock, the sun was retreating and people were moving briskly, wrapped in their heavy coats against the cold that was to come. But now the window was full in the beam of the dying sunlight, and Barry stood there, illuminated in its golden warmth for a whole minute, knowing it would soon be gone.

---

3. **taint:** trace of something harmful or bad.

Responding to the Story

1. How does the shaving bowl represent two different parts of Barry's relationship with his father over the years?
2. The author describes the preparing and putting away of the shaving tools as *ritualistic* and *ceremonial.* Are these words appropriate to these simple acts? Explain.
3. What prompts the father to "let go all his authority" and hand it over to his son?

Exploring the Author's Craft

1. Writers often imply more than they say directly. Explain what is implied in each of the following lines or passages.
   a. "It's comforting," he said. "You'd be surprised how comforting it is."
   b. "You're young," his father said, "to have this happen." "Not too young," Barry said. "I'm bigger than most men." "I think you are," his father said.
   c. "But now the window was full in the beam of the dying sunlight, and Barry stood there, illuminated in its golden warmth for a whole minute, knowing it would soon be gone."
2. **Diction** is an author's choice of words or phrases, and those words intrinsically contribute to the **mood** or atmosphere of a story. In "Shaving" a tender, delicate, and warm mood is conveyed by words such as *cradled* as the boy holds his father's head. Identify five more single words that contribute to the mood you think the story portrays. (A story may have more than one mood.)

Writer's Workshop

This extraordinary story is centered on one seemingly simple activity: a boy shaving his sick father. The story's richness far transcends a simple activity, of course, but the writer first captured, in minute detail, all the actions of the one shave.

1. Observe someone performing an extended action, either in your own home, or in a classroom, gym, restaurant, store, or office. Record in as much detail as you can how that action is performed.
2. Write a prose selection in which you tell about a parent and child involved in an activity together. Guide the reader through the action so that the reader feels that she or he is there with the parent and child.

Budge Wilson

Budge Wilson, who was born in 1927, has published a novel and two collections of short stories, *The Leaving*, which won the Canadian Library Association's Young Adult Book Award in 1991, and *The Dandelion Garden*. Many of her stories are set in the Canadian province of Nova Scotia, but they deal with issues young people everywhere can relate to. A critic gives Wilson the ultimate compliment by saying that her stories are "universal in theme." This, of course, is what every author wants to achieve, universality.

"I have to tell you how I hate this cardboard father of yours"

My Mother and Father

I was born in Grace Maternity Hospital in Halifax, entering the world noisily and with confidence, to greet a mother who was already a widow. Far from her home in the south of France, she spent eight solitary days in the hospital, and then wrapped me in a blue blanket and took me home to an empty house.

It was early November when we entered that house, and France must have seemed a hundred light-years away. My mother had come to Nova Scotia as a young war bride in 1919, and after ten childless years had finally given birth to her first and last baby. The next several months of my life in that home must have been terrible indeed for her. She and my father had moved from Wolfville to Halifax shortly before he died, and she was therefore living in a strange city as well as in a foreign land. Although she had an almost perfect mastery of English, she retained a slight French accent, and was considered strange, alien, too exotic for safety. As a result, she had few acquaintances, no close friends, and of course no husband. Furthermore, it would be six months before one could expect any semblance of summer to soften Canada's stern, uncompromising East Coast. It was fifteen years before I gave more than a few passing thoughts to these matters. Now I often think about them.

However, during my childhood I did think a great deal about my father. As a preschooler, I looked about me and noted that other houses contained fathers who left in the morning and returned at night. These same men took their children to the Halifax Exhibition, mended their bicycles, carried out the garbage, and put on the storm windows. "Where," I asked my mother, at age three, "is my father?" Long ago though that was, I can remember the scene well. She was washing the dishes at the time, and suddenly the sloshing and clatter stopped. I watched her as she stood silent and still, her wet hands clasping the edge of the sink. I even remember that she was wearing a black-and-white checked apron.

Finally, she shook her hands, dried them on the towel that was draped over her shoulder, and sat down beside me at the kitchen table. Her face was completely blank, telling me nothing. Taking my small hand in hers, she said, "Jeanne, my dear, I am sorry, but your father is dead." I asked if he would come back again, but she said no, he would not. Not ever. I thought about that, and then I went out to play. My mother returned to the dishes. I did not grieve or cry. There had been no face to love or miss, no presence to be significant by its absence. I simply lacked something I had never had—like a two-wheeled bike, a pet dog, or curly hair.

My mother maintained a silence on the subject of my father, and it was not until I started school that I asked any further questions. One day in the schoolyard, a small group of children lined up against the swings, chanting:

"The girl in red
Is a girl we know.
She hasn't got a father.
Ho! Ho! Ho!"

I was wearing a red coat; they were obviously referring to me. This nasty rhyme was a familiar one; I am sorry to say that I had already used it myself on other people. One day it might be:

"The girl in the freckles
   Is a girl we know.
   Her teeth are all crooked.
   Ho! Ho! Ho!"

or one I remember forty years later with residual[1] shame:

"The boy who smells
   Is a boy we know.
   His underwear is dirty.
   Ho! Ho! Ho!"

When I returned home from school that noon, my mother was busy preparing dinner. We talked of this and that—unimportant friendly things. Yes, the spelling test was easy. No, I didn't want to take the class piano lessons. Yes, I still liked my teacher very much. But I saved the important question until she was seated, fully occupied with nothing except me. I knew that my question was not a casual one.

As we settled down to our chicken and fried potatoes (I remember that very clearly), I spoke to her with no warning or preamble whatsoever. "How," I asked, as she raised her fork for the first bite, "did my father die?"

She lowered her fork slowly. She seemed to be thinking. Raising her left hand, she bit her thumbnail. Once again, there was no expression on her face. This was characteristic of her: you could never tell what she was thinking. Nowadays they talk a lot about people's vibrations—their vibes—and how we all should be alert to recognize and respond to them. My mother gave off no vibes. She had a masklike, expressionless face that registered love, but almost nothing else. This was both a good thing and a bad thing. I did not have to worry about her looking angry or worried. She never did. On the other hand, apart from what she actually said to me, I knew nothing about her whatsoever. She was a dutiful and in many ways a talented mother. She made me feel loved and secure; she also provided space and materials for creative and independent activities, encouragement for my efforts, interest in my life, and a consistent and

---

1. **residual:** remaining; left over from the past.

dependable routine. But I had no idea who *she* was. Possibly this was fine, too. I *thought* I knew who she was: she was my mother.

I waited for her to reply. Then she pushed aside her fork and clasped her hands together in her lap.

"Your father," she said, "was a brave man. He fought for four years in the war and returned to Canada safe and sound." She sounded as though she were reciting a piece of prose as a school assignment. There was a sing-song quality to her voice, and I could detect no feeling in it. "Ten years later, two months before you were born, we went for a picnic to Lawrencetown Beach. There had been a bad storm the previous day, and the waves were very high. A friend of his went in swimming, and was swept out to sea by the undertow. Your father swam out to try to save him, but the other man grabbed him and dragged him under the water. They both drowned." She then rose and dumped her entire untouched dinner into the garbage. "That," she said, her French accent suddenly very marked, "was the way it was." Then she added. "I hope this will not be making you in fear of the water."

No indeed, it would not be making me in fear of the water. Or of anything else, for that matter. I now had my father, and he would be at my side from then on, whenever I needed him. What I did not know about him I would invent. Unlike my mother, I hungrily attacked my dinner. With elation I gobbled down my chicken and my fried potatoes and asked for a second helping. Then I dashed out the back door, taking the short cut to school through a vacant lot. I knew exactly what I was going to do.

I waited until recess, and then I strode out to the swing set. In as loud a voice as I could muster, I chanted:

"The girl in red
Is a girl you know.
Her father was a *hero*.
Ho! Ho! Ho!"

It was the first time the rhyme had been used as a rebuttal.[2] The children gathered around me, full of questions. What do you mean?

---

2. **rebuttal:** a response to disprove a statement or argument.

What *kind* of hero? What did he *do?* I could see skepticism on some faces, grudging envy on others. So I told them my story—not without embellishment and flair. I did not have French ancestry for nothing. Gesticulating dramatically, I described the beach, the gigantic waves, the cries of the endangered friend. I told how my father, tall, strong, and magnificently built, tossed off his sweater and raced fearlessly into the raging sea, without a thought or backward glance. I lingered over the pursuit of the drowning man, speaking of the power of my father's swimming stroke, of his struggle with his friend, of the way the other man finally dragged him down to the cruel sea bottom. Looking about me, I could see that my audience was a receptive one. I then added a touching postscript, describing the scene on the shore, the sorrowing wives, the arrival of ambulances and stretchers, and the eventual funeral of that doomed heroic man.

From that day on, the vision of my father grew and flourished, and inside my head, he became taller and more handsome. His features were strong and firm, and he was gentle and brave all at the same time. He did not lose his temper or scold, like Alena Marriot's father. He did not belch at the dinner table like Mr. Rankin, nor did he sit around on a deck chair on Sunday afternoons with a fat stomach hanging out. He did not have a fat stomach to begin with, and he also did not sit around. He was too busy taking me to circuses and on camping trips, fixing broken toys, and treating us to Popsicles and double deckers at the ice-cream store. He became my private prop, and I leaned on him often and confidently when the going was not smooth.

I talked a lot about this new father of mine at home. I described what he looked like, what he did, what kind of person he was. My mother listened passively, adding nothing, but also taking nothing away. When the summer months came, I would say to Mother, who had no car, "Dad would have taken us on picnics." When my swing set broke, I said to her, "My *father* could have fixed that." When I had difficulty with my math and she could not help me, I commented, "I'll bet *Dad* could have shown me how this worked." My father was as present in my life as if he had left at eight-thirty and would return again at six.

Gradually, as I started the perverse journey into my teens, I compared my mother more and more to my father and found her wanting. Why was she not more exciting? People from France are supposed to be passionate and fascinating. My father, who was only a *Canadian*, for heaven's sake, was *far* more interesting. Why didn't she have more friends, why couldn't she get rid of that accent, why didn't she buy a car? My father would have had a white convertible, and he would have been forever bringing his friends home for dinner, taking them out for drives, inviting them for the weekend. Why did my mother have to look so *drab?* Why did she pull her hair back from her face in a chignon,[3] and why was she always dressed in black—black sweaters and black slacks, slim black skirts, simple little black dresses? I was tired of her perpetual single strand of pearls. My dad would have worn red plaid shirts on weekends and a blue sweatshirt for fishing. On formal occasions he would have sported a bright striped tie with his navy jacket and his grey flannels. There would have been variety and color to his appearance.

My criticisms—spoken or silent—had little outward effect on my mother, except to make her a little more quiet, a little more sad. This was worse than the still and mysterious dignity that I was used to, and it infuriated me. I did not want to hurt her. I even loved her. But what I really wanted was for her to change. Why couldn't she? Or why *wouldn't* she? I couldn't understand it. To me it seemed so simple. I had pointed out to her the flaws that marred her image to me and to the world. Why did she not at least *argue?* I wanted a mother who was lively, passionate, responsive. I looked at her carefully, objectively. She was very pretty. Her features were small, regular, and well defined; her eyes were enormous. Her hair was thick and still black. In my mind, I refashioned her. Closing my eyes, I put her in a fiery red dress; I curled her hair; I had her dance a jig in the living room. But when I opened my eyes she was still there, features composed, sitting quietly, knitting a pair of argyle socks for her brother in France. She looked up at me and asked gently, "Would you like fish or meat patties for supper?"

I sighed. "Fish," I replied, and went upstairs to finish my homework. The click of her knitting needles get on my nerves.

One Saturday in 1944, when I was a brittle, tense fifteen years of age, I woke up at 8:00 A.M. and contemplated the coming day. I would call my best friend, Judy, and arrange to go shopping with her in the afternoon; later, we would have Cokes at the counter in Diana Sweets, and talk about school and life and boys. Jerry McInnis and his friends

---

3. **chignon** (shēnʹyon): a knot of hair worn at the back of the head.

might be there, too, and someone might ask us to the Hi-Y dance. I jumped out of bed and started dressing. Clothed in bra and panties, I scrutinized myself in the mirror. Not great, I thought, but not bad. My figure was slim but not shapeless. I had small, firm breasts, a tiny waist, and tidy hips. Built like my mother, I thought wryly. I had a lot of jet-black hair; a Veronica Lake hairstyle[4] covered one-half of my small white face. I looked at myself and the world out of one eye.

Enough of this, I thought, and poked around in my bureau for my stockings. These were pre-jeans days. If you wanted to cut a dash in Diana Sweets or on Barrington Street or in Mills Brothers clothing store, you wore a pleated skirt, a baggy sweater, and stockings. It was still wartime, and nylons were non-existent except through something called the black market; panty hose had yet to be invented. But we did have stockings that were less utilitarian than lisle[5] ones, and I searched feverishly for what I knew was my last pair. I opened drawer after drawer and suddenly remembered that I had torn them last week on that stupid broken chair rung. Dad would have fixed that long ago, I thought savagely. He was dead, and my mother was no good at fixing things, and I couldn't go downtown without stockings, and I was furious. I stalked into my mother's room and stared at her bureau drawers. I could hear her downstairs moving about in the kitchen, and I felt that I was safe. I would have done bodily injury to anyone who so much as touched my dresser drawers, but I coldly and systematically explored drawer after drawer, in my search for a pair of stockings I could steal. It was as though I were thinking, If you can't provide me with a father, at least supply me with some stockings.

At last I found the right drawer. It was very small and it was in a night table that I would not have expected to hold clothing. The drawer contained about five pairs, and I looked them over to consider a size, shade, texture. Underneath the stockings was a small envelope on which was written "PRIVATE." I opened it without hesitation.

Inside the envelope were seven photographs. There was one snapshot of a little girl with long black hair and a big grin, hamming it up for the

---

4. **Veronica Lake hairstyle:** Veronica Lake was an American film star in the 1940s known for the lock of hair that usually covered one of her eyes.
5. **lisle:** a fine, strong cotton or linen.

camera in an extravagant pose. Was it me, or was it my mother? She looked like both of us; but this picture was yellow and old. There was another shot of a young woman in a long white dress; she was small, radiant, and very elegant. Her hair was pulled back from her exquisite little face, and she held herself like a duchess. I knew who she was. Next came a studio portrait of a young man. Apart from an expression of almost oppressive cheerfulness, he was singularly unattractive. He had pale eyes, a poorly defined chin, and a lot of over-large teeth. I wondered if this was the brother for whom she knitted those complicated argyle socks. Probably, because he was in each of the next three pictures. I picked them up one by one. The first showed my mother and him standing on the deck of a ship. They were laughing, and they looked very happy. His hat was off, and his thin wispy hair was blowing every which way, doing nothing to improve his indifferent features. The next picture was of him alone, standing on a beach in an old-fashioned bathing suit. His shoulders were narrow, his thin hair was plastered down on his head and parted in the middle, and his knees were nobby. Then there was a snapshot of him in uniform, saluting in an exaggerated military manner, grinning into the camera. Silly, I thought. No wonder my mother had never bothered to visit her brother.

The sixth picture was like a physical blow to me. I looked at it for a full minute before I was ready to accept its significance. My mother, still radiant, was standing in the center of the picture, dressed once more in the elegant white dress. She held a large bouquet of flowers. Beside her, looking at her and thus revealing to the camera his unfortunate chin line, was the same man. He stood perhaps half an inch taller than my mother. To the left were a middle-aged man and woman; to the right was a young couple in formal dress.

If indeed this was a wedding picture, and it certainly was, my mother had married that seedy-looking little stranger. And if she had married him, he was my father.

I tried to absorb the enormity of my discovery. Frantically my mind clutched at the vision of my tall, imposing father—compassionate, dependable. But apparently he was not, after all, either compassionate or dependable, because he was already fading. As I stood there in my mother's bedroom, dressed only in my underwear and garter belt, he bade me a dim farewell. In his place stood this terrible man, this wispy interloper[6] with too many teeth. Numb shock gave way to fury, and grabbing the pictures, I slammed the drawer shut and fled to my room. My mind was a confusion of swiftly revolving wheels, interlocking, relentlessly turning. I could focus on nothing. As I dressed, I stole anxious looks in the mirror, looking for signs of my new parentage. I inspected my eyes, my chin line, my mouth, my hair, even my shoulders. It was all right. I was entirely my mother's child. Evidently my father's genes had made no mark upon me. Having no stockings (who cared?) I ripped off my garter belt and pulled on sweater, skirt, socks, and saddle shoes. Savagely I brushed my hair, stopping periodically to inspect that insipid stranger who had sent my real father away. My wheels turned and turned and found no track. My wrath was terrible, but I could not center it. My mother's husband, as I chose to think of him, received his share. How *dared* he be my father, presenting to me his unwelcome inheritance, hiding for all those years and then appearing among my mother's stockings to mock me, evicting my real father. Some of my rage was directed at that imaginary father, too—for not existing, for leaving me to this dead and unattractive man, for betraying me. And my mother: my anger mounted, and my heart pounded against my rib cage. How could she have let me live this lie for so long? I stalked out of the room and prepared to join battle in the kitchen.

When I entered the room, my mother was making pancakes at the far counter, and her back was to me. She turned around and welcomed me with her gentle smile, which abruptly faded. I made up for my mother's lack of vibrations. Even in those days before the invention of vibes, I vibrated with an intensity that was unmistakable. On that morning, a blind person would have known that something was wrong.

"What is wrong, Jan?" asked my mother, who had long ago adopted the English version of my French name. She waited, still and impassive, for my answer.

I slammed the pictures down on the kitchen counter beside the mixing bowl. I swung around and faced her, pointing a shaking finger at the little pile of photographs. "What's wrong?" I cried, "What's *wrong! Everything's* wrong! My whole *life* is wrong! Who is that *man?* That awful *man?* Why is he my father? How could you hide these things for

---

6. **interloper:** person who intrudes or interferes.

so long? How could you *do* this to me?" I searched in my mind for the comfort of my former father. But he had departed, and I was alone. I pounded the table, the counter, and then clutched both sides of my head. Absurdly I shouted, "What have you done with my father?"

My mother watched me, her face unreadable. She wiped her hands on her apron. She took it off. She looked at me in silence for a few moments. Then she picked up an empty bottle from the counter and hurled it against the opposite wall, smashing it into countless pieces. My tempest stilled as quickly as if she had fired a rifle into the air, and I watched her, transfixed, my wheels stopped and still and waiting.

"How dare you!" She spoke at first quietly, through her teeth, and then gradually her voice gathered force and volume. "How dare you," she repeated savagely, "open my private drawer and put your nosy little self-centered hands on my past?" She had never spoken to me like this before. Never. "How dare you," she went on, "pass judgment on my choice of husband. Or on his merits? You who have lived with a cardboard father for these nine long years. What do you know about pain or about patience or about the need to hold your tongue?"

There was a pause, while she caught her breath. I was too stunned to be frightened, too fascinated to be quiet. "But why didn't you *tell* me?" I pleaded.

"Why didn't I tell you?" She had found her breath, and was launched once more upon her defense. It was as though she could speak forever, as though the bottle, when it broke, had released the locked-up voice and pain of fifteen years. "Because *you* told *me*. You told me who he was, what he looked like, the nature of his personality." As she continued, her French accent intensified, fracturing her impeccable[7] and bloodless English, revealing the passion behind her words. Sometimes she retained her *th*'s, sometimes not. Her sentences were convoluted and peppered with French words. "What was I to be doing?" she asked, throwing her arms wide. "You were loving this figure *du papier*[8] long before you ever made mention of his existence. I have known always that a child needs two parents, and you seemed to be so happy with this nothing-man you made into your *papa*. He seemed to make you strong

---

7. **impeccable:** without fault; perfect.
8. ***du papier:*** of paper. [French]

even, to make you think we were a family *complète*, not just a *toi et moi.
Mon Dieu!*[9] Do you think I wanted this stranger in our house?" She was
pacing the kitchen now like a panther in a cage, back and forth, around,
across. She pointed, spread her arms, pounded her fists on the counter.
"But when he was presented to me, this *étranger*, this *inconnu*[10] you were
too young, I thought, too fragile, to disappoint. He was the big hero, the
Superman of your life, and what is more, all your friends were believing
the reality of this big lie. How could I take him away from you? So I hid
your father under my stockings, where I assumed"—she raised her
lovely chin and looked at me sideways—"I assumed that nobody would
have the very bad breeding to be going."

"Oh, *Maman!*" I said, slipping oddly, naturally, into my childhood
name for her, reaching out to touch her as she swept by. "What was he,
the *real* he, really like?"

"Just one little moment!" she cried, still pacing. "I have not even begin
to finish. I have to tell you how I hate this cardboard father of yours. I
let him live here because you need him, but I feel many times like I
could kill him dead. He was always better than me. More exciting. *Plus
vivant. Plus beau.*[11] Me, I was the silent one, the dull one. I could not fix
the bicycles, the chairs. It is a very bad thing to be jealous. But to be
jealous of a person who does not even exist is an agony. And a mother,"
she added bleakly, "loves very hard."

"Come on, *Maman*," I coaxed, rising and taking her hand, stopping
her pacing. "Please. I'm ready now. I'm even sorry. Tell me. Tell me about
your husband."

She sat down then. She looked more like her old composed self. "I
was seventeen," she said, "and it was France and the war, and *même s'il
faisait*[12] very warm and sunny, it was a time of fear and hunger, too.
Then came this soldier man, an *officier* even, and me so young, and he
came from a land so far away, and it was a romantic thing. You think
he does not look so handsome like your paper father, but he was not so
bad as he look in the pictures. He was very fun and always laughing,

---

9. *toi et moi. Mon Dieu:* you and me. My God! [French]
10. *étranger . . . inconnu:* stranger . . . unknown person. [French]
11. *Plus vivant. Plus beau:* More lively. More attractive. [French]
12. *meme s'il faisait:* at the same time the weather was . . . [French]

and *un peu*[13] reckless, you know, and not afraid of things. Or seemed like that. Now I wonder. I think maybe he was afraid of so much that he had to prove things all the time. He got medals in the war. I even think now that maybe I was one of his medals, his trophies. It was not a prudent thing to bring back to Canada—*English* Canada—a French wife. But I was unique. I was pretty, I was *chic*. He could say, 'Look. I am not tall or handsome or even very clever. But I have capture this young girl along with my medals, and she is the only one exactly like herself. She is special. So maybe *I* am too.' And *souvent*[14] I think that people believed him."

There was a silence. She was sitting quietly now, staring sadly into space. I felt I should say something—something kind. "And what about the drowning?" I asked gently. "I guess he was a hero after all."

She rose swiftly and continued her pacing. "A hero!" she cried scornfully. "What makes a hero? A hero is living with your own bad things and staring them in the face. That beach and that drowning I will never forgive. *Never.* To begin with, you do not take a seven-month pregnant wife and friends with four tiny children to a beach in a raging wind when everyone know the beach is dangerous. But no. He want to go, so we all go. I learn very early that what he say, we do. Then the foolish other man go to swim in that terrible sea, because your father *dare* him to go. He call him a coward if he do not go. So he start to drown. And what do my husband do? There are other people on the beach, some of them big men, and life preservers on a pole. There is even a boat not far away. But no. This so reckless man just jump in the water and be the big hero to save his friend, who is twice as big as he is. He leave on the shore his wife and his unborn child, and the other woman and her four children. Not one of us could swim. Not one. And we have to stand there and watch it all happening. I won't tell you all the bad parts, but how you like to be those little children and see their daddy brought in dead by the other men? Stupid! Stupid! I can never forgive it!"

And my mother sat down and put her face into her hands and cried like a child. I picked up my chair and took it over beside her. I put my

13. *un peu:* a little. [French]
14. *souvent:* often. [French]

arms around her and hugged her and let her cry and cry. She had fifteen years of crying to do, and I was in no rush to stop her. My frozen mother had thawed, and there was no way I was going to interrupt the process.

Finally, she stopped crying, and gazed at me, red-eyed. She seemed to have regained her mastery of English. "I'm sorry," she said, "that I wouldn't try to change, to make you proud of me. But I had put the rest of myself in a box and pulled down the lid. I refused to change my hair and my clothes, too. And," she added, "I still do."

"*Maman,*" I said, my throat tight, "I'm sorry. You're beautiful. *Comme tu es belle.*"[15] And strangely, I believed it. I looked at her sad, distinguished little face with its lovely bones, enhanced by the simplicity of her hair. I admired her trim figure in her tasteful little black dress. "My dad was right," I said. "You *were* special. One of a kind. A real trophy."

We talked for a long time that day. The years fell away, and she seemed young again—animated, released, a person as well as a mother. I moved out of childhood, and put one foot into the adult world.

As for my mother, she took off her apron and accepted a job as a translator in a government department. Discovering French-Canadian women who were strangers in Halifax, she befriended them, making them feel welcome in a chilly environment. At the age of fifty, *Maman* met and married a Québécois[16] university teacher, and went to live in Montreal. At seventy-eight, he is a lively and sensitive person, warm, sophisticated, and a good father to me. My mother's hair is white now, but still thick, and she wears it drawn back from her lovely old face in a chignon. She stands proud, erect, and her figure, in her simple black dress, is still slender. She nearly always wears a single strand of pearls.

---

15. *Comme tu es belle:* How beautiful you are. [French].
16. Québécois: person from the Canadian province of Quebec.

Responding to the Story

1. At age three, after the narrator learns that her father is dead, she tells us, "I did not grieve or cry. There had been no face to love or miss, no presence to be significant by its absence. I simply lacked something I had never had—like a two-wheeled bike, a pet dog, or curly hair." Do you find this response believable? Explain.
2. After she learns how her father died, Jeanne creates a vision of him. What does that vision consist of? Can you understand why Jeanne creates it?
3. Summarize the mother's reaction when she finally explodes after "these nine long years." What point does she make about the father Jeanne had created in her mind? Do you consider the mother's views valid? Explain.

Exploring the Author's Craft

1. **Irony** is a term that refers to the difference between what is expected and what really is. What is ironic about Jeanne's mother's story about her husband's death?
2. **Description** involves using nouns and adjectives to paint a vivid picture of a place, person, or object. As with all good writing, being specific and tangible is crucial to good description. Precise nouns are even more important than adjectives.

   Budge Wilson is a master of description. Point out lines in the story in which Wilson describes Jeanne's mother.

Writer's Workshop

Here's a chance to try out your own descriptive skills. Describe a person or a place you know well. Bring the person or place alive by naming as many specifics as you can. Use precise nouns and include adjectives where appropriate. Avoid compiling strings of adjectives to pile onto every noun.

Alternate Media Response

Draw these three faces. Make strong distinctions among the three.

a. The romanticized father that Jeanne has imagined for years.

b. Jeanne's image of her father once she sees the photographs of him.

c. The way Jeanne's mother envisions her late husband.

Frederick Pollack

Frederick Pollack's story won first prize for the short story in the 1963 Scholastic Writing Awards. He was a senior at Palo Alto California Senior High School at the time.

Father and son react very differently to the discovery that "you can't go home again."

Asphalt

We neither love nor hurt because we do not try to reach each other.
Edward Albee, *The Zoo Story*

Kroch's and Brentano's in Chicago advertises itself as the Largest Bookstore in the World but apparently can't afford air conditioning. Luckily, the paperbacks—all the books I usually have enough money to buy casually—are in the basement, where it is damp and relatively cool. The New Arrivals rack is right at the bottom of the stairwell, and I was standing there, engrossed in the new Ballantine edition of H. G. Wells' stories, when my father came up behind me and tapped me on the shoulder.

I'd told him over the phone that I'd meet him in Kroch's, but hadn't said exactly where—and Kroch's is a big place. I suppose I should have stayed near the entrance waiting for him. But I wanted to browse, and all that's near the entrance is the Psychiatry section, with Freud's eyes staring unblinkingly at me from the covers of his *Collected Works* spread across the top shelf. I always tell myself I should read more in that field, but somehow I can never become interested. At any rate, I'd drifted away from the entrance, and when Pop came in at noon I was downstairs. He'd been looking for me for ten minutes.

He was angry, of course. I knew that as soon as he tapped me on the shoulder and growled my name—even before I'd turned around and glanced at his flushed, heavy face. "Hi, Pop," I said and then kept trying to make him be quiet. I've always hated being embarrassed, especially in public, and having people stare at me. Fortunately, there weren't many people downstairs in Kroch's that day. Eventually he ground to a halt, told me to come long, and started up the stairs. I followed about three steps behind. It was the first time I'd seen him in five months.

He had the use of his brother's massive Oldsmobile for the day, and had parked it illegally right in front of the bookstore. He never worries about cops, especially not those of his home town. We got in. He gunned the motor with less anger than I'd expected, and we drove off. I watched the marble front of Kroch's recede into the surrounding cityscape, reflecting that his brief tirade had at least served some purpose: we'd in effect said hello already . . . I didn't have to kiss him. Not that I mind kissing him, mind you, it's just that I feel a bit self-conscious about it. I suppose it would seem too cold if we just shook hands.

There was nothing I especially needed to tell him; he'd ask later how school was, and how things were at home, and I'd tell him that my grades so far this year were mediocre but I hoped to make a comeback with a few big tests and reports, that the teachers were especially bad this year, and the other kids were as usual, that Mom was feeling okay, that Sis was sick with a virus. So there was silence as we drove down Wabash and across the river into the Near North Side, silence like someone sprawled across us in the front seat. I looked out the window at the baking city.

Abruptly he began to talk—about his job, his contacts, the vagaries of his friends, the difficulties posed by certain of his relationships, the Kandinsky retrospective at the Guggenheim.[1] I wanted to hear more about the Kandinsky show, but he didn't have much to say about it. I chuckled or grunted at appropriate intervals and eventually he attained such a peak of good humor that I asked him how his flight in from New York had been and how was Uncle Max with whom he was staying. Fine, and fine.

---

1. **Kandinsky . . . Guggenheim:** Wassily Kandinsky (1866–1944): Russian painter whose works were being shown at the Guggenheim Museum in New York City.

I asked him where we were going. Usually his response to that question is "Keep quiet and follow me," but today was different for some reason. He said he thought we might go see his friend Jacobson. I'd expected that might be it—Pop doesn't have too many friends on the North Side and Jake's the one he usually visits when he comes back to Chicago. But was there any place I'd rather go first? he asked. Surprised, I turned and looked at him. He was staring at me with his gray eyes (mine are black, like my mother's). "Why, no," I said, ". . . we usually go visiting and I like your friends. Whatever you want to do." He grunted, and very shortly we parked.

Jacobson is a short man of about fifty with large eyes and a scraggly beard. He is a moderately successful painter who belongs to no school, certainly not abstract expressionism.[2] His style and subject matter have changed often in the years I've known him. I saw him the last time Pop visited Chicago; at that time Jake was painting harsh, angular semiabstractions of cities. Pop said they had little subtlety and less variation, but I liked the bright harsh surface they presented to my mind. As we climbed to his studio I hoped to see more of these paintings.

We knocked; he opened the door, and as Pop and he embraced I wandered into the cool, whitewashed cavern where his easel stood and his new painting hung. It was immediately evident that he had ended his "City" series.

The two men stood somewhere behind me, discussing the new development. Pop was praising it warmly; Jake was expressing his great hopes. I stared disconsolately at his newest work braced on his easel, a picture for which the new pictures hanging on the walls were obviously prototypes. They were all landscapes, many with skeletal trees which writhed like those of van Gogh,[3] but painted in misty pastels. There were people in the pictures, many of them girls . . . their sad eyes begged companionship, and something about them made one want to be beside them. But of course one could not . . . I don't think I'll ever like this new tack of Jacobson's; these pictures confuse me, make me feel uneasy.

---

2. **abstract expressionism:** style of painting that conveys emotions and feelings through nonrepresentational images.

3. **van Gogh** (van gō´): Vincent van Gogh(1853–1890), Dutch painter.

We ate lunch. I was grateful to Jacobson when he asked me how school was; my ambiguous, vaguely confident generalities satisfied him, and Pop too. I wouldn't have to talk to him about it later, to *explain* the situation, to *analyze* things. I sat by an open window overlooking the small garden court for some hours while they talked. Jacobson has a large library which includes a good selection of science fiction. I started Bester's *The Demolished Man*. A cool wind trickled occasionally over my face. I was annoyed by the chirping of birds and the thick smell of warm grass rising from the garden, but the window was the coolest place in the studio.

Around three-thirty Pop sat down next to me; Jacobson was, I think, on the phone. He asked me hesitantly whether I was enjoying myself. Sure, I said. He said he hadn't seen Jake in some time and wouldn't have a chance tomorrow, but that he felt guilty seeing him on my time. Was I angry? Not a bit, I said. It must be pretty boring for you, he said. No, I muttered, I'm reading. What book? he asked. You wouldn't like it, I said. It's escapist. He moved away and I returned to the book.

We left about ten minutes later. The sun was lower in the sky and appeared larger. The air was like dishwater; the city stank of heat and settling soot. Pop asked me if there was a film I wanted to see. No, I said, the only one in the area was that Italian film *L'Avventura*, which I'd already seen. Albee's *The Zoo Story* was playing on the same bill as Beckett's *Krapp's Last Tape* in a theatre downtown. He hadn't seen them, but I'd read the reviews and they sounded depressing, so that was out.

We went down to Twelfth Street where goods are sold through customer peddling. Pop wanted to buy me something; I now have a beautiful pair of Italian shoes, I'll only be able to war them for dress-up because I need arch supports, but still they're nice to have. I thanked him.

I knew where we were going next, although he'd said nothing. We go there whenever he comes back to Chicago. I never argue, you know. I don't like to "thrash things out" with him because there's nothing I want to "thrash out," nothing I think really *has* to be "thrashed out," but if I *had* to discuss something with him I'd tell him I don't like going south of Twelfth. I pity the underprivileged wretches down there as much as the next liberal, but I get no charge out of looking at them and their sordid surroundings. But he goes back there every time and takes me with him. He used to live in that area when he was a boy.

Things are at their worst three blocks south of Twelfth. This is
Maxwell Street. Maxwell Street used to be the melting pot of Chicago
in the early part of this century, but the Poles and the Irish bubbled
away, and the Jews—including my parents—made the grade and rose
like steam into the middle class, into West Rogers Park, Evanston, and
the suburbs. Maxwell Street is a slum, the property of a few odd men
out of the great ethnic migrations to the other parts of the city, and of
the Negroes and Puerto Ricans who are trapped here. Today the streets
and sidewalks were crowded with stands and pushcarts, dispensing
goods of every description—wormy cabbages, picture frames, mink
stoles made from synthetic fibers, old mattresses, damaged boxes of
cereals, hot dogs, hamburgers 60 per cent pork. From a loudspeaker,
over a plate-glass window bearing the legend *BODEGA*, flowed *"Que
bonita bandera"* like mellifluous, brightly colored oil-slick. Pop.,
rummaging through one of the displays, said that you can save hundreds
here if you know *how* to buy. I grunted and sucked air through my
teeth. The smell was like melting sulphur. *"Que bonita bandera, que
bonita bandera. . . ."*

Pop said my name; I turned and looked at him. He had found a box
of spectacles, the nineteenth century kind: two glass octagons and thin
brown wires. He had placed a pair on the bridge of his nose and was
staring at me. I laughed dutifully but felt uneasy; they gave his face an
unwonted benignity.[4] I told him to take them off; he'd never look like
Benjamin Franklin. He chuckled at this.

We wandered through the neighborhood. There is a department store
on the corner of Halsted Street, one of those institutions which makes it
so expensive to be poor. Like Field's and Sears, its rich cousins uptown,
it had been built in the last century. Unlike them, it had been allowed to
deteriorate. Pop stood on the corner for an interminable time, staring at
the building.

"I used to work here during the Depression," he said.

"I know," I said. "You told me about it the last time we were here."

I suppose he didn't hear me, for he began to tell me about his
employer, the owner of the store when he had worked there, a German
who admired Hitler and made life tough for Pop in accordance with the

---

4. **unwonted benignity:** unusual kindly feeling.

historical traditions of the Fatherland. We walked north; there was a boarded-up building, sooty and rotting.

"That was once the best restaurant on the South Side," he said.

"You and Mom ate there sometimes in the old days."

"Yes. When I was taking her out, in the old days."

A streetcar clanged past us as we walked, one of the last of its kind in the city. He told me about Kelly, the conductor, who had become one of his fellow officers in the E.T.O.[5] Every building and street corner in this neighborhood spurred him on to more reminiscences of his childhood and young manhood. I had never known him to be so garrulous about the subject. We turned on some street whose name I've forgotten and passed the bar, still in operation, where the big-time gangsters had hung out once. We turned north again and walked several blocks into an area which was undergoing considerable alteration. And then, on a deserted middle-of-nowhere street corner, he stopped.

"That brown building over there was my school," he said, and stopped. He looked at me. I was trying to stifle a yawn.

"Sorry," I said.

"Tired?" he ask angrily.

"Not a bit," I said. "I bet you were the only one in your class who made good."

"Yes, but that's not the point," he said vaguely.

"Point of what?" I asked, rather irritated now.

He said nothing, but turned and walked a few feet away from me at a diagonal. Half the block was nothing but a flat field of black asphalt, a parking lot. Across from it was an electrical powerhouse and, incredibly enough, a few trees.

"I used to live here."

"On this asphalt?" I asked with what I thought was great good humor.

"There used to be a house here. I lived here with my mother and father, three brothers and three sisters. It was crowded and hot and wretched. We all had a certain affection for each other. Three blocks from here is where I first met your mother. I could show you the place."

"What's the point?" I said firmly. Suddenly I was tired. All the discomfort of this hot day was clinging to me like grease, like loathsome

---

5. E.T.O.: in World War II, European Theater of Operations.

grease. I was irritated with his unfathomable talk, with his stare, with the obvious depression which was twisting his eyebrows and lips. I wanted to leave, and I made him know it. I think I told him I was getting a bit hungry. He nodded, and muttered something, I think it was "I guess there is no point." We went back to the car and drove quickly out of the South Side.

We ate at the Red Star Inn, a *gemütlich*[6] German restaurant on the Near North Side. He told me he was leaving tomorrow, sometime around ten P.M. I wouldn't be able to see him, of course; I had homework and he had plenty of people he had to see. He told me to give his regards to Mom and to Sis, who had been in bed for a week with a virus. I said I would. He asked me how school was. "Fine," I said. I told him it had been a pleasure seeing him, that this Wienerschnitzel was delicious and thanks for the Italian shoes. We finished simultaneously and he drove me home.

It was dusk now, a humid summer twilight in Chicago. We drove north on the Outer Drive, which borders Lake Michigan. There were still many people on the beaches—teenage boys and girls, mostly, lying unashamedly in each other's arms, sweating on each other. I turned and looked past my father's head at the beautiful apartment houses of the Gold Coast. The hum of the air conditioners was almost audible above the whoosh of the cars. Lights were going on in the windows of the sumptuous apartments, yellow lights, warm and inviting. Pop turned on the radio and twisted the station-selector knob with increasing irritation, searching for a symphony, finding only the harsh, bright whine of rock 'n' roll. I rested my arm on the ledge of the open window and looked out at the lake. The breeze dried the sweat on my forehead, whipped through my hair. It was cooler here.

---

6. *gemütlich* (gə müt′lik): pleasant, congenial. [German]

Responding to the Story

1. "What is the point?" the narrator asked his father at one moment. What do you see as the point of this story?
2. How did you feel about this father and son and their relationship?
3. Why do you think Frederick Pollack entitled his story "Asphalt"?

Exploring the Author's Craft

The **setting** is the time and place in which a narrative occurs. Frederick Pollack shows extraordinary skill in making a relationship come alive and does the same with the Chicago setting of "Asphalt." Without looking at the story again, recall and write down as many details of the setting as you can.

Writer's Workshop

A comparison and contrast essay touches upon similarities (comparisons) and differences (contrasts) between whatever two things are being discussed. Write a comparison and contrast essay about "Asphalt" and either "Shaving" or "Guess What? I Almost Kissed My Father Goodnight!"

   You might want to structure your essay by first writing about similarities between the two stories and then writing about the differences. Before you begin, jot down in two lists the similarities and differences.

Making Connections in
PART TWO

Complete one or more of the following assignments as your teacher directs.

1. In a comparison and contrast essay we look for similarities (comparisons) and differences (contrasts). In both "Why Can't They Tell You Why? and "My Mother and Father" a young person is dealing with a missing father. Write an essay in which you point out similarities and differences between the two stories.
2. Write an essay about the importance of families and friends in our lives. Refer to three of the stories in Part Two to support your main idea.
3. Of the characters in Part Two other than narrators, which one is the most appealing to you? Why?

COMING OF AGE

PART THREE

Falling in Love

A 14-year-old boy is entranced with Sheila Mant, "at seventeen, all but out of reach, " but our hero likes to fish for bass, too. Can romance blossom in a canoe that has a fishing line trailing out its back? In a story by humorist Jean Shepherd, a boy moans and groans about having to do a friend a favor and take out a girl as his blind date for the evening. He's in for a big surprise. Alfonso in Gary Soto's "Broken Chain" hates the way he looks, does 50 push-ups a day and studies "the magazine pictures of rock stars for a hair style." Sound familiar?

Most collections of stories for students don't even *acknowledge* the essential part of coming-of-age that involves romance and all its manifestations. Enjoy this section of the book, which deals with infatuations and the various hesitant steps along the intriguing but erratic journey called love.

Gary Soto

Gary Soto was born in 1952 in Fresno, California. A prolific writer, he has produced nine poetry collections for adults, including *New and Selected Poems*, a 1995 finalist for the National Book Award. He has also written nonfiction for young adults, a play, and a movie script. Most interestingly, one of his recent projects was an opera called *Nerd-landia* commissioned by the Los Angeles Opera. Soto creates works that are fresh, alive, and vivid, evoking his Mexican heritage and the California of his youth. Taken together, his books for adults and young people have sold over a million copies; one can almost see and hear and taste and touch the places Gary Soto evokes in them.

Alfonso didn't want to be the handsomest kid at school, but he was determined to be better looking than average.

Broken Chain

Alfonso sat on the porch trying to push his crooked teeth to where he thought they belonged. He hated the way he looked. Last week he did fifty sit-ups a day, thinking that he would burn those already apparent ripples on his stomach to even deeper ripples, dark ones, so when he went swimming at the canal next summer, girls in cut-offs would notice. And the guys would think he was tough, someone who could take a punch and give it back. He wanted "cuts" like those he had seen on a calendar on an Aztec warrior standing on a pyramid with a woman in his arms. (Even she had cuts he could see beneath her thin dress.) The calendar hung above the cash register at La Plaza. Orsua, the owner, said Alfonso could have the calendar at the end of the year if the waitress, Yolanda, didn't take it first.

Alfonso studied the magazine pictures of rock stars for a hairstyle. He liked the way Prince looked—and the bass player from Los Lobos. Alfonso thought he would look cool with his hair razored into a V in the back and streaked purple. But he knew his mother wouldn't go for it. And his father, who was *puro Mexicano*, would sit in his chair after work, sullen as a toad, and call him "sissy."

Alfonso didn't dare color his hair. But one day he had had it butched on the top, like in the magazines. His father had come home that evening from a softball game, happy that his team had drilled four homers in a thirteen-to-five bashing of Color Tile. He'd swaggered into the living room, but had stopped cold when he saw Alfonso and asked, not joking but with real concern, "Did you hurt your head at school? *Qué pasó?*"[1]

Alfonso had pretended not to hear his father and had gone to his room, where he studied his hair from all angles in the mirror. He liked what he saw until he smiled and realized for the first time that his teeth were crooked, like a pile of wrecked cars. He grew depressed and turned away from the mirror. He sat on his bed and leafed through the rock magazine until he came to the rock star with the butched top. His moth was closed, but Alfonso was sure his teeth weren't crooked.

Alfonso didn't want to be the handsomest kid at school, but he was determined to be better looking than average. The next day he spent his lawn-mowing money on a new shirt, and, with a pocketknife, scooped the moons of dirt from under his fingernails.

He spent hours in front of the mirror trying to herd his teeth into place with his thumb. He asked his mother if he could have braces, like Frankie Molina, her godson, but he asked at the wrong time. She was at the kitchen table licking the envelope to the house payment. She glared up at him, "Do you think money grows on trees?"

His mother clipped coupons from magazines and newspapers, kept a vegetable garden in the summer, and shopped at Penney's and Kmart. Their family ate a lot of frijoles, which was OK because nothing else tasted so good, though one time Alfonso had had Chinese pot stickers and thought they were the next best food in the world.

He didn't ask his mother for braces again, even when she was in a better mood. He decided to fix his teeth by pushing on them with his

---

1. *Qué pasó:* What happened? [Spanish]

thumbs. After breakfast that Saturday he went to his room, closed the door quietly, turned the radio on, and pushed for three hours straight.

He pushed for ten minutes, rested for five, and every half hour, during a radio commercial, checked to see if his smile had improved. It hadn't.

Eventually he grew bored and went outside with an old gym sock to wipe down his bike, a ten-speed from Montgomery Ward. His thumbs were tired and wrinkled and pink, the way they got when he stayed in the bathtub too long.

Alfonso's older brother, Ernie, rode up on *his* Montgomery Ward bicycle looking depressed. He parked his bike against the peach tree and sat on the back steps, keeping his head down and stepping on ants that came too close.

Alfonso knew better than to say anything when Ernie looked mad. He turned his bike over, balancing it on the handlebars and seat, and flossed the spokes with the sock. When he was finished, he pressed a knuckle to his teeth until they tingled.

Ernie groaned and said, "Ah, man."

Alfonso waited a few minutes before asking, "What's the matter?" He pretended not to be too interested. He picked up a wad of steel wool and continued cleaning the spokes.

Ernie hesitated, not sure if Alfonso would laugh. But it came out. "Those girls didn't show up. And you better not laugh."

"What girls?"

Then Alfonso remembered his brother bragging about how he and Frostie met two girls from Kings Canyon Junior High last week on Halloween night. They were dressed as gypsies, the costume for all poor Chicanas—they just had to borrow scarves and gaudy red lipstick from their *abuelitas*.[2]

Alfonso walked over to his brother. He compared their two bikes: his gleamed like a handful of dimes, while Ernie's looked dirty.

"They said we were supposed to wait at the corner. But they didn't show up. Me and Frostie waited and waited like *pendejos*.[3] They were playing games with us.

Alfonso thought that was a pretty dirty trick but sort of funny too. He would have to try that some day.

---

2. *abuelitas:* little grandmothers. [Spanish]
3. *pendejos:* silly, stupid ones. [Spanish]

"Were they cute?" Alfonso asked.

"I guess so."

"Do you think you could recognize them?"

"If they were wearing red lipstick, maybe."

Alfonso sat with his brother in silence, both of them smearing ants with their floppy high tops. Girls could sure act weird, especially the ones you meet on Halloween.

Later that day, Alfonso sat on the porch pressing on his teeth. Press, relax; press, relax. His portable radio was on, but not loud enough to make Mr. Rojas come down the steps and wave his cane at him.

Alfonso's father drove up. Alfonso could tell by the way he sat in his truck, a Datsun with a different-colored front fender, that his team had lost their softball game. Alfonso got off the porch in a hurry because he knew his father would be in a bad mood. He went to the backyard, where he unlocked his bike, sat on it with the kickstand down, and pressed on his teeth. He punched himself in the stomach, and growled, "Cuts." Then he patted his butch and whispered, "Fresh."

After a while Alfonso pedaled up the street, hands in his pockets, toward Foster's Freeze, where he was chased by a ratlike Chihuahua. At his old school, John Burroughs Elementary, he found a kid hanging upside down on the top of a barbed-wire fence with a girl looking up at him. Alfonso skidded to a stop and helped the kid untangle his pants from the barbed wire. The kid was grateful. He had been afraid he would have to stay up there all night. His sister, who was Alfonso's age, was also grateful. If she had to go home and tell her mother that Frankie was stuck on a fence and couldn't get down, she would get scolded.

"Thanks," she said. "What's your name?"

Alfonso remembered her from his school and noticed that she was kind of cute, with ponytails and straight teeth. "Alfonso. You go to my school, huh?"

"Yeah. I've seen you around. You live nearby?"

"Over on Madison."

"My uncle used to live on that street, but he moved to Stockton."

"Stockton's near Sacramento, isn't it?"

"You been there?"

"No." Alfonso looked down at his shoes. He wanted to say something clever the way people do on TV. But the only thing he could think to say was that the governor lived in Sacramento. As soon as he shared this observation, he winced inside.

Alfonso walked with the girl and the boy as they started for home. They didn't talk much. Every few steps, the girl, whose name was Sandra, would look at him out of the corner of her eye, and Alfonso would look away. He learned that she was in seventh grade, just like him, and that she had a pet terrier named Queenie. Her father was a mechanic at Rudy's Speedy Repair, and her mother was a teacher's aide at Jefferson Elementary.

When they came to the street, Alfonso and Sandra stopped at her corner, but her brother ran home. Alfonso watched him stop in the front yard to talk to a lady he guessed was their mother. She was raking leaves into a pile.

"I live over there," she said, pointing.

Alfonso looked over her shoulder for a long time, trying to muster enough nerve to ask her if she'd like to go bike riding tomorrow.

Shyly, he asked, "You wanna go bike riding?"

"Maybe." She played with a ponytail and crossed one leg in front of the other. "But my bike has a flat."

"I can get my brother's bike. He won't mind."

She thought a moment before she said, "OK. But not tomorrow. I have to go to my aunt's."

"How about after school on Monday?"

"I have to take care of my brother until my mom comes home from work. How 'bout four-thirty?"

"OK," he said. "Four-thirty." Instead of parting immediately, they talked for a while, asking questions like "Who's your favorite group?" "Have you ever been on the Big Dipper at Santa Cruz?" and "Have you ever tasted pot stickers?" But the question-and-answer period ended when Sandra's mother called her home.

Alfonso took off as fast as he could on his bike, jumped the curb, and cool as he could be, raced way with his hands stuffed in his pockets. But when he looked back over his shoulder, the wind raking through his butch, Sandra wasn't even looking. She was already on her lawn, heading for the porch.

That night he took a bath, pampered his hair into place, and did more than his usual set of exercises. In bed, in between the push-and-rest on his teeth, he pestered his brother to let him borrow his bike.

"Come on, Ernie," he whined. "Just for an hour."

"*Chale*, I might want to use it."

"Come on, man, I'll let you have my trick-or-treat candy."

"What you got?"

"Three baby Milky Ways and some Skittles."

"Who's going to use it?"

Alfonso hesitated, then risked the truth. "I met this girl. She doesn't live too far."

Ernie rolled over on his stomach and stared at the outline of his brother, whose head was resting on his elbow. "*You* got a girlfriend?"

"She ain't my girlfriend, just a girl."

"What does she look like?"

"Like a girl."

"Come on, what does she look like?"

"She's got ponytails and a little brother."

"Ponytails! Those girls who messed with Frostie and me had ponytails. Is she cool?"

"I think so."

Ernie sat up in bed. "I bet you that's her."

Alfonso felt his stomach knot up. "She's going to be my girlfriend, not yours!"

"I'm not going to get even with her!"

"You better not touch her," Alfonso snarled, throwing a wadded Kleenex at him. "I'll run you over with my bike."

For the next hour, until their mother threatened them from the living room to be quiet or else, they argued whether it was the same girl who had stood Ernie up. Alfonso said over and over that she was too nice to pull a stunt like that. But Ernie argued that she lived only two blocks from where those girls had told them to wait, that she was in the same grade, and, the clincher, that she had ponytails. Secretly, however, Ernie was jealous that his brother, two years younger than himself, might have found a girlfriend.

Sunday morning, Ernie and Alfonso stayed away from each other, though over breakfast they fought over the last tortilla. Their mother, sewing at the kitchen table, warned them to knock it off. At church they made faces at one another when the priest, Father Jerry, wasn't looking. Ernie punched Alfonso in the arm, and Alfonso, his eyes wide with anger, punched back.

Monday morning they hurried to school on their bikes, neither saying a word, though they rode side by side. In first period, Alfonso worried himself sick. How would he borrow a bike for her? He considered asking his best friend, Raul, for his bike. But Alfonso knew Raul, a paper boy with dollar signs in his eyes, would charge him, and he had less than sixty cents, counting the soda bottles he could cash.

Between history and math, Alfonso saw Sandra and her girlfriend huddling at their lockers. He hurried by without being seen.

During lunch Alfonso hid in metal shop so he wouldn't run into Sandra. What would he say to her? If he weren't mad at his brother, he could ask Ernie what girls and guys talk about. But he *was* mad, and anyway, Ernie was pitching nickels with his friends.

Alfonso hurried home after school. He did the morning dishes as his mother had asked and raked the leaves. After finishing his chores, he did a hundred sit-ups, pushed on his teeth until they hurt, showered, and combed his hair into a perfect butch. He then stepped out to the patio to clean his bike. On an impulse, he removed the chain to wipe off the gritty oil. But while he was unhooking it from the back sprocket, it snapped. The chain lay in his hand like a dead snake.

Alfonso couldn't believe his luck. Now, not only did he not have an extra bike for Sandra, he had no bike for himself. Frustrated, and on the verge of tears, he flung the chain as far as he could. It landed with a hard slap against the back fence and spooked his sleeping cat, Benny. Benny looked around, blinking his soft gray eyes, and went back to sleep.

Alfonso retrieved the chain, which was hopelessly broken. He cursed himself for being stupid, yelled at his bike for being cheap, and slammed the chain onto the cement. The chain snapped in another place and hit him when it popped up, slicing his hand like a snake's fang.

"Ow!" he cried, his mouth immediately going to his hand to suck on the wound.

After a dab of iodine, which only made his cut hurt more, and a lot of thought, he went to the bedroom to plead with Ernie, who was changing to his after-school clothes.

"Come on, man, let me use it," Alfonso pleaded. "Please, Ernie, I'll do anything."

Although Ernie could see Alfonso's desperation, he had plans with his friend Raymundo. They were going to catch frogs at the Mayfair canal.

He felt sorry for his brother, and gave him a stick of gum to make him feel better, but there was nothing he could do. The canal was three miles away, and the frogs were waiting.

Alfonso took the stick of gum, placed it in his shirt pocket, and left the bedroom with his head down. He went outside, slamming the screen door behind him, and sat in the alley behind his house. A sparrow landed in the weeds, and when it tried to come close, Alfonso screamed for it to scram. The sparrow responded with a squeaky chirp and flew away.

At four he decided to get it over with and started walking to Sandra's house, trudging slowly, as if he were waist-deep in water. Shame colored his face. How could he disappoint his first date? She would probably laugh. She might even call him *menso*.[4]

He stopped at the corner where they were supposed to meet and watched her house. But there was no one outside, only a rake leaning against the steps.

Why did he have to take the chain off? he scolded himself. He always messed things up when he tried to take them apart, like the time he tried to repad his baseball mitt. He had unlaced the mitt and filled the pocket with cotton balls. But when he tried to put it back together, he had forgotten how it laced up. Everything became tangled like kite string. When he showed the mess to his mother, who was at the stove cooking dinner, she scolded him but put it back together and didn't tell his father what a dumb thing he had done.

Now he had to face Sandra and say, "I broke my bike, and my stingy brother took off on his."

He waited at the corner a few minutes, hiding behind a hedge for what seemed like forever. Just as he was starting to think about going home, he heard footsteps and knew it was too late. His hands, moist from worry, hung at his sides, and a thread of sweat raced down his armpit.

He peeked through the hedge. She was wearing a sweater with a checkerboard pattern. A red purse was slung over her shoulder. He could see her looking for him, standing on tiptoe to see if he was coming around the corner.

---

4. *menso:* stupid. [Spanish]

What have I done? Alfonso thought. He bit his lip, called himself *menso*, and pounded his palm against his forehead. Someone slapped the back of his head. He turned around and saw Ernie.

"We got the frogs, Alfonso," he said, holding up a wiggling plastic bag. "I'll show you later."

Ernie looked through the hedge, with one eye closed, at the girl. "She's not the one who messed with Frostie and me," he said finally. "You still wanna borrow my bike?"

Alfonso couldn't believe his luck. What a brother! What a pal! He promised to take Ernie's turn next time it was his turn to do the dishes. Ernie hopped on Raymundo's handlebars and said he would remember that promise. Then he was gone as they took off without looking back.

Free of worry now that his brother had come through, Alfonso emerged from behind the hedge with Ernie's bike, which was mud-splashed but better than nothing. Sandra waved.

"Hi," she said.

"Hi," he said back.

She looked cheerful. Alfonso told her his bike was broken and asked if she wanted to ride with him.

"Sounds good," she said, and jumped on the crossbar.

It took all of Alfonso's strength to steady the bike. He started off slowly, gritting his teeth, because she was heavier than he thought. But once he got going, it got easier. He pedaled smoothly, sometimes with only one hand on the handlebars, as they sped up one street and down another. Whenever he ran over a pothole, which was often, she screamed with delight, and once, when it looked like they were going to crash, she placed her hand over his, and it felt like love.

Responding to the Story

1. Does Gary Soto have it right about being in seventh grade and being in love, which is what it "felt like" at this story's end? List all of Alfonso's behaviors that strike you as accurate about being in seventh grade and infatuated, or in love.
2. What other aspects of being in seventh grade does the author understand? List them and explain why you think Gary Soto portrayed them correctly. Is there anything in the story that doesn't ring true? Explain.

Exploring the Author's Craft

This story is filled with the "stuff" of daily life, including references to performers who were popular at the time the story was written. What kind of world does Gary Soto evoke?

Writer's Workshop

In Gary Soto's California, Alfonso "liked the way Prince looked—and the bass player from Los Lobos." Alfonso's mother shopped at Penney's and Kmart. Write about daily life for a character in a contemporary setting that you are familiar with. Write several hundred words. You can get a plot started, but you don't have to finish it; the main thing is to create your atmosphere—alive with contemporary energy and action. What kind of notes will you make before starting to write?

William Stafford

In his prose work *You Must Revise Your Life*, William Stafford (1914–1993) wrote, "A person writes by means of that meager and persistent little self he has within him all the time." Stafford had a long and distinguished career as a poet. He was born in 1914 in Hutchinson, Kansas, the oldest of three children. During the Depression in the 1930s, the family moved often within Kansas, and Stafford delivered papers and worked as a field hand and an electrician's assistant to help support the family.

He worked his way through the University of Kansas, and at the start of World War II, registered as a pacifist. During the war he worked in various camps for conscientious objectors. At the end of the war, he married Dorothy Frantz (they had four children) and finished his M.S. degree at the University of Kansas. He received his Ph.D. in 1954 from the University of Iowa.

He began teaching in 1948 at Lewis and Clark College in Portland, Oregon, and remained there until his retirement in 1980. *Down in My Heart*, an autobiographic work, was published in 1947 while he worked for a relief agency near San Francisco. Stafford's poetry collections include *West of Your City* (1960); *Traveling Through the Dark* (1962), which won a National Book Award in 1963; *The Rescued Year* (1966); *Allegiances* (1970); *Someday, Maybe* (1973); *Stories That Could Be True: New and Collected Poems* (1977); and *An Oregon Message* (1987).

"Every night—or almost every night—the girl was there."

The Osage Orange Tree

On that first day of high school in the prairie town where the tree was, I stood in the sun by the flagpole and watched, but pretended not to watch, the others. They stood in groups and talked and knew each other, all except one—a girl though—in a faded blue dress, carrying a sack lunch and standing near the corner looking everywhere but at the crowd.

I might talk to her, I thought. But of course it was out of the question.

That first day was easier when the classes started. Some of the teachers were kind; some were frightening. Some of the students didn't care, but I listened and waited; and at the end of the day I was relieved, less conspicuous from then on.

But that day was not really over. As I hurried to carry my new paper route, I was thinking about how in a strange town, if you are quiet, no one notices, and some may like you, later. I was thinking about this when I reached the north edge of town where the scattering houses dwindle. Beyond them to the north lay just openness, the plains, a big swoop of nothing. There, at the last house, just as I cut across a lot and threw to the last customer, I saw the girl in the blue dress coming along the street, heading on out of town, carrying books. And she saw me.

"Hello."

"Hello."

And because we stopped we were friends. I didn't know how I could stop, but I didn't hurry on. I stood. There was nothing to do but to act as if I were walking on out too. I had three papers left in the bag, and I frantically began to fold them—box them, as we called it—for throwing. We had begun to walk and talk. The girl was timid; I became more bold. Not much, but a little.

"Have you gone to school here before?" I asked.

"Yes, I went here least year."

A long pause. A meadowlark sitting on a fencepost hunched his wings and flew. I kicked through the dust of the road.

I began to look ahead. Where could we possibly be walking to? I couldn't be walking just because I wanted to be with her.

Fortunately, there was one more house, a gray house by a sagging barn, set two hundred yards from the road.

"I thought I'd see if I could get a customer here," I said, waving toward the house.

"That's where I live."

"Oh."

We were at the dusty car tracks that turned off the road to the house. The girl stopped. There was a tree at that corner, a straight but little tree with slim branches and shiny dark leaves.

"I could take a paper tonight to see if my father wants to buy it."

A great relief, this. What could I have said to her parents? I held out a paper, dropped it, picked it up, brushing off the dust. "No, here's a new one"—a great action, putting the dusty paper in the bag over my shoulder and pulling out a fresh one. When she took the paper we stood there a minute. The wind was coming in over the grass. She looked out with a tranquil expression.

She walked away past the tree, and I hurried quickly back toward town. Could anyone in the houses have been watching? I looked back once. The girl was standing on the small bridge halfway in to her house. I hurried on.

The next day at school I didn't ask her whether her father wanted to take the paper. When the others were there I wouldn't say anything. I stood with the boys. In American history the students could choose their seats, and I saw that she was too quiet and plainly dressed for many to notice her. But I crowded in with the boys, pushing one aside, scrambling for a seat by the window.

That night I came to the edge of town. Two papers were left, and I walked on out. The meadowlark was there. By some reeds in a ditch by the road a dragonfly—snake feeders, we called them—glinted. The sun was going down, and the plains were stretched out and lifted, some way, to the horizon. Could I go on up to the house? I didn't think so, but I walked on. Then, by the tree where her road turned off, she was standing. She was holding her books. More confused than ever, I stopped.

"My father will take the paper," she said.

She told me always to leave the paper at the foot of the tree. She insisted on that, saying their house was too far; and it is true that I was far off my route, a long way, a half-mile out of my territory. But I didn't think of that.

And so we were acquainted. What I remember best in that town is those evening walks to the tree. Every night—or almost every night—

the girl was there. Evangeline was her name. We didn't say much. On Friday night of the first week she gave me a dime, the cost of the paper. It was a poor newspaper, by the way, cheap, sensational, unreliable. I never went up to her house. We never talked together at school. But all the time we knew each other; we just happened to meet. Every evening.

There was a low place in the meadow by that corner. The fall rains made a pond there, and in the evenings sometimes ducks would be coming in—a long line with set wings down the wind, and then a turn, and a skimming glide to the water. The wind would be blowing and the grass bent down. The evenings got colder and colder. The wind was cold. As winter came on the time at the tree was dimmer, but not dark. In the winter there was snow. The pond was frozen over; all the plains were white. I had to walk down the ruts of the road and leave the paper in the crotch of the tree, sometimes, when it was cold. The wind made a sound through the black branches. But usually, even on cold evenings, Evangeline was there.

At school we played ball at noon—the boys did. And I got acquainted. I learned that Evangeline's brother was janitor at the school. A big dark boy he was—a man, middle-aged I thought at the time. He didn't ever let on that he knew me. I would see him sweeping the halls, bent down, slow. I would see him and Evangeline take their sack lunches over to the south side of the building. Once I slipped away from the ball game and went over there, but he looked at me so steadily, without moving, that I pretended to be looking for a book, and quickly went back, and got in the game and struck out.

You don't know about those winters, and especially that winter. Those were the dust years. Wheat was away down in price. Everyone was poor—poor in a way that you can't understand. I made two dollars a week, or something like that, on my paper route. I could tell about working for ten cents an hour—and then not getting paid; about families that ate wheat, boiled, for their main food, and burned wheat for fuel. You don't know how it would be. All through that hard winter I carried a paper to the tree by the pond, in the evening, and gave it to Evangeline.

In the cold weather Evangeline wore a heavier dress, a dark, straight, heavy dress, under a thick black coat. Outdoors she wore a knitted cap that fastened under her chin. She was dressed this way when we met and she took the paper. The reeds were broken now. The meadowlark was gone.

And then came the spring. I have forgotten to tell just how Evangeline looked. She was of medium height, and slim. Her face was pale, her forehead high, her eyes blue. Her tranquil face I remember well. I remember her watching the wind come in over the grass. Her dress was long, her feet small. I can remember her by the tree, with her books, or walking on up the road toward her house and stopping on the bridge halfway up there, but she didn't wave, and I couldn't tell whether she was watching me or not. I always looked back as I went over the rise toward town.

And I can remember her in the room at school. She came into American history one spring day, the first really warm day. She had changed from the dark heavy dress to the dull blue one of the last fall; and she had on a new belt, a gray belt, with blue stitching along the edges. As she passed in front of Jane Wright, a girl who sat on the front row, I heard Jane say to the girl beside her, "Why look at Evangeline— that old dress of hers has a new belt!"

"Stop a minute, Evangeline," Jane said, "let me see your new dress."

Evangeline stopped and looked uncertainly at Jane and blushed. "It's just made over," she said, "it's just . . ."

"It's cute, Dear," Jane said; and as Evangeline went on Jane nudged her friend in the ribs and the friend smothered a giggle.

Well, that was a good year, Commencement time came, and—along with the newspaper job—I had the task of preparing for finals and all. One thing, I wasn't a student who took part in the class play or anything like that. I was just one of the boys—twenty-fourth in line to get my diploma.

And graduation was bringing an end to my paper-carrying. My father covered a big territory in our part of the state, selling farm equipment; and we were going to move at once to a town seventy miles south. Only because of my finishing the school year had we stayed till graduation.

I had taught another boy my route, always leaving him at the end and walking on out, by myself, to the tree. I didn't really have to go around with him that last day, the day of graduation, but I was going anyway.

At the graduation exercises, held that May afternoon, I wore my brown Sunday suit. My mother was in the audience. It was a heavy day. The girls had on new dresses. But I didn't see her.

I suppose that I did deserve old man Sutton's "Shhh!" as we lined up to march across the stage, but I for the first time in the year forgot my caution, and asked Jane where Evangeline was. She shrugged, and I could see for myself that she was not there.

We marched across the stage; our diplomas were ours; our parents filed out; to the strains of a march on the school organ we trailed to the hall. I unbuttoned my brown suit coat, stuffed the diploma in my pocket, and sidled out of the group and upstairs.

Evangeline's brother was emptying wastebaskets at the far end of the hall. I sauntered toward him and stopped. I didn't know what I wanted to say. Unexpectedly, he solved my problem. Stopping in his work, holding a partly empty wastebasket over the canvas sack he wore over his shoulder, he stared at me, as if almost to say something.

"I noticed that your sister wasn't here," I said. The noise below was dwindling. The hall was quiet, an echoey place; my voice sounded terribly loud. He emptied the rest of the wastebasket and shifted easily. He was a man, in big overalls. He stared at me.

"Evangeline couldn't come," he said. He stopped, looked at me again, and said, "She stole."

"Stole?" I said. "Stole what?"

He shrugged and went toward the next wastebasket, but I followed him.

"She stole the money from her bank—the money she was to use for her graduation dress," he said. He walked stolidly on, and I stopped. He deliberately turned away as he picked up the next wastebasket. But he said something else, half to himself. "You knew her. You talked to her . . . I know." He walked away.

I hurried downstairs and outside. The new carrier would have the papers almost delivered by now; so I ran up the street toward the north. I took a paper from him at the end of the street and told him to go back. I didn't pay any more attention to him.

No one was at the tree, and I turned, for the first time, up the road to the house. I walked over the bridge and on up the narrow, rutty tracks. The house was gray and lopsided. The ground of the yard was packed; nothing grew there. By the back door, the door to which the road led, there was a grayish-white place on the ground where the dishwater had been thrown. A gaunt shepherd dog trotted out growling.

And the door opened suddenly, as if someone had been watching me come up the track. A woman came out—a woman stern-faced, with a shawl over her head and a dark lumpy dress on—came out on the back porch and shouted, "Go 'way, go 'way! We don't want no papers!" She waved violently with one hand, holding the other on her shawl, at her throat, She coughed so hard that she leaned over and put her hand against one of the uprights of the porch. Her face was red. She glanced toward the barn and leaned toward me. "Go 'way!"

Behind me a meadowlark sang. Over all the plains swooped the sky. The land was drawn up somehow toward the horizon.

I stood there, half-defiant, half-ashamed. The dog continued to growl and to pace around me, stiff-legged, his tail down. The windows of the house were all blank, with blinds drawn. I couldn't say anything.

I stood a long time and then, lowering the newspaper I had held out, I stood longer, waiting, without thinking of what to do. The meadowlark bubbled over again, but I turned and walked away, looking back once or twice. The old woman continued to stand, leaning forward, her head out. She glanced at the barn, but didn't call out any more.

My heels dug into the grayish place where the dishwater had been thrown; the dog skulked along behind.

At the bridge, halfway to the road, I stopped and looked back. The dog was lying down again; the porch was empty; and the door was closed. Turning the other way, I looked toward town. Near me stood our ragged little tree—an Osage orange tree it was. It was feebly coming into leaf, green all over the branches, among the sharp thorns. I hadn't wondered before how it grew there, all alone, in the plains country, neglected. Over our pond some ducks came slicing in.

Standing there on the bridge, still holding the folded-boxed-newspaper, that worthless paper, I could see everything. I looked out along the road to town. From the bridge you would see the road going away, to where it went over the rise.

Glancing around, I flipped that last newspaper under the bridge and then bent far over and looked where it had gone. They were there—a pile of boxed newspapers, thrown in a heap, some new, some worn and weathered, by rain, by snow.

Responding to the Story

1. It's a scene we don't see and can only imagine: What do you think Evangeline might have been thinking and doing when the narrator came up to her house that last time?
2. "In a strange town, if you are quiet, no one notices, and some may like you, later." Do you agree or disagree with this statement? Comment.

Exploring the Author's Craft

1. The term *imagery* refers to the sensory details in a literary work. Find passages that appeal to one or more of the five senses. What would have been lost if these passages had been omitted?
2. Analyze what William Stafford did in this story to make you sympathetic to both the narrator and Evangeline.

Writer's Workshop

The setting—"openness, the plains, a big swoop of nothing" and that forlorn house—is as much a character as the people in this story. Now, capture your own setting using vivid imagery. In three or four paragraphs bring alive an outdoor place you know well. Tell not only what it looks like but how it smells, the sounds you hear, the textures you feel, and even what you might taste. Immerse the reader in details that create a truly distinctive place. Read your paper to the class.

W. D. Wetherell

W. D. Wetherell is the author of eight books, including *The Man Who Loved Levittown*, a story collection that won the Drue Heinz Literature Prize in 1985; *Checkhov's Sister*, a novel that was selected by *The New York Times* as one of the best dozen novels of 1990; and a collection of essays, *Upland Stream*. Wetherell's most recent novel is *The Wisest Man in America*, published in 1995.

He was born in 1948 on Long Island and now lives in rural New Hampshire, the setting for "The Bass, the River, and Sheila Mant." Wetherell says that when writing the story, "being the fisherman I am, it was very difficult not to let the boy catch the bass—not to have him dump the girl out of the boat instead. But the demands of fiction are tougher than the demands of life—the girl must stay, the bass go. What's especially important is to realize that having a heartbreaking crush on a girl isn't a tragedy, far from it; the tragedy would be to go through adolescence and not have a crush, a helpless crush, on someone, and learn what painful lessons are there."

What's more important to fourteen-year-old boy—a beautiful girl or a largemouth bass?

The Bass, the River, and Sheila Mant

There was a summer in my life when the only creature that seemed lovelier to me than a largemouth bass was Sheila Mant. I was fourteen. The Mants had rented the cottage next to ours on the river; with their parties, their frantic games of softball, their constant comings and goings, they appeared to me denizens[1] of a brilliant existence. "Too noisy by half," my mother quickly decided, but I would have given anything to be invited to one of their parties, and when my parents went to bed I would sneak through the woods to their hedge and stare enchanted at the candlelit swirl of white dresses and bright, paisley skirts.

Sheila was the middle daughter—at seventeen, all but out of reach. She would spend her days sunbathing on a float my Uncle Siebert had moored in their cove, and before July was over I had learned all her moods. If she lay flat on the diving board with her hand trailing idly in the water, she was pensive, not to be disturbed. On her side, her head propped up by her arm, she was observant, considering those around her with a look that seemed queenly and severe. Sitting up, arms tucked around her long, suntanned legs, she was approachable, but barely, and it was only in those glorious moments when she stretched herself prior to entering the water that her various suitors found the courage to come near.

These were many. The Dartmouth heavyweight crew[2] would scull by her house on their way upriver, and I think all eight of them must have been in love with her at various times during the summer; the coxswain[3] would curse at them through his megaphone, but without effect—there was always a pause in their pace when they passed Sheila's float. I suppose to these jaded twenty-year-olds she seemed the incarnation of innocence and youth, while to me she appeared unutterably suave, the epitome of sophistication. I was on the swim

---

1. **denizens:** inhabitants.
2. **Dartmouth . . . crew:** the men from Dartmouth College in New Hampshire rowing in a racing shell—a long, narrow boat.
3. **coxswain** (kok′ sən): person who steers a racing shell and gives directions to the crew.

team at school, and to win her attention would do endless laps between my house and the Vermont shore, hoping she would notice the beauty of my flutter kick, the power of my crawl. Finishing, I would boost myself up onto our dock and glance casually over toward her, but she was never watching, and the miraculous day she was, I immediately climbed the diving board and did my best tuck and a half for her, and continued diving until she had left and the sun went down and my longing was like a madness and I couldn't stop.

It was late August by the time I got up the nerve to ask her out. The tortured will-I's, won't-I's, the agonized indecision over what to say, the false starts toward her house and embarrassed retreats—the details of these have been seared from my memory, and the only part I remember clearly is emerging from the woods toward dusk while they were playing softball on their lawn, as bashful and frightened as a unicorn.

Sheila was stationed halfway between first and second, well outside the infield. She didn't seem surprised to see me—as a matter of fact, she didn't seem to see me at all.

"If you're playing second base, you should move closer," I said.

She turned—I took the full brunt of her long red hair and well-spaced freckles.

"I'm playing outfield," she said, "I don't like the responsibility of having a base."

"Yeah, I can understand that," I said, though I couldn't.

"There's a band in Dixford tomorrow night at nine. Want to go?"

One of her brothers sent the ball sailing over the leftfielder's head; she stood and watched it disappear toward the river.

"You have a car?" she said, without looking up.

I played my master stroke. "We'll go by canoe."

I spent all of the following day polishing it. I turned it upside down on our lawn and rubbed every inch with Brillo, hosing off the dirt, wiping it with chamois until it gleamed as bright as aluminum ever gleamed. About five, I slid it into the water, arranging cushions near the bow so Sheila could lean on them if she was in one of her pensive moods, propping up my father's transistor radio by the middle thwart so we could have music when we came back. Automatically, without thinking about it, I mounted my Mitchell reel on my Pfleuger spinning rod and stuck it in the stern.

I say automatically, because I never went anywhere that summer without a fishing rod. When I wasn't swimming laps to impress Sheila, I was back in our driveway practicing casts, and when I wasn't practicing casts, I was tying the line to Tosca, our springer spaniel, to test the reel's drag, and when I wasn't doing any of those things, I was fishing the river for bass.

Too nervous to sit at home, I got in the canoe early and started paddling in a huge circle that would get me to Sheila's dock around eight. As automatically as I brought along my rod, I tied on a big Rapala plug, let it down into the water, let out some line and immediately forgot all about it.

It was already dark by the time I glided up to the Mants' dock. Even by day the river was quiet, most of the summer people preferring Sunapee or one of the other nearby lakes, and at night it was a solitude difficult to believe, a corridor of hidden life that ran between banks like a tunnel. Even the stars were part of it. They weren't as sharp anywhere else; they seemed to have chosen the river as a guide on their slow wheel toward morning, and in the course of the summer's fishing, I had learned all their names.

I was there ten minutes before Sheila appeared. I heard the slam of their screen door first, then saw her in the spotlight as she came slowly down the path. As beautiful as she was on the float, she was even lovelier now—her white dress went perfectly with her hair, and complimented her figure even more than her swimsuit.

It was her face that bothered me. It had on its delightful fullness a very dubious expression.

"Look," she said. "I can get Dad's car."

"It's faster this way," I lied. "Parking's tense up there. Hey, it's safe. I won't tip it or anything."

She let herself down reluctantly into the bow. I was glad she wasn't facing me. When her eyes were on me, I felt like diving in the river again from agony and joy.

I pried the canoe away from the dock and started paddling upstream. There was an extra paddle in the bow, but Sheila made no move to pick it up. She took her shoes off, and dangled her feet over the side.

Ten minutes went by.

"What kind of band?" she said.

"It's sort of like folk music. You'll like it."

"Eric Caswell's going to be there. He strokes number four."

"No kidding?" I said. I had no idea who she meant.

"What's that sound?" she said, pointing toward shore.

"Bass. That splashing sound?"

"Over there."

"Yea, bass. They come into the shallows at night to chase frogs and moths and things. Big largemouths. *Micropetrus salmonides*," I added, showing off.

"I think fishing's dumb," she said, making a face. "I mean, it's boring and all. Definitely dumb."

Now I have spent a great deal of time in the years since wondering why Sheila Mant should come down so hard on fishing. Was her father a fisherman? Her antipathy toward fishing nothing more than normal filial rebellion? Had she tried it once? A messy encounter with worms? It doesn't matter. What does, is that at that fragile moment in time I would have given anything not to appear dumb in Sheila's severe and unforgiving eyes.

She hadn't seen my equipment yet. What I *should* have done, of course, was push the canoe in closer to shore and carefully slide the rod into some branches where I could pick it up again in the morning. Failing that, I could have surreptitiously dumped the whole outfit overboard, written off the forty or so dollars as love's tribute. What I actually *did* do was gently lean forward, and slowly, ever so slowly, push the rod back through my legs toward the stern where it would be less conspicuous.

It must have been exactly what the bass was waiting for. Fish will trail a lure sometimes, trying to make up their mind whether or not to attack, and the slight pause in the plug's speed caused by my adjustment was tantalizing enough to overcome the bass's inhibitions. My rod, safely out of sight at last, bent double. The line, tightly coiled, peeled off the spool with the shrill, tearing zip of a high-speed drill.

Four things occurred to me at once. One, that it was a bass. Two, that it was a big bass. Three, that it was the biggest bass I had ever hooked. Four, that Sheila Mant must not know.

"What was that?" she said, turning half around.

"Uh, what was what?"

"That buzzing noise."

"Bats."

She shuddered, quickly drew her feet back into the canoe. Every instinct I had told me to pick up the rod and strike back at the bass, but there was no need to—it was already solidly hooked. Downstream, an awesome distance downstream, it jumped clear of the water, landing with a concussion heavy enough to ripple the entire river. For a moment, I thought it was gone, but then the rod was bending again, the tip dancing into the water. Slowly, not making any motion that might alert Sheila, I reached down to tighten the drag.

While all this was going on, Sheila had begun talking and it was a few minutes before I was able to catch up with her train of thought.

"I went to a party there. These fraternity men. Katherine says I could get in there if I wanted. I'm thinking more of UVM or Bennington. Somewhere I can ski."

The bass was slanting toward the rocks on the New Hampshire side by the ruins of Donaldson's boathouse. It had to be an old bass—a young one probably wouldn't have known the rocks were there. I brought the canoe back out into the middle of the river, hoping to head it off.

"That's neat," I mumbled. "Skiing. Yeah, I can see that."

"Eric said I have the figure to model, but I thought I should get an education first. I mean, it might be a while before I get started and all. I was thinking of getting my hair styled, more swept back? I mean, Ann-Margret? Like hers, only shorter."

She hesitated. "Are we going backwards?"

We were. I had managed to keep the bass in the middle of the river away from the rocks, but it had plenty of room there, and for the first time a chance to exert its full strength. I quickly computed the weight necessary to draw a fully loaded canoe backwards—the thought of it made me feel faint.

"It's just the current," I said hoarsely. "No sweat or anything."

I dug in deeper with my paddle. Reassured, Sheila began talking about something else, but all my attention was taken up now with the fish. I could feel its desperation as the water grew shallower. I could sense the extra strain on the line, the frantic way it cut back and forth in the water. I could visualize what it looked like—the gape of its mouth, the flared gills and thick, vertical tail. The bass couldn't have encountered many forces in its long life that it wasn't capable of handling, and the unrelenting tug at its mouth must have been a source of great puzzlement and mounting panic.

Me, I had problems of my own. To get to Dixford, I had to paddle up a sluggish stream that came into the river beneath a covered bridge. There was a shallow sandbar at the mouth of this stream—weeds on one side, rocks on the other. Without doubt, this is where I would lose the fish.

"I have to be careful with my complexion. I tan, but in segments. I can't figure out if it's even worth it. I wouldn't even do it probably. I saw Jackie Kennedy in Boston and she wasn't tan at all."

Taking a deep breath, I paddled as hard as I could for the middle, deepest part of the bar. I could have threaded the eye of a needle with the canoe, but the pull on the stern threw me off and I overcompensated—the canoe veered left and scraped bottom. I pushed the paddle down and shoved. A moment of hesitation . . . a moment more . . . The canoe shot clear into the deeper water of the stream. I immediately looked down at the rod. It was bent in the same, right arc—miraculously, the bass was still on.

The moon was out now. It was low and full enough that its beam shone directly on Sheila there ahead of me in the canoe, washing her in a creamy, luminous glow. I could see the lithe, easy shape of her figure. I could see the way her hair curled down off her shoulders, the proud, alert tilt of her head, and all theses things were as a tug on my heart. Not just Sheila, but the aura she carried about her of parties and casual touchings and grace. Behind me, I could feel the strain of the bass, steadier now, growing weaker, and this was another tug on my heart, not just the bass but the beat of the river and the slant of the stars and the smell of the night, until finally it seemed I would be torn apart between longings, split in half. Twenty yards ahead of us was the road, and once I pulled the canoe up on shore, the bass would be gone, irretrievably gone. If instead I stood up, grabbed the rod and started pumping, I would have it—as tired as the bass was, there was no chance it could get away. I reached down for the rod, hesitated, looked up to where Sheila was stretching herself lazily toward the sky, her small breasts rising beneath the soft fabric of her dress, and the tug was too much for me, and quicker than it takes to write down, I pulled a penknife from my pocket and cut the line in half.

With a sick, nauseous feeling in my stomach, I saw the rod unbend.

"My legs are sore," Sheila whined. "Are we there yet?"

Through a superhuman effort of self-control, I was able to beach the canoe and help Sheila off. The rest of the night is much foggier. We walked to the fair—there was the smell of popcorn, the sound of guitars. I may have danced once or twice with her, but all I really remember is her coming over to me once the music was done to explain that she would be going home in Eric Caswell's Corvette.

"Okay," I mumbled.

For the first time that night she looked at me, really looked at me.

"You're a funny kid, you know that?"

Funny. Different. Dreamy. Odd. How many times was I to hear that in the years to come, all spoken with the same quizzical, half-accusatory tone Sheila used then. Poor Sheila! Before the month was over, the spell she cast over me was gone, but the memory of that lost bass haunted me all summer and haunts me still. There would be other Sheila Mants in my life, other fish, and though I came close once or twice, it was these secret hidden tuggings in the night that claimed me, and I never made the same mistake again.

Responding to the Story

1. How did you like this story? For once, we have an author who sees some humor—not just agony—in the various tensions of adolescence. The big question is, did you see humor in the boy's dilemma?
2. Why does Sheila Mant appeal to the narrator?
3. What kind of person is Sheila? Give a portrait of her based entirely on what she says.

Exploring the Author's Craft

Here is a tough analytical question: How does W. D. Wetherell make this story amusing? Start by analyzing the major conflict in the story. You will be analyzing one short story in particular but commenting, really, on the nature of comic writing.

Writer's Workshop

It's much easier to see the humor in a painful situation when you're looking back at it from some distance in time. The summer when he was 14 (assuming this story is at least somewhat autobiographical), the narrator probably saw no humor in that canoe ride.

Tell a story of some aspect of your own "coming of age" that looks amusing to you now. Don't just write that it was amusing; show what made it amusing.

Alternate Media Response

1. Analyze a current situation comedy on television. Is it funny? If it is, where does the humor lie? Are the lines amusing? Is the humor chiefly of the slapstick or physical variety? Is the plot (situation) funny? Report to the class.

2. Study videos or reruns of some famous movie and television comedians of the past such as the Marx Brothers, Charlie Chaplin, Abbott and Costello, Lucille Ball and Desi Arnaz, and others. If you think these people are funny, tell why in a short paper. Be specific with references to what you saw. If they are not funny to you, analyze why they are not.

Richard Peck

One of the most popular young adult novelists, Peck has written over twenty books, including adult novels. He was born in Decatur, Illinois, in 1934 and attended the University of Exeter in 1954–55, received his B.A. degree from DePauw in 1956, and his M.A. degree from Southern Illinois University in 1959. He has been a college instructor in English, a high school English teacher, a textbook editor, and, since 1971, a full-time writer.

His books for younger readers include *Dreamland Lake, Blossom Culp and the Sleep of Death, Don't Look and It Won't Hurt*, and *The Dreadful Future of Blossom Culp.*

Some of Peck's most popular books for older readers include *Secrets of the Shopping Mall, Remembering the Good Times, Those Summer Girls I Never Met, Through a Brief Darkness*, and *Unfinished Portrait of Jessica.* Many of his books have won awards from the American Library Association. *Are You in the House Alone?* and *Father Figure* were made-for-TV movies. Peck has also written poetry and short stories and frequently visits schools, libraries, and teachers' organizations to speak with young adults and teachers. His novels deal with the serious problems of growing up but also offer humorous situations and witty dialogue.

Sometimes, we're in the wrong class.

I Go Along

Anyway, Mrs. Tibbetts comes into the room for second period, so we all see she's still in school. This is the spring she's pregnant, and there are some people making some bets about when she's due. The smart money says she'll make it to Easter, and after that we'll have a sub teaching us. Not that we're too particular about who's up there at the front of the room, not in this class.

Being juniors, we also figure we know all there is to know about sex. We know things about sex no adult ever heard of. Still, the sight of a pregnant English teacher slows us down some. But she's married to Roy Tibbetts, a plumber who was in the service and went to jump school, so that's okay. We see him around town in his truck.

And right away Darla Craig's hand is up. It's up a lot. She doesn't know any more English than the rest of us, but she likes to talk.

"Hey, Mrs. Tibbetts, how come they get to go and we don't?"

She's talking about the first-period people, the Advanced English class. Mrs. Tibbetts looks like Darla's caught her off base. We never hear what a teacher tells us, but we know this. At least Darla does.

"I hadn't thought," Mrs. Tibbetts says, rubbing her hand down the small of her back, which may have something to do with being pregnant. So now we're listening, even here in the back row. "For the benefit of those of you who haven't heard," she says, "I'm taking some members of the—other English class over to the college tonight, for a program."

The college in this case is Bascomb College at Bascomb, a thirty-mile trip over an undivided highway.

"We're going to hear a poet read from his works."

Somebody halfway back in the room says, "Is he living?" And we all get a big bang out of this.

But Mrs. Tibbetts just smiles. "Oh, yes," she says, "he's very much alive." She reaches for her attendance book, but this sudden thought strikes her. "Would anyone in this class like to go too?" She looks up at us, and you see she's being fair, and nice.

Since it's only the second period of the day, we're all feeling pretty good. Also it's a Tuesday, a terrible TV night. Everybody in the class puts up their hands. I mean everybody. Even Marty Crawshaw, who's already married. And Pink Hohenfield, who's in class today for the first time this month. I put up mine. I go along.

Mrs. Tibbetts looks amazed. She's never seen this many hands up in our class. She's never seen anybody's hand except Darla's. Her eyes get wide. Mrs. Tibbetts has really great eyes, and she doesn't put anything on them. Which is something Darla could learn from.

But then she sees we have to be putting her on. So she just says, "Anyone who would like to go, be in the parking lot at five-thirty. And eat first. No eating on the bus."

Mrs. Tibbetts can drive the school bus. Whenever she's taking the advanced class anywhere, she can go to the principal for the keys. She can use the bus anytime she wants to, unless the coach needs it.

Then she opens her attendance book, and we tune out. And at five-thirty that night I'm in the parking lot. I have no idea why. Needless to say, I'm the only one here from second period. Marty Crawshaw and Pink Hohenfield will be out on the access highway about now, at 7-Eleven, sitting on their hoods. Darla couldn't make it either. Right offhand I can't think of anybody who wants to ride a school bus thirty miles to see a poet. Including me.

The advanced-English juniors are milling around behind school. I'm still in my car, and it's almost dark, so nobody sees me.

Then Mrs. Tibbetts wheels the school bus in. She's got the amber fogs flashing, and you can see the black letters along the yellow side: CONSOLIDATED SCHOOL DIST. She swings in and hits the brakes, and the doors fly open. The advanced class starts to climb aboard. They're more orderly than us, but they've got their groups too. And a couple of smokers. I'm settling behind my dashboard. The last kid climbs in the bus.

And I seem to be sprinting across the asphalt. I'm on the bus, and the door's hissing shut behind me. When I swing past the driver's seat, I don't look at Mrs. Tibbetts, and she doesn't say anything. I wonder where I'm supposed to sit.

They're still milling around in the aisle, but there are plenty of seats. I find an empty double and settle by the window, pulling my ball cap down in front. It doesn't take us long to get out of town, not this town. When we go past 7-Eleven, I'm way down in the seat with my hand shielding my face on the window side. Right about then, somebody sits down next to me. I flinch.

"Okay?" she says, and I look up, and it's Sharon Willis.

I've got my knee jammed up on the back of the seat ahead of me. I'm bent double, and my hand's over half my face. I'm cool, and it's Sharon Willis.

"Whatever," I say.

"How are you doing, Gene?"

I'm trying to be invisible, and she's calling me by name.

"How do you know me?" I ask her.

She shifts around. "I'm a junior, you're a junior. There are about fifty-three people in our whole year. How could I not?"

Easy, I think, but don't say it. She's got a notebook on her lap. Everybody seems to, except me.

"Do you have to take notes?" I say, because I feel like I'm getting into something here.

"Not really," Sharon says, "but we have to write about it in class tomorrow. Our impressions."

I'm glad I'm not in her class, because I'm not going to have any impressions. Here I am riding the school bus for the gifted on a Tuesday night with the major goddess girl in school, who knows my name. I'm going to be clean out of impressions because my circuits are starting to fail.

Sharon and I don't turn this into anything. When the bus gets out on the route and Mrs. Tibbetts puts the pedal to the metal, we settle back. Sharon's more or less in with a group of the top girls around school. They're not even cheerleaders. They're a notch above that. The rest of them are up and down the aisle, but she stays put. Michelle Burkholder sticks her face down by Sharon's ear and says, "We've got a seat for you back here. Are you coming?"

But Sharon just says, "I'll stay here with Gene." Like it happens every day.

I look out the window a lot. There's still some patchy snow out in the fields, glowing gray. When we get close to the campus of Bascomb college, I think about staying on the bus.

"Do you want to sit together," Sharon says, "at the program?"

I clear my throat. "You go ahead and sit with your people."

"I sit with them all day long," she says.

At Bascomb College we're up on bleachers in a curtained-off part of the gym. Mrs. Tibbetts says we can sit anywhere we want to, so we get very groupy. I look up, and here I am sitting in these bleachers, like we've gone to State in the play-offs. And I'm just naturally here with Sharon Willis.

We're surrounded mainly by college students. The dean of Bascomb college gets up to tell us about the grant they got to fund their poetry program. Sharon has her notebook flipped open. I figure it's going to be like a class, so I'm running out when the poet comes in.

First of all, he's only in his twenties. Not even a beard, and he's not dressed like a poet. In fact, he's dressed like me: Levi's and Levi's jacket. Big heavy-duty belt buckle. Boots, even. A tall guy, about a hundred and eighty pounds. It's weird, like there could be poets around and you wouldn't realize they were there.

But he's got something. Every girl lens forward. College girls, even. Michelle Burkholder bobs up to zap him with her flash camera. He's got a few loose-leaf pages in front of him. But he just begins.

"I've written a poem for my wife," he says, "about her."

Then he tells us this poem. I'm waiting for the rhyme, but it's more like talking, about how he wakes up and the sun's bright on the bed and his wife's still asleep. He watches her.

"Alone," he says, "I watch you sleep
Before the morning steals you from me,
Before you stir and disappear
Into the day and leave me here
To turn and kiss the warm space
You leave beside me."

He looks up and people clap. I thought what he said was a little too personal, but I could follow it. Next to me Sharon's made a note. I look down at her page and see it's just an exclamation point.

He tells us a lot of poems, one after another. I mean, he's got poems on everything. He even has one about his truck:

"Old buck-tooth, slow-to-start mama,"

something like that. People laugh, which I guess is okay. He just keeps at it, and he really jerks us around with his poems. I mean, you don't know what the next one's going to be about. At one point they bring him a glass of water, and he takes a break. But mainly he keeps going.

He ends up with one called "High School."

"On my worst nights," he says, "I dream myself back.
I'm the hostage in the row by the radiator, boxed in,
Zit-blasted, and they're popping quizzes at me.
I'm locked in there, looking for words
To talk myself out of being this young
While every girl in the galaxy
Is looking over my head, spotting for a senior.
On my really worst nights it's last period
On a Friday and somebody's fixed the bell
So it won't ring:
    And I've been cut from the team,
    And I've forgotten my locker combination,
    And I'm waiting for something damn it to hell
    To happen."

And the crowd goes wild, especially the college people. The poet just gives us a wave and walks over to sit down on the bottom bleacher. People swarm down to get him to sign their programs. Except Sharon and I stay where we are.

"That last one wasn't a poem," I tell her. "The others were, but not that one."

She turns to me and smiles. I've never been this close to her before, so I've never seen the color of her eyes.

"Then write a better one," she says.

We sit together again on the ride home.

"No, I'm serious," I say. "You can't write poems about zits and your locker combination."

"Maybe nobody told the poet that," Sharon says.

"So what are you going to write about him tomorrow?" I'm really curious about this.

"I don't know," she says. "I've never heard a poet reading before, not in person. Mrs. Tibbetts shows us tapes of poets reading."

"She doesn't show them to our class."

"What would you do if she did?" Sharon asks.

"Laugh a lot."

The bus settles down on the return trip. I picture all these people going home to do algebra homework, or whatever. When Sharon speaks again, I almost don't hear her.

"You ought to be in this class," she says.

I pull my ball cap down to my nose and lace my fingers behind my head and kick back in the seat. Which should be answer enough.

"You're as bright as anybody on this bus. Brighter than some."

We're rolling on through the night, and I can't believe I'm hearing this. Since it's dark, I take a chance and glance at her. Just the outline of her nose and her chin, maybe a little stubborn.

"How do you know I am?"

"How do you know you're not?" she says. "How will you ever know?"

But then we're quiet because what else is there to say? And anyway, the evening's over. Mrs. Tibbetts is braking for the turnoff, and we're about to get back to normal. And I get this quick flash of tomorrow, in second period with Marty and Pink and Darla, and frankly it doesn't look that good.

Responding to the Story

1. Is this story appropriately placed in a section called "Falling in Love"? Explain.
2. What do you think the narrator means by the last line?

Exploring the Author's Craft

In some short stories, the main character wrestles with physical challenges, but in others, like this one, the main character simply gains new insight or changes in some way. Does the author provide sufficient motivation for Gene's new insight in your opinion? Discuss.

Writer's Workshop

1. Write about the next day in the narrator's life from Gene's point of view.
2. In a paragraph or two, fill in some additional details of Gene's life based on what you know about him. What kind of car does he drive? Does he now have, or has he had, a girlfriend? If so, what is, or was, she like? Does he have a part-time job? If so, where? What kind of parents does he have? Will he graduate? What will he do when he's out of high school? Compare your character sketch with those written by others in your class.

Jean Shepherd

Humorist Jean Shepherd was born in Chicago in the 1920s (various dates have been reported) and grew up in Hammond, Indiana. He appeared on the radio six nights a week for over twenty years, telling funny stories of his youth; later he had a show on public television called *Jean Shepherd's America*. His short stories have been collected in books with unusual titles such as *In God We Trust, All Others Pay Cash* and *Wanda Hickey's Night of Golden Memories*. Shepherd adapted one of his tales into the very popular movie *A Christmas Story* (1983), which has become a holiday classic.

"The fourteenth summer is a magic one for all kids."

The Endless Streetcar Ride into the Night, and the Tinfoil Noose

There are about four times in a man's life, or a woman's, too, for that matter, when unexpectedly, from out of the darkness, the blazing carbon lamp, the cosmic searchlight of Truth shines full upon them. It is how we react to those moments that forever seals our fate. One crowd simply puts on its sunglasses, lights another cigar, and heads for the nearest plush French restaurant in the jazziest section of town, sits down and orders a drink, and ignores the whole thing. While we, the Doomed, caught in the brilliant glare of illumination, see ourselves inescapably for what we are, and from that day on skulk in the weeds, hoping no one else will spot us.

Those moments happen when we are least able to fend them off. I caught the first one full in the face when I was fourteen. The fourteenth summer is a magic one for all kids. You have just slid out of the pupa stage,[1] leaving your old baby skin behind, and have not yet become a grizzled, hardened, tax-paying beetle. At fourteen you are made out of cellophane. You curl easily and everyone can see through you.

When I was fourteen, Life was flowing through me in a deep, rich torrent of Castoria.[2] How did I know that the first rocks were just ahead, and I was about to have my keel ripped out on the reef? Sometimes you feel as thought you are alone in a rented rowboat, bailing like mad in the darkness with a leaky bailing can. It is important to know that there are at least two billion other ciphers[3] in the same boat, bailing with the same leaky can. They all think they are alone and are crossed with an evil star. They are right.

I'm fourteen years old, in my sophomore year at high school. One day Schwartz, my purported best friend, sidled up to me edgily outside of school while we were waiting on the steps to come in after lunch. He proceeded to outline his plan:

"Helen's old man won't let me take her out on a date on Saturday night unless I get a date for her girlfriend. A double date. The old coot figures, I guess, that if there are four of us there won't be no monkey business. Well, how about it? Do you want to go on a blind date with this chick? I never seen her."

Well. For years I had this principle—absolutely *no* blind dates. I was a man of perception and taste, and life was short. But there is a time in your life when you have to stop taking and begin to give just a little. For the first time the warmth of sweet Human Charity brought the roses to my cheeks. After all, Schwartz was my friend. It was little enough to do, have a blind date with some no doubt skinny, pimply girl for your best friend. I would do it for Schwartz. He would do as much for me.

"Okay. Okay, Schwartz."

Then followed the usual ribald[4] remarks, feckless boasting, and dirty jokes about dates in general and girls in particular. It was decided that

---

1. **pupa stage:** stage of development for many insects between a larva and a full-fledged adult.
2. **Castoria:** a commercial brand of castor oil, a foul-smelling and -tasting liquid once commonly used as a health tonic.
3. **ciphers:** people of no importance.
4. **ribald:** off-color; vulgar.

next Saturday we would go all the way. I had a morning paper route at the time, and my life savings stood at about $1.80. I was all set to blow it on one big night.

I will never forget that particular Saturday as long as I live. The air was as soft as the finest of spun silk. The scent of lilacs hung heavy. The catalpa trees rustled in the early evening breeze from off the Lake. The inner Me itched in that nameless way, that indescribable way that only the fourteen-year-old Male fully knows.

All that afternoon I had carefully gone over my wardrobe to select the proper symphony of sartorial brilliance. That night I set out wearing my magnificent electric blue sport coat, whose shoulders were so wide that they hung out over my frame like vast, drooping eaves, so wide I had difficulty going through an ordinary door head-on. The electric blue sport coat that draped voluminously almost to my knees, its wide lapels flapping soundlessly in the slightest breeze. My pleated gray flannel slacks began just below my breastbone and indeed chafed my armpits. High-belted, cascading down finally to grasp my ankles in a vise-like grip. My tie, indeed one of my most prized possessions, had been a gift form my Aunt Glenn upon the state occasion of graduation from eighth grade. It was of a beautiful silky fabric, silvery pearly colored, four inches wide at the fulcrum, and of such a length to endanger occasionally my zipper in moments of haste. Hand-painted upon it was a magnificent blood-red snail.

I had spent fully two hours carefully arranging and rearranging my great mop of wavy hair, into which I had rubbed fully a pound and a half of Greasy Kid Stuff.[5]

Helen and Schwartz waited on the corner under the streetlight at the streetcar stop near Junie Jo's home. Her name was Junie Jo Prewitt. I won't forget it quickly, although she has, no doubt, forgotten mine. I walked down the dark street alone, past houses set back off the street, through the darkness, past privet hedges, under elm trees, through air rich and ripe with promise. Her house stood back from the street even farther than the others. It sort of crouched in the darkness, looking out at me, kneeling. Pregnant with Girldom. A real Girlfriend house.

---

5. **Greasy Kid Stuff:** a phrase from advertising originally intended to criticize other, "inferior" brands of hair treatments; later often used to refer to all male hair grooming products.

The first faint touch of nervousness filtered through the marrow of my skullbone as I knocked on the door of the screen-enclosed porch. No answer. I knocked again, louder. Through the murky screens I could see faint lights in the house itself. Still no answer. Then I found a small doorbell button buried in the sash. I pressed. From far off in the bowels of the house I heard two chimes "Bong" politely. It sure didn't sound like our doorbell. We had a real ripper that went off like a broken buzz saw, more of a BRRRAAAAKKK than a muffled Bong. This was a rich people's doorbell.

The door opened and there stood a real, genuine, gold-plated Father: potbelly, underwear shirt, suspenders, and all.

"Well?" he asked.

For one blinding moment of embarrassment I couldn't remember her name. After all, she was a blind date. I couldn't just say:

"I'm here to pick up some girl."

He turned back into the house and hollered:

"JUNIE JO! SOME KID'S HERE!"

"Heh, heh. . . ." I countered.

He led me into the living room. It was an itchy house, sticky stucco walls of a dull orange color, and all over the floor this Oriental rug with the design crawling around, making loops and sworls. I sat on an overstuffed chair covered in stiff green mohair that scratched even through my slacks. Little twisty bridge lamps stood everywhere. I instantly began to sweat down the back of my clean white shirt. Like I said, it was a very itchy house. It had little lamps sticking out of the walls that looked like phony candles, with phony glass orange flames. The rug started moaning to itself.

I sat on the edge of the chair and tried to talk to this Father. He was a Cub fan. We struggled under water for what seemed like an hour and a half, when suddenly I heard someone coming down the stairs. First the feet; then those legs, and there she was. She was magnificent! The greatest-looking girl I ever saw in my life! I have hit the double jackpot! And on a blind date! Great Scot!

My senses actually reeled as I clutched the arm of that bilge-green chair for support. Junie Jo Prewitt made Cleopatra look like a Girl Scout!

Five minutes later we are sitting in the streetcar, heading toward the bowling alley. I am sitting next to the most fantastic creation in the Feminine department known to Western man. There are the four of us in that long, yellow-lit streetcar. No one else was aboard; just us four. I, naturally, being a trained gentleman, sat on the aisle to protect her from candy wrappers and cigar butts and such. Directly ahead of me, also on the aisle, sat Schwartz, his arm already flung affectionately in a death grip around Helen's neck as we boomed and rattled through the night.

I casually flung my right foot up onto my left knee so that she could see my crepe-soled, perforated, wing-toed, Scotch bluchers[6] with the two-toned laces. I started to work my famous charm on her. Casually, with my practiced offhand, cynical, cutting, sardonic humor I told her about how my Old Man had cracked the block in the Oldsmobile, how the White Sox were going to have a good year this year, how my kid brother wet his pants when he saw a snake, how I figured it was going to rain, what a great guy Schwartz was, what a good second baseman I was, how I figured I might go out for football. On and on I rolled, like Old Man River, pausing significantly for her to pick up the conversation. Nothing.

Ahead of us Schwartz and Helen was almost indistinguishable one from the other. They giggled, bit each other's ears, whispered, clasped hands, and in general made me itch even more.

From time to time Junie Jo would bend forward stiffly from the waist and say something I could never quite catch into Helen's right ear.

I told her my great story of the time that Uncle Carl lost his false teeth down the airshaft. Still nothing. Out of the corner of my eye I could see that she had her coat collar turned up, hiding most of her face as she sat silently, looking forward past Helen Weathers into nothingness.

I told her about this old lady on my paper route who chews tobacco, and roller skates in the backyard every morning. I still couldn't get through to her. Casually I inched my right arm up over the back of the seat behind her shoulders. The acid test. She leaned forward, avoiding my arm, and stayed that way.

"Heh, heh, heh. . . ."

As nonchalantly as I could, I retrieved it, battling a giant cramp in my right shoulder blade. I sat in silence for a few seconds, sweating heavily as ahead Schwartz and Helen are going at it hot and heavy.

---

6. bluchers: shoes with a tongue and front made from one piece of leather.

It was then that I became aware of someone saying something to me. It was an empty car. There was no one else but us. I glanced around, and there it was. Above us a line of car cards looked down on the empty streetcar. One was speaking directly to me, to me alone.

DO YOU OFFEND?[7]

Do I *offend?!*

With no warning, from up near the front of the car where the motorman is steering I see this thing coming down the aisle directly toward *me*. It's coming closer and closer. I can't escape it. It's this blinding, fantastic, brilliant, screaming blue light. I am spread-eagled in it. There's a pin sticking through my thorax. I see it all now.

I AM THE BLIND DATE!

ME!!

I'M the one they're being nice to!

I'm suddenly getting fatter, more itchy. My new shoes are like bowling balls with laces; thick, rubber-crepe bowling balls. My great tie that Aunt Glenn gave me is two feet wide, hanging down to the floor like some crinkly tinfoil noose. My beautiful hand-painted snail is seven feet high, sitting up on my shoulder, burping. Great Scot! It is all clear to me in the searing white light of Truth. My friend Schwartz, I can see him saying to Junie Jo:

"I got this crummy fat friend who never has a date. Let's give him a break and. . . ."

I AM THE BLIND DATE!

They are being nice to *me!* She is the one who is out on a Blind Date. A Blind Date that didn't make it.

In the seat ahead, the merriment rose to a crescendo. Helen tittered; Schwartz cackled. The marble statue next to me stared gloomily out into the darkness as our streetcar rattled on. The ride went on and on.

I AM THE BLIND DATE!

I didn't say much the rest of the night. There wasn't much to be said.

---

7. **DO YOU OFFEND:** advertising slogan for a deodorant company of the period.

Responding to the Story

1. Did you anticipate the story's ending? If so, at what point? Which details gave you a clue to where the story was heading?
2. The reference source *Current Biography* has stated that one of Shepherd's purposes in writing is "to preserve the way of life of 'the great unrecorded'"—the people and events writers don't think to document because they *are* so typical and average. How does this description apply to this short story?

Exploring the Author's Craft

Though the end of this story is less than happy, there are humorous touches throughout. One way that the writer uses humor is by creating an exaggeratedly self-important attitude in the narrator. Find at least three lines in the story that convey this attitude.

Writer's Workshop

Your job is to capture your world the same way Jean Shepherd captured his, which was middle-class America in the 1930s and 1940s. Write three paragraphs focusing on a small aspect of your world that actually reveals a lot about what living in it is like. Name objects. Be concrete and specific. Use a little exaggeration for comic effect if you wish.

Alternate Media Response

For his date with Junie Jo the narrator wore a "zoot suit"—an exaggerated style of suit first popularized in the early 1940s. Find pictures from the era of young men wearing these suits, and note what the stylish young women who accompany them are wearing. Then draw the narrator and Junie Jo in proper period style.

Susie Kretschmer

Susie Kretschmer was a senior at Talawanda High School in Oxford, Ohio, when her story won a Scholastic Writing Award in 1986.

Amy and David had a special friendship—that couldn't last.

And Summer Is Gone

We're both sophomores in high school now. I'm fifteen; she'll be sixteen in a week. I know when her birthday is, of course, just as she knows mine. Birthdays don't change.

Almost sixteen, yea, but I can still see her the summer I turned twelve; the day we first met, the day I moved into the newly built house at the end of her street. I was standing half-asleep in the sunlight, looking in despair at the expanse of bare dirt that purported to be our lawn. And suddenly she was there in front of me, all buck teeth and gangling legs and tumbling, tangled blond-brown hair, tall as I was and unafraid to claim every inch of it.

"Hi, I'm Amy," she said, jumping agilely over the exposed water meter and looking right into my face.

"I'm David," I mumbled, but I couldn't help smiling, answering her frankly appraising stare with my own.

Two hours later we were covered with mud, in the midst of a great canal-digging project in the bare gravelly dirt of my "lawn." She landscaped it with wildflowers from the drainage ditch behind our houses and asked if I'd ever been to the creek. I said no, and she showed it to me.

We were friends from then on, best friends that summer. She lived three houses down from me: If I knelt on the edge of the sink in the upstairs bathroom and craned my neck, I could see the lights of her house. I knew how far it was exactly, because with two tin cans and three balls of string we had once run a message line from her house to mine.

The phones hadn't worked, of course, and the irate lady who lived in the house in between ordered it dismantled at once—pieces of it are still probably tangled in the weeds of the drainage ditch—but I remember how it felt to have that line stretching between us, connecting us even though we were apart, for that was how I always felt with her.

She showed me the creek and we spent most of our summers there, wading in the current, catching crawdads and minnows with my parents' abducted spaghetti colander, building dams and then pushing out the one stone that would send the water flooding through. We dug up creek clay and made pots, and painted ourselves wildly with its blue streaks, pretending to be Indians, Aztecs, or Mayas. I remember her standing in the algae-green water that first summer, her long, tanned legs half wet and shiny, half dry with the cracking clay stripes and dots of an Aztec king.

We took out every book in the library on Aztecs and Mayas. I was an artist, always had been, and I would paint in their style—in reds, oranges, and rusts, on the rocks by the creek—geometric designs and the Nine Lords of the Night. Amy would build little pyramids of clay. My tempera always washed away with the next rain, and Amy's pyramids would dissolve when the water rose, but we were content to make them new each time.

And sometimes we would just sit by the creek in the sun. When she grinned, her newly acquired braces would gleam; she'd sit patiently with her mouth open while I peered into it with clinical interest, and we'd shoot her rubber bands at each other. In the summer, she was mine alone, and I was hers.

But she hardly spoke to me at school, ever. I thought a million times that I understood why. Her female friends were the sort that are almost popular, those who get invited to every party but never give any, those who carry gossip but never provoke it, extras surrounding the popular ones for atmosphere and dramatic staging. All of them had names that ended in *-i*, and they all dotted their *i*'s with circles: Kelli, Lori, Shelli, Tammi, Lani, Terri—and Ami. Though Amy wore cutoffs and grungy T-shirts in the summer, during the school year her clothes were the same as theirs.

She moved differently, when she came back to me that summer between seventh and eighth grade. She'd always been more agile than I was, scrambling up on the bluffs far ahead of me, but the way she moved was different now. No buck-toothed, lanky colt-girl now, but curvy and lithe, proportioned as a woman, not a child. And it disturbed me, upset my world—and I liked it. So I would follow her on the bluffs despite my paralyzing fear of heights, and when she took my hand to pull me up over the edge I liked her touch. It was no longer merely the pleasant, reassuring touch of a friend, but something electric as well.

Yet as her body changed, she herself changed. No longer would she wade with me, or wrestle on the couch, and she refused to play pretend games any more. She got rid of her dress-up clothes some time in seventh grade, and by this, the third summer, they were gone. Well, I hid mine, too—my Dracula capes and Arabian turbans; and I hid away my wooden swords since she'd no longer duel with me. She stopped eating around me, too. We had both been famous for the amount of food we could consume and had demolished entire bags of chocolate chips and monstrous salads together. But now she complained she was fat and affected to eat little. She didn't look fat to me, but she said she was. Increasingly, the popular names crept into her conversation. She always wanted to talk about the people in our grade, but only the ones she knew—and I hardly knew any of them. She stopped listening to her Simon and Garfunkel records, replacing them with Duran Duran.

So we lay on her living room floor and watched old movies, and I learned to curb my satirical remarks, for what she would once have laughed at had become serious to her now. We went less and less often to the creek.

I spent more time on my art, alone, and didn't show it to her, for she didn't want to see it anymore. And in August she went away to camp. She came back the day before school started and never did call me. And I was alone.

I'd always been alone at school, with a few acquaintances good enough to talk to between classes, or to get assignments from. But for friendship, I had looked to her. And I saw that she had not spoken to me at school, or dared to associate with me in public. I thought, that eighth-grade year, that it was because Amy had grown up, had left behind childhood while I was still immature.

So the first Christmas went by that I didn't give her a present, and soon after, her fourteenth birthday went by, too. I lived in the worlds that I drew.

Amy's grades slipped. We had both been bright, straight-A's, but now she was getting B's and C's. I didn't keep close track, for I never saw her except when we passed on the way to school in the morning. I'd see her leave her house every evening—there seemed no night when she didn't go out. After a while, I stopped watching.

The less said about the summer before high school, the better. I was alone. But when it was over, we went to high school, Amy and I. She joined the flag corps—I joined the newspaper. She was in my top-level English class but dropped down after a week, and I never had her in a class again. I hung around with some guys from the swim team—I'd joined my freshman year—and went through the motions of studying, dreaming of college.

So we lived, separate. I didn't date at all—she dated ten guys a month. I hid alone—she went to every party, every football game, every prestigious event at school. I was pretty surprised to see her, then, sophomore year, at the local art exhibit where I'd won for the second year in a row. Masquerading as a museum, the local library was filled with people milling about with juice and cookies at the reception for the winners.

Why she was there, I don't really know. I think perhaps some friends of hers had gotten an honorable mention, and they had stopped by to pick her up. But she was there, and she was with her friends.

I was standing next to Danny, otherwise known as fourth honorable mention for his loving depiction of a souped-up red Maserati, when she came to my picture. I had painted a great Aztec pyramid under oily black storm clouds, with nine masque-hideous faces upon it, one face for each tier. The lighting was angry and hellish and red, and an uneasy orange fire burned in each masque-face's eyes. The picture was called "The Nine Lords of the Night."

Amy saw it. One slender hand to her feathered blond hair, the nails polished in coral, a boy's class ring on one finger, she saw it. As she turned around, I met her blue eyes with a level calm stare. Electric our glance, for she knew. She remembered. I had not thought she would forget. And I saw in her eyes that she knew that I saw.

We held it but a moment, for her friend broke in with a mocking harsh laugh. "What a *gay* picture. But everyone knows that all artists are gay anyway."

"Yeah," replied the other one, bored, "and the more they win, the gayer they are."

Amy turned her back on me, but not before I heard her assenting "Yeah, I know." And they left laughing.

And I stood in silence, and I knew I had lost her. She had been more truly mine than I had ever known, for the person she'd been for me had not existed for anyone else. I watched her go, and I cried within, for I understood that it was I who had grown up and she who had gotten lost. For I have kept who I am, and it is what I always be. And Amy is gone.

Responding to the Story

1. Is it believable that a boy and girl at age 12 could be as good friends as Amy and David were? Discuss.
2. Did you sympathize with the narrator's plight? Why or why not?

Exploring the Author's Craft

Identify two places in the story where you feel the author should have dramatized a scene rather than told us that it had occurred. What would be gained by having these scenes dramatized—that is, having us see the characters in action?

Writer's Workshop

1. "All of them had names that ended in -*i*, and they all . . ." This sentence appears in a particularly telling paragraph; here the author captures, with examples, behavioral customs of the teenage world. Now you do the same. In one simple paragraph, describe the behavioral customs of the teenagers you know.
2. Author Susie Kretschmer created a male first-person narrator. Take on that same challenging task; create the voice of someone of the opposite sex. Do the start, or more, of a narrative. Write four or five paragraphs in that voice. Brainstorm with a small group to come up with a topic for your paragraphs.

Sherwood Anderson

Sherwood Anderson, who lived from 1876 to 1941, is most famous for the book *Winesburg, Ohio*, a loosely connected group of short stories about small-town life in the Midwest. "Sophistication" is one of the stories that make up that book. Critic Malcolm Cowley says of Anderson's writing in *Winesburg, Ohio*, "That single moment of aliveness . . . that sudden reaching out of two characters through walls of inarticulateness and misunderstanding—is the effect that Anderson is trying to create for his readers." That sentence applies very much to "Sophistication."

"There is a time in the life of every boy when he for the first time takes the backward view of life."

Sophistication

It was early evening of a day in the late fall and the Winesburg County Fair had brought crowds of country people into town. The day had been clear and the night came on warm and pleasant. On the Trunion Pike, where the road after it left town stretched away between berry fields now covered with dry brown leaves, the dust from passing wagons arose in clouds. Children, curled into little balls, slept on the straw scattered on wagon beds. Their hair was full of dust and their fingers black and sticky. The dust rolled away over the fields and the departing sun set it ablaze with colors.

In the main street of Winesburg crowds filled the stores and the sidewalks. Night came on, horses whinnied, the clerks in the stores ran madly about, children became lost and cried lustily, an American town worked terribly at the task of amusing itself.

Pushing his way through the crowds in Main Street, young George Willard concealed himself in the stairway leading to Doctor Reefy's office and looked at the people. With feverish eyes he watched the faces drifting past under the store lights. Thoughts kept coming into his head and he did not want to think. He stamped impatiently on the wooden steps and looked sharply about. "Well, is she going to stay with him all day? Have I done all this waiting for nothing?" he muttered.

George Willard, the Ohio village boy, was fast growing into manhood and new thoughts had been coming into his mind. All that day, amid the jam of people at the Fair, he had gone about feeling lonely. He was about to leave Winesburg to go away to some city where he hoped to get work on a city newspaper and he felt grown-up. The mood that had taken possession of him was a thing known to men and unknown to boys. He felt old and a little tired. Memories awoke in him. To his mind his new sense of maturity set him apart, made of him a half-tragic figure. He wanted someone to understand the feeling that had taken possession of him after his mother's death.

There is a time in the life of every boy when he for the first time takes the backward view of life. Perhaps that is the moment when he crosses the line into manhood. The boy is walking through the street of his town. He is thinking of the future and of the figure he will cut in the world. Ambitions and regrets awake within him. Suddenly something happens; he stops under a tree and waits as for a voice calling his name. Ghosts of old things creep into his consciousness; the voices outside of himself whisper a message concerning the limitations of life. From being quite sure of himself and his future he becomes not at all sure. If he be an imaginative boy a door is torn open and for the first time he looks out upon the world, seeing, as though they marched in procession before him, the countless figures of men who before his time have come out of nothingness into the world, lived their lives and again disappeared into nothingness. The sadness of sophistication has come to the boy. With a little gasp he sees himself as merely a leaf blown by the wind through the streets of his village. He knows that in spite of all the stout talk of his fellows he must live and die in uncertainty, a thing blown by the winds, a thing destined like corn to wilt in the sun. He shivers and looks eagerly about. The eighteen years he has lived seem but a moment, a breathing space in the long march of humanity. Already he hears death calling. With all his heart he wants to come close to some other human, touch someone with his hands, be touched by the hand of another. If he prefers that the other be a woman, that is because he believes that a woman will be gentle, that she will understand. He wants, most of all, understanding.

When the moment of sophistication came to George Willard his mind turned to Helen White, the Winesburg banker's daughter. Always he had been conscious of the girl growing into womanhood as he grew into manhood. Once on a summer night when he was eighteen, he had walked with her on a country road and in her presence had given way to an impulse to boast, to make himself appear big and significant in her eyes. Now he wanted to see her for another purpose. He wanted to tell her of the new impulses that had come to him. He had tried to make her think of him as a man when he knew nothing of manhood and now he wanted to be with her and to try to make her feel the change he believed had taken place in his nature.

As for Helen White, she also had come to a period of change. What George felt, she in her young woman's way felt also. She was no longer a girl and hungered to reach into the grace and beauty of womanhood. She had come home from Cleveland, where she was attending college, to spend a day at the Fair. She also had begun to have memories. During the day she sat in the grandstand with a young man, one of the instructors from the college, who was a guest of her mother's. The young man was of a pedantic[1] turn of mind and she felt at once he would not do for her purpose. At the Fair she was glad to be seen in his company as he was well dressed and a stranger. She knew that the fact of his presence would create an impression. During the day she was happy, but when night came on she began to grow restless. She wanted to drive the instructor away, to get out of his presence. While they sat together in the grandstand and while the eyes of former schoolmates were upon them, she paid so much attention to her escort that he grew interested. "A scholar needs money. I should marry a woman with money," he mused.

Helen White was thinking of George Willard even as he wandered gloomily through the crowds thinking of her. She remembered the summer evening when they had walked together and wanted to walk with him again. She thought that the months she had spent in the city, the going to theaters and the seeing of great crowds wandering in

---

1. **pedantic:** scholarly in a narrow, dull way.

lighted thoroughfares, had changed her profoundly. She wanted him to feel and be conscious of the change in her nature.

The summer evening together that had left its mark on the memory of both the young man and woman had, when looked at quite sensibly, been rather stupidly spent. They had walked out of town along a country road. Then they had stopped by a fence near a field of young corn and George had taken off his coat and let it hang on his arm. "Well, I've stayed here in Winesburg—yes—I've not yet gone away but I'm growing up," he had said. "I've been reading books and I've been thinking. I'm going to try to amount to something in life.

"Well," he explained, "that isn't the point. Perhaps I'd better quit talking."

The confused boy put his hand on the girl's arm. His voice trembled. The two started to walk back along the road toward town. In his desperation George boasted, "I'm going to be a big man, the biggest that ever lived here in Winesburg," he declared. "I want you to do something, I don't know what. Perhaps it is none of my business. I want you to try to be different from other women. You see the point. It's none of my business I tell you. I want you to be a beautiful woman. You see what I want."

The boy's voice failed and in silence the two came back into town and went along the street to Helen White's house. At the gate he tried to say something impressive. Speeches he had thought out came into his head, but they seemed utterly pointless. "I thought—I used to think—I had it in my mind you would marry Seth Richmond. Now I know you won't," was all he could find to say as she went through the gate and toward the door of her house.

On the warm fall evening as he stood in the stairway and looked at the crowd drifting through Main Street, George thought of the talk beside the field of young corn and was ashamed of the figure he had made of himself. In the street the people surged up and down like cattle confined in a pen. Buggies and wagons almost filled the narrow thoroughfare. A band played and small boys raced along the sidewalk, diving between the legs of men. Young men with shining red faces walked awkwardly about with girls on their arms. In a room above one of the stores, where a dance was to be held, the fiddlers tuned their instruments. The broken sounds floated down through an open window and out across the murmur of voices and the loud blare of the horns of the band. The medley of sounds got on young Willard's nerves. Everywhere, on all sides, the sense of crowding, moving life closed in about him. He wanted to run away by himself and think. "If she wants to stay with that fellow she may. Why should I care? What difference does it make to me?" he growled and went along Main Street and through Hern's grocery into a side street.

George felt so utterly lonely and dejected that he wanted to weep but pride made him walk rapidly along, swinging his arms. He came to Westley Moyer's livery barn[2] and stopped in the shadows to listen to a group of men who talked of a race Westley's stallion, Tony Tip, had won at the Fair during the afternoon. A crowd had gathered in front of the barn and before the crowd walked Westley, prancing up and down and boasting. He held a whip in his hand and kept tapping the ground. Little puffs of dust arose in the lamplight. "Hell, quit your talking," Westley exclaimed. "I wasn't afraid, I knew I had 'em beat all the time. I wasn't afraid."

Ordinarily George Willard would have been intensely interested in the boasting of Moyer, the horseman. Now it made him angry. He turned and hurried away along the street. "Old windbag," he sputtered. "Why does he want to be bragging? Why don't he shut up?"

George went into a vacant lot and, as he hurried along, fell over a pile of rubbish. A nail protruding from an empty barrel tore his trousers. He sat down on the ground and swore. With a pin he mended the torn place and then arose and went on. "I'll go to Helen White's house, that's what I'll do. I'll walk right in. I'll say that I want to see her. I'll walk right in and sit down, that's what I'll do," he declared, climbing over a fence and beginning to run.

On the veranda of Banker White's house Helen was restless and distraught. The instructor sat between the mother and daughter. His talk wearied the girl. Although he had also been raised in an Ohio town, the instructor began to put on the airs of the city. He wanted to appear cosmopolitan. "I like the chance you have given me to study the background out of which most of our girls come," he declared. "It was good of you, Mrs. White, to have me down for the day." He turned to Helen and laughed. "Your life is still bound up with the life of this

---

2. **livery barn:** place where horses might be boarded or rented out.

town?" he asked. "There are people here in whom you are interested?" To the girl his voice sounded pompous and heavy.

Helen arose and went into the house. At the door leading to a garden at the back she stopped and stood listening. Her mother began to talk. "There is no one here fit to associate with a girl of Helen's breeding," she said.

Helen ran down a flight of stairs at the back of the house and into the garden. In the darkness she stopped and stood trembling. It seemed to her that the world was full of meaningless people saying words. Afire with eagerness she ran through a garden gate and turning a corner by the banker's barn, went into a little side street. "George! Where are you, George?" she cried, filled with nervous excitement. She stopped running, and leaned against a tree to laugh hysterically. Along the dark little street came George Willard, still saying words. "I'm going to walk right into her house. I'll go right in and sit down, " he declared as he came up to her. He stopped and stared stupidly. "Come on," he said and took hold of her hand. With hanging heads they walked away along the street under the trees. Dry leaves rustled under foot. Now that he had found her George wondered what he had better do and say.

At the upper end of the fairground, in Winesburg, there is a half-decayed old grandstand. It has never been painted and the boards are all warped out of shape. The fairground stands on top of a low hill rising out of the valley of Wine Creek and from the grandstand one can see at night, over a cornfield, the lights of the town reflected against the sky.

George and Helen climbed the hill to the fairground, coming by the path past Waterworks Pond. The feeling of loneliness and isolation that had come to the young man in the crowded streets of his town was both broken and intensified by the presence of Helen. What he felt was reflected in her.

In youth there are always two forces fighting in people. The warm unthinking little animal struggles against the thing that reflects and remembers, and the older, the more sophisticated thing had possession of George Willard. Sensing his mood, Helen walked beside him filled with respect. When they got to the grandstand they climbed up under the roof and sat down on one of the long benchlike seats.

There is something memorable in the experience to be had by going into a fairground that stands at the edge of a Middle Western town on a night after the annual fair has been held. The sensation is one never to be forgotten. On all sides are ghosts, not of the dead, but of living people. Here, during the day just passed, have come the people pouring in from the town and the country around. Farmers with their wives and children and all the people from the hundreds of little frame houses have gathered within these board walls. Young girls have laughed and men with beards have talked of the affairs of their lives. The place has been filled to overflowing with life. It has itched and squirmed with life and now it is night and the life has all gone away. The silence is almost terrifying. One conceals oneself standing silently beside the trunk of a tree and what there is of a reflective tendency in his nature is intensified. One shudders at the thought of the meaninglessness of life while at the same instant, and if the people of the town are his people, one loves life so intensely that tears come into the eyes.

In the darkness under the roof of the grandstand, George Willard sat beside Helen White and felt very keenly his own insignificance in the scheme of existence. Now that he had come out of town where the presence of the people stirring about, busy with a multitude of affairs, had been so irritating the irritation was all gone. The presence of Helen renewed and refreshed him. It was as though her woman's hand was assisting him to make some minute³ readjustment of the machinery of his life. He began to think of the people in the town where he had always lived with something like reverence. He had reverence for Helen. He wanted to love and to be loved by her, but he did not want at the moment to be confused by her womanhood. In the darkness he took hold of her hand and when she crept close put a hand on her shoulder. A wind began to blow and he shivered. With all his strength he tried to hold and to understand the mood that had come upon him. In that high place in the darkness the two oddly sensitive human atoms held each other tightly and waited. In the mind of each was the same thought. "I have come to this lonely place and here is this other," was the substance of the thing felt.

In Winesburg the crowded day had run itself out into the long night of the late fall. Farm horses jogged away along lonely country roads pulling their portion of weary people. Clerks began to bring samples of goods in off the sidewalks and lock the doors of stores. In the Opera

---

3. **minute:** very small.

House a crowd had gathered to see a show and further down Main Street the fiddlers, their instruments tuned, sweated and worked to keep the feet of youth flying over a dance floor.

In the darkness in the grandstand Helen White and George Willard remained silent. Now and then the spell that held them was broken and they turned and tried in the dim light to see into each other's eyes. They kissed but that impulse did not last. At the upper end of the fairground a half dozen men worked over horses that had raced during the afternoon. The men had built a fire and were heating kettles of water. Only their legs could be seen as they passed back and forth in the light. When the wind blew the little flames of the fire danced crazily about.

George and Helen arose and walked away into the darkness. They went along a path past a field of corn that had not yet been cut. The wind whispered among the dry corn blades. For a moment during the walk back into town the spell that held them was broken. When they had come to the crest of Waterworks Hill they stopped by a tree and George again put his hands on the girl's shoulders. She embraced him eagerly and then again they drew quickly back from that impulse. They stopped kissing and stood a little apart. Mutual respect grew big in them. They were both embarrassed and to relieve their embarrassment dropped into the animalism of youth. They laughed and began to pull and haul at each other. In some way chastened and purified by the mood they had been in they became, not man and woman, not boy and girl, but excited little animals.

It was so they went down the hill. In the darkness they played like two splendid young things in a young world. Once, running swiftly forward, Helen tripped George and he fell. He squirmed and shouted. Shaking with laughter, he rolled down the hill. Helen ran after him. For just a moment she stopped in the darkness. There was no way of knowing what woman's thoughts went through her mind but, when the bottom of the hill was reached and she came up to the boy, she took his arm and walked beside him in dignified silence. For some reason they could not have explained they had both got from their silent evening together the thing needed. Man or boy, woman or girl, they had for a moment taken hold of the thing that makes the mature life of men and women in the modern world possible.

Responding to the Story

1. What has caused George in paragraph 5 to "[take] the backward view of life"? What needs does he have at this point?
2. Why does the writer refer to the experience in question 1 as "the sadness of sophistication"?
3. How have both Helen and George changed since the last time they walked together?
4. Are Helen and George "sophisticated" at the end of the story? Explain your ideas.

Exploring the Author's Craft

This story is built around a serious idea, but it is not simply an essay. Instead, Anderson has taken the idea and dramatized it with real people in real settings.

Reread the paragraph beginning "There is something memorable in the experience to be had by going into a fairground. . . ." Considering what you have learned in discussing this story, explain how the description in this paragraph brings to life the ideas Anderson is writing about.

Writer's Workshop

As Sherwood Anderson did in "Sophistication," create a story built around an insight into life. Think about some realization about life, or people, that you have recently come to. Then create two or three characters—keep it simple—and dramatize your insight in a short piece of fiction. Have the insight occur to one of the characters and write about that character in the third person, as Anderson did.

Alternate Media Response

Create a video script for the later portion of this story, when George and Helen are speaking at the fair grandstand. Show both the tenderness and uncertainty of their relationship. Now tape the scene. Try to capture exactly what is in Anderson's short story. You may want to update the story by placing it in a contemporary setting, but remain true to the tone and themes of "Sophistication."

Making Connections in
PART THREE

Complete one or more of the following assignments as your teacher directs.

1. What views of infatuation, romance, and love are shown in the stories in Part Three? In your answer, refer to at least five of the stories and discuss the variety of portraits of lovers and observations about love that are presented here.
2. Which two of the fourteen or so main characters who appear in the stories in Part Three seem the most real to you? Explain your reaction.
3. Do any of these depictions of youthful infatuation and love seem quite *unrealistic* to you? If so, why?

COMING OF AGE

Out in the World

A visit to a nursing home. Losing a friend because of your color. The first experience of death in one's life. A girl's attempt to be initiated into a soriority.

These are just a few of the subjects explored in this section of the book as young people encounter the world beyond their homes, families, and friends. As most students would readily acknowledge, our learning about life occurs in far more places that just the school classroom. In the stories in Part Four, we meet characters who are out in the classroom of daily living, discovering what life has to offer—and learning about themselves.Of course, this is what we hope has been happening for you with this book all along.

Carrie A. Young

Carrie A. Young was born in Lynchburg, Virginia, and currently lives in Florida. She was formerly employed as a social worker with a foster care agency in New York City. "Adjö Means Good-bye" was her first published story.

Why should two friends stop seeing each other?

Adjö Means Good-bye

It has been a long time since I knew Marget Swenson. How the years have rushed by! I was a child when I knew her, and now I myself have children. The circle keeps turning, keeps coming full.

The mind loses many things as it matures, but I never lost Marget; she has remained with me, like the first love and the first hurt. The mind does not lose what is meaningful to one's existence. Marget was both my first love and first hurt. I met her when she joined our sixth-grade class.

She stood before the class holding tightly to the teacher's hand, her blue, frightened eyes sweeping back and forth across the room until they came to rest on my face. From that very first day we became friends. Marget, just fresh from Sweden, and me, a sixth-generation American. We were both rather shy and quiet and perhaps even lonely, and that's why we took to each other. She spoke very little English, but somehow we managed to understand each other. We visited one another at home practically every day. My young life had suddenly become deliciously complete. I had a dear friend.

Sometimes we talked and laughed on the top of the big, dazzling green hill close to the school. We had so much to talk about; so many things were new to her. She asked a thousand questions and I—I, filled to bursting with pride that it was from me that she wished to learn, responded eagerly and with excesses of superlatives.[1]

Now, sometimes, when I drive my children to school and watch them race up the walks to the doors, I wonder what lies ahead in the momentary darkness of the hall corridors, and think of Marget once more, I think of how she came out of a dark corridor one day, the day she really looked at my brother when she was visiting me. I saw her following him with new eyes, puzzled eyes, and a strange fear gripped me. "Your brother," she whispered to me, "is African?"

I was a little surprised and a little hurt. Didn't we cheer for Tarzan when we went to the movies? Were not the Africans always frightened and cowardly? But I answered, "No silly," and I continued to wait.

"He looks different from you."

"He should," I said, managing to laugh. My brother was darker than anyone else in the family. "He's a boy and I'm a girl. But we're both Negro, of course."

She opened her mouth to say something else, then closed it and the fear slipped away.

Marget lived up on the hill. That was the place where there were many large and pretty houses. I suppose it was only in passing that I knew only white people lived there. Whenever I visited, Marget's mother put up a table in their garden, and Marget and I had milk and *kaka*, a kind of cake. Mrs. Swenson loved to see me eat. She was a large, round woman, with deep blue eyes and very red cheeks. Marget, though much smaller, of course, looked quite like her. We did our homework after we had the cake and milk, compositions or story reading. When we finished, Mrs. Swenson hugged me close and I knew I was loved in that home. A child knows when it is loved or only tolerated. But I was loved. Mrs. Swenson thanked me with a thick, Swedish accent for helping Marget.

Marget and I had so much fun with words, and there were times when we sat for hours in my garden or hers, or on the hilltop, surrounded by grass and perhaps the smell of the suppers being prepared for our fathers still at work downtown. Her words were

---

1. **superlatives:** the highest degree of comparisons of adjectives or adverbs, such as *finest, best, greatest.*

Swedish, mine, English. We were surprised how much alike many of them sounded, and we laughed at the way each of us slid our tongues over the unfamiliar words. I learned the Swedish equivalents of mother, father, house, hello, friend, and good-bye.

One day Marget and I raced out of school as soon as the ringing bell released us. We sped down the hill, flashed over gray concrete walks and green lawns dotted with dandelions and scattered daisies, our patent leather buckled shoes slapping a merry tattoo[2] as we went, our long stockings tumbling down our legs. We were going to Marget's to plan her birthday party. Such important business for ten-year-olds!

Eventually, after much planning and waiting, the day of the party came. I put on my pink organdy dress with the big bertha collar[3] and a new pair of patent leather shoes that tortured my feet unbearably. Skipping up the hill to Marget's I stopped at a lawn which looked deserted. I set down my gift and began to pick the wild flowers that were growing there. Suddenly, from out of nowhere, an old man appeared. "What do you think you're doing, pulling up my flowers?" he shouted. Once again I held myself tightly against the fear, awaiting that awful thing that I felt must come. "I wanted to take them to my friend," I explained. "She's having a birthday today."

The old man's eyes began to twinkle. "She is, is she? Well, you must wait a minute, young lady." He went away and came back with garden shears and cut a handful and then an armful of flowers, and with a smile sent me on my way. My childish fears had been ambushed by a kindness.

I arrived at the party early and Marget and I whizzed around, putting the finishing touches on the decorations. There were hardly enough vases for all the flowers the old man had given me. Some fifteen minutes later the doorbell rang and Marget ran around to the front, saying, "Oh, here they come!"

But it was Mary Ann, another girl in our class, and she was alone. She put her present for Marget on the table and the three of us talked. Occasionally, Marget got up and went around to the front to see who had come unheralded[4] by the doorbell. No one.

---

2. **tattoo:** series of taps.
3. **big bertha collar:** wide collar that covers the shoulders.
4. **unheralded:** unannounced.

"I wonder what's taking them so long?" Mary Ann asked.

Growing more upset by the minute, Marget answered, "Maybe they didn't remember what time the party was."

How does a child of ten describe a sense of foreboding, the feeling that the bad things have happened because of herself? I sat silently, waiting.

When it got to be after five, Mrs. Swenson called Marget inside; she was there for a long time, and when she came out, she looked very, very sad. "My mother does not think they are coming," she said.

"Why not?" Mary Ann blurted.

"Betty Hatcher's mother was here last night and she talked a long time with my mother. I thought it was about the party. Mother kept saying, 'Yes, yes, she is coming.'"

I took Marget's hand. "Maybe they were talking about me," I said. Oh! I remember so painfully today how I wanted her quick and positive denial to that thrust of mine into darkness where I knew something alive was lurking. Although she did it quite casually, I was aware that Marget was trying to slip her hand from mine, as though she might have had the same thought I had voiced aloud. I opened my hand and let her go. "Don't be silly," she said.

No one came. The three of us sat in the middle rows and rows of flowers and ate our ice cream and cake. Our pretty dresses, ribbons, and shoes were dejected blobs of color. It was as if the world had swung out around us and gone past, leaving us whole, but in some way indelibly stamped forever.

It was different between Marget and me after her birthday. She stopped coming to my house, and when at school I asked her when she would, she looked as though she would cry. She had to do something for her mother, was her unvarying excuse. So, one day, I went to her house, climbed up the hill where the old man had picked the flowers, and a brooding, restless thing grew within me at every step, almost a *knowing*. I had not, after all, been invited to Marget's. My throat grew dry and I thought about turning back, and for the first time the hill and all the homes looked alien, even threatening to me.

Marget almost jumped when she opened the door. She stared at me in shock. then, quickly, in a voice I'd never heard before, she said, "My mother says you can't come to my house anymore."

I opened my mouth, and closed it without speaking. The awful thing had come; the knowing was confirmed. Marget, crying, closed the door in my face. When I turned to go down the stairs and back down the hill to my house, my eyes, too, were filled with tears. No one had to tell me that the awful thing had come because Marget was white and I was not. I just *knew* it deep within myself. I guess I expected it to happen. It was only a question of when.

June. School was coming to a close. Those days brimmed with strange, uncomfortable moments when Marget and I looked at each other and our eyes darted quickly away. We were little pawns,[5] one white, one colored, in a game over which we had no control then. We did not speak to each other at all.

On the last day of school, I screwed up a strange and reckless courage and took my autograph book to where Marget was sitting. I handed it to her. She hesitated, then took it, and without looking up, wrote words I don't remember now; they were quite common words, the kind everyone was writing in everyone else's book. I waited. Slowly, she passed her book to me and in it I wrote with a slow, firm hand some of the words she had taught me. I wrote *Adjö min vän*. Good-bye, my friend. I released her, let her go, told her not to worry; told her that I no longer needed her. *Adjö*.

Whenever I think of Marget now, and I do at the most surprising times, I wonder if she ever thinks of me, if she is married and has children, and I wonder if she has become a queen by now, instead of a pawn.

---

5. **pawns:** in chess, the pieces of lowest value; here, an unimportant person who is used to gain some advantage.

Responding to the Story

1. Explain why Marget was the narrator's "first love and first hurt."
2. What does the author mean when she says of Marget, "I wonder if she ever thinks of me . . . and I wonder if she has become a queen by now, instead of a pawn"?

Exploring the Author's Craft

The narrator implies from the beginning that this story will have an unhappy ending. Trace the steps that move this story from happiness to sadness. The technique of providing clues to future action is called *foreshadowing*. Does the foreshadowing in this story spoil the ending? Why or why not?

Writer's Workshop

1. Does prejudice still exist in our society today? Write an essay in which you explain your opinion; support your position with anecdotes of personal experience if possible.
2. Write a diary entry from Marget's point of view after she tells the narrator that she can't come to Marget's house anymore.

Amy Boesky

"A Veil of Water" won a Scholastic Writing Award in 1977 when Boesky was a senior at Seaholm Senior High School in Birmingham, Michigan. As Boesky explains, "I have always loved reading and writing, but I preferred to do both on my own—I was frustrated with school assignments, and writing fiction became an important outlet for me during high school. The feelings which inspired this story (feelings of sorrow and loss) were both real and personal, but the tragedy at the center of the story was imagined. Though I was hesitant at first about sending stories and poems to magazines, I found the idea of an 'audience' encouraged me to write. I published a short story in *Seventeen* magazine before I graduated from high school but in college began to concentrate on poetry."

Boesky published individual poems and a book in verse for children while in college. She went on to graduate school in Renaissance English literature, first at Oxford University in England and then at Harvard. After completing her doctorate she taught at Georgetown University, and she is currently teaching English at Boston College.

The narrator's first experience of grief changes her world.

A Veil of Water

It is cold out. We are standing outside on the lawn, which is stiff and crunching under our boots. My aunt is crying. No one asks why. My aunt is a big woman, and the tears seem silly. It is as solemn and inappropriate as if a man were crying. My brother is tired, there are circles under his eyes, and the circles look artificial—like dark makeup on his thin face. I am reminded of Halloween. Last year I was a ballerina. My aunt says it is time to come inside, out of the cold.

We sit down at the kitchen table. My aunt's house is smaller than ours, and noisier. She has three sons, my cousins. We can hear them making odd sounds in the other rooms, the other rooms of their house. The heat makes my fingers tingle. My cousins are named Jamie, Bob, and Eddie. None of them is kind to me. On other days they have tormented me, pulling my hair, making mean jokes about my dress. (Usually I wear blue jeans, like my brother, but when we come to visit, my mother tells me to wear a dress.) There is lace on the collar and it is scratching my neck. Today we sit alone at the table, my aunt, my brother, myself. My aunt makes hot chocolate and pours it into plastic cups. She forgets to put marshmallows in it. Joshua, who is my brother and older than me, drinks his. I don't.

My aunt leans back in her chair, and the chair sways back with her. She looks huge and somehow blurred. She stretches her arms out to me, offering me something. I stare at her and wait for something to become clear. I am tired. I can feel the floor moving uncertainly beneath my feet. My uncle comes in the room. He is a huge man, his stomach shakes when he walks. He puts his arms around me and I am entirely hidden, a party of nothing. "We're going to sleep now, princess," he says to me, into my ear. His voice is too strong to hear all at once. Then I am up in the air, floundering, the floor is a million miles away. "Just hold on!" my uncle booms. I clutch at his shirt with hysterical fingers. I can smell pipe tobacco on him, on his neck and collar. My legs grab at the empty air, kicking for support. We bump our way up the short stairway. He lays me down on a bed that is too big for me, and I squirm away into the wide expanse of blankets. He does not undress me. He turns the lights out, and he closes the door behind him. A minute later he pushes the door open a little. The light from the hall slips fuzzily through the crack. I sleep. I m dreaming about a bird, a big black bird that is somehow familiar to me, and somehow terrible. In my sleep I am exhausted and not frightened. Then a door opens, and a light turns on, and I wake in terror to see my aunt leaning over me, unfastening the buttons on my dress. I cry out, jerking away from her. Her hands are cold. She reaches for me again, and I scream at her. I can feel the rush of wings near me. She moves away, and the light is gone, and I am alone in the darkness.

When I wake again I am utterly drained, as if I had walked for hours in my sleep. I am lying in a tangle of rumpled sheets, still in my navy dress. My tights have slid down low on my legs. My shoes are gone. I feel stiff and bleary-eyed, as if I had cried in my sleep. I have no clear idea where I am, or what I am doing here. Joshua is next to me in bed, asleep, breathing hard through his mouth. There is spittle on his cheek. He is wearing pajamas, but they are not his. The pajamas are light blue with little brown footballs on them. I decide they are Eddie's, and I inch away from him, feeling betrayed. I'm not certain where I am. I don't remember anything that happened yesterday, or before that.

I help my aunt with the breakfast dishes. She has red blotches on her face. "all my life I've wanted a daughter," she says. Her voice sounds the way Joshua's does when he has done something very bad. She does not look at me. We are alone in the kitchen and the heat of the water rises up at us, eager for escape. My aunt says she is worried about me. She wants me to see the doctor. She says she is afraid I am sick, but I can tell from the way she says it that she doesn't really believe it. I nod at her anyway. I know there is nothing wrong with me.

My aunt talks to me about school. She says that she has called my teacher, and she understands that it will take me a while to adjust. She waits for me to say something but I don't. I listen to her talk and I wipe the steaming dishes with a yellow towel.

After breakfast I sit on the couch and watch TV. There are two cartoons, Bugs Bunny and another one I don't recognize. In the cartoons the animals and people are always getting hurt, but in the next scene they re better again. after the cartoons there are game shows. Sometimes the dog comes and rubs slowly against the sides of my legs. My mother never wanted a dog. She told Joshua they make muddy messes.

My aunt comes in and sits down next to me. "I want to talk to you about what happened," she says. There is something in her voice that I don't like.

"What happened? Nothing happened," I say stubbornly. I don't know what she's talking about.

My uncle comes home from work in the middle of the day. "We're going out," he says to me. I nod at him. My head feels light and funny, like a helium balloon bobbing at the end of a piece of limp yarn. He takes me by the hand and we walk together. It is snowing, and the motion of the whiteness is so fast and constant it is as if the sky were turning inside out. Inside my mittens my fingers are numbed with cold.

We take the bus. My boots leak snow, and two small puddles form under my feet. I read the ads over my head, and my uncle smokes a pipe. When the bus stops we get off again. I trip a little on the second step, but my uncle catches me. We walk for a long time. The snow is in my face. When I breathe the air dragons out of my mouth in a pale white fume, like pipe smoke. My uncle holds my hand so tightly it hurts. "Am I walking too fast?" he asks me, and his voice is high up and lost in whiteness. "I'm not used to holding hands with a girl."

We are inside a building now, and we are wet and tired of walking. My uncle shakes the snow from his gloves and takes some loose coins from his pocket. He hands them to the lady behind the desk and she gives him two paper tickets, one pink and one yellow.

We are in the aquarium. I have been here before. My uncle leads me by the hand and we walk slowly from glass to glass. Inside the tiny aqua squares the fish are swimming awkwardly, their bubble faces pushing out at us.

My uncle stoops, putting his face against the glass. He blows his face out at the fish, and they dart away, terrified. "I used to come here," he says. His voice is low. "When I was growing up, your father used to take me here almost every Sunday. There was something magic here, some magic that was only here when he was."

We keep walking. There is something aching at the back of my throat.

"I remember how our parents used to tease him," he says. He looks down at me. Then he laughs. His voice is not happy, but the laughter is in it, and the sadness too. "I never knew a man with that much color inside of him."

I blink. The air is alive, pushing me back. "Sometimes he would say stories . . ." I say brokenly. My uncle looks down at me, waiting.

"Sometimes he would make stories," I say lamely. "He would make stories up about the fish—which one was the father, and which one was his little girl. Sometimes . . ."

A week ago, or two weeks ago, or more, my father had stood here next to me, and I had pressed my nose to the glass while he laughed. I used to think the fish could hear his voice. "Look, they're dancing for you now," my father would say, and when I looked I could see that he was right. I want to tell my uncle this now, but there is something else he is waiting to hear. I stare at him, and now he looks different; I am seeing him through a veil of water, he bubbles before me brokenly, like a fish. I m crying. He holds me, holds me with both his arms. I am not crying very hard, but I am crying.

We leave soon. There is no reason to stay. We walk outside awkwardly, bumping into each other and into other people, and my eyes are blinded with my tears. The world looks different suddenly. I am seeing it through water, and it will never look the same again.

Responding to the Story

1. What has happened to the characters in this story? Once you have determined that, do you believe that the narrator's behavior and reactions are understandable? Explain.
2. What clues are there about the ages of the narrator and her brother?

Exploring the Author's Craft

1. Writers often mean more than what they seem to say. For example, they will often use something concrete—an object, place, character, or event—as a **symbol** of some abstract quality or idea. What does the "big black bird" symbolize? How are the cartoons the narrator watches symbolic?
2. A **motif** is an idea, element, incident, or object that recurs in a literary work. What is the motif in "A Veil of Water"? Is it appropriate to the story? Discuss.

Writer's Workshop

Amy Boesky, who wrote this story as a senior in high school, hadn't experienced a death close to her when she wrote "A Veil of Water." Your job now as a budding writer is to create a similarly believable and compelling first-person narrative. Imagine your circumstances exactly ten years from now. Write a diary entry that conveys where you are and what you have done on that day.

Alternate Media Response

In any medium you wish, illustrate a moment in this story that you find especially gripping or dramatic.

Eugenia Collier

Eugenia Collier won the Gwendolyn Brooks Award for Fiction from *Negro Digest* for "Marigolds" in 1969. Since then, the story has been widely reprinted.

Collier was born in Baltimore, Maryland, in 1928. She graduated magna cum laude from Howard University in 1948 and received an M.A. degree from Columbia University in 1950. She was a caseworker in Baltimore for five years and then became an assistant instructor at Morgan State College in 1955. She became a professor at the Community College of Baltimore in 1970 and now chairs the English Department at Morgan State. She married in 1948 and has three sons.

Sometimes there is an impulse to destroy what seems too beautiful.

Marigolds

When I think of the hometown of my youth, all that I seem to remember is dust—the brown, crumbly dust of late summer—arid, sterile dust that gets into the eyes and makes them water, gets into the throat and between the toes of bare brown feet. I don't know why I should remember only the dust. Surely there must have been lush green lawns and paved streets under leafy shade trees somewhere in town; but memory is an abstract painting—it does not present things as they are, but rather as they *feel*. And so, when I think of that time and that place, I remember only the dry September of the dirt roads and grassless yards of the shantytown where I lived. And one other thing I remember, another incongruency of memory—a brilliant splash of sunny yellow against the dust—Miss Lottie's marigolds.

Whenever the memory of those marigolds flashes across my mind, strange nostalgia comes with it and remains long after the picture has faded. I feel again the chaotic emotions of adolescence, illusive as smoke, yet as real as the potted geranium before me now. Joy and rage and wild animal gladness and shame become tangled together in the multicolored skein of fourteen-going-on-fifteen as I recall that devastating moment when I was suddenly more woman than child, years ago in Miss Lottie's yard. I think of those marigolds at the strangest times; I remember them vividly now as I desperately pass away the time waiting for you, who will not come.

I suppose that futile waiting was the sorrowful background music of our impoverished little community when I was young. The Depression that gripped the nation was no new thing to us, for the black workers of rural Maryland had always been depressed. I don't know what it was that we were waiting for; certainly not for the prosperity that was "just around the corner," for those were white folks' words, which we never believed. Nor did we wait for hard work and thrift to pay off in shining success as the American Dream promised, for we knew better than that, too. Perhaps we waited for a miracle, amorphous in concept but necessary if one were to have the grit to rise before dawn each day and labor in the white man's vineyard until after dark, or to wander about in the September dust offering one's sweat in return for some meager share of bread. But God was chary[1] with miracles in those days, and so we waited—and waited.

We children, of course were only vaguely aware of the extent of our poverty. Having no radios, few newspapers, and no magazines, we were somewhat unaware of the world outside our community. Nowadays we would be called "culturally deprived" and people would write books and hold conferences about us. In those days everybody we knew was just as hungry and ill-clad as we were. Poverty was the cage in which we all were trapped, and our hatred of it was still the vague, undirected restlessness of the zoo-bred flamingo who knows that nature created him to fly free.

As I think of those days I feel most poignantly the tag end of summer, the bright dry times when we began to have a sense of shortening days and the imminence of the cold.

---

1. **chary:** careful.

By the time I was fourteen my brother Joey and I were the only children left at our house, the older ones having left home for early marriage or the lure of the city, and the two babies having been sent to relatives who might care for them better than we. Joey was three years younger than I, and a boy, and therefore vastly inferior. Each morning our mother and father trudged wearily down the dirt road and around the bend, she to her domestic job, he to his daily unsuccessful quest for work. After our few chores around the tumbledown shanty, Joey and I were free to run wild in the sun with other children similarly situated.

For the most part, those days are ill-defined in my memory, running together, combining like a fresh watercolor painting left out in the rain. I remember squatting in the road drawing a picture in the dust, a picture which Joey gleefully erased with one sweep of his dirty foot. I remember fishing for minnows in a muddy creek and watching sadly as they eluded my cupped hands, while Joey laughed uproariously. And I remember, that year, a strange restlessness of body and of spirit, a feeling that something old and familiar was ending, and something unknown and therefore terrifying was beginning.

One day returns to me with special clarity for some reason, perhaps because it was the beginning of the experience that in some inexplicable way marked the end of innocence. I was loafing under the great oak tree in our yard, deep in some reverie which I have now forgotten except that it involved some secret, secret thoughts of one of the Harris boys across the yard. Joey and a bunch of kids were bored now with the old tire suspended from an oak limb which had kept them entertained for awhile.

"Hey, Lizabeth," Joey yelled. He never talked when he could yell. "Hey, Lizabeth, let's us go somewhere."

I came reluctantly from my private world. "Where at, Joey?"

The truth was that we were becoming tired of the formlessness of our summer days. The idleness whose prospect had seemed so beautiful during the busy days of spring now had degenerated to an almost desperate effort to fill up the empty midday hours.

"Let's go see can we find us some locusts on the hill," someone suggested.

Joey was scornful. "Ain't no more locusts there. Y'all got 'em all while they was still green."

The argument that followed was brief and not really worth the effort. Hunting locust trees wasn't fun any more by now.

"Tell you what," said Joey finally, his eyes sparkling. "Let's us go over to Miss Lottie's."

The idea caught on at once, for annoying Miss Lottie was always fun. I was still child enough to scamper along with the group over rickety fences and through bushes that tore our already raggedy clothes, back to where Miss Lottie lived. I think now that we must have made a tragicomic spectacle, five or six kids of different ages, each of us clad in only one garment—the girls in faded dresses that were too long or too short, the boys in patchy pants, their sweaty brown chests gleaming in the hot sun. A little cloud of dust followed our thin legs and bare feet as we tramped over the barren land.

When Miss Lottie's house came into view we stopped, ostensibly to plan our strategy, but actually to reinforce our courage. Miss Lottie's house was the most ramshackle of all our ramshackle homes. The sun and rain had long since faded its rickety frame siding from white to a sullen gray. The boards themselves seemed to remain upright not from being nailed together but rather from leaning together like a house that a child might have constructed from cards. A brisk wind might have blown it down, and the fact that it was still standing implied a kind of enchantment that was stronger than the elements. There it stood, and as far as I know is standing yet—a gray rotting thing with no porch, no shutters, no steps, set on a cramped lot with no grass, not even any weeds—a monument to decay.

In front of the house in a squeaky rocking chair sat Miss Lottie's son, John Burke, completing the impression of decay. John Burke was what was known as "queer-headed." Black and ageless, he sat, rocking day in and day out in a mindless stupor, lulled by the monotonous squeak-squawk of the chair. A battered hat atop his shaggy head shaded him from the sun. Usually John Burke was totally unaware of everything outside his quiet dream world. But if you disturbed him, if you intruded upon his fantasies, he would become enraged, strike out at you, and curse at you in some strange enchanted language which only he could understand. We children made a game of thinking of ways to disturb John Burke and then to elude his violent retribution.

But our real fun and our real fear lay in Miss Lottie herself. Miss Lottie seemed to be at least a hundred years old. Her big frame still held traces

of the tall, powerful woman she must have been in youth, although it
was now bent and drawn. Her smooth skin was a dark reddish-brown,
and her face had Indianlike features and the stern stoicism that one
associates with Indian faces. Miss Lottie didn't like intruders either,
especially children. She never left her yard, and nobody ever visited her.
We never knew how she managed those necessities which depend on
human interaction—how she ate, for example, or even whether she ate.
When we were tiny children, we thought Miss Lottie was a witch and
we made up tales, that we half believed ourselves, about her exploits. We
were far too sophisticated now, of course, to believe the witch nonsense.
But old fears have a way of clinging like cobwebs, and so when we
sighted the tumbledown shack, we had to stop to reinforce our nerves.

"Look, there she is," I whispered, forgetting that Miss Lottie could not
possibly have heard me from that distance. "She's fooling with them
crazy flowers."

'Yeh, look at' er."

Miss Lottie's marigolds were perhaps the strangest part of the picture.
Certainly they did not fit in with the crumbling decay of the rest of her
yard. Beyond the dusty brown yard, in front of the sorry gray house, rose
suddenly and shockingly a dazzling strip of bright blossoms, clumped
together in enormous mounds, warm and passionate and sun-golden. The
old black witch-woman worked on them all summer, every summer,
down on her creaky knees, weeding and cultivating and arranging, while
the house crumbled and John Burke rocked. For some perverse reason,
we children hated those marigolds. They interfered with the perfect
ugliness of the place; they were too beautiful; they said too much that
we could not understand; they did not make sense. There was something
in the vigor with which the old woman destroyed the weeds that
intimidated us. It should have been a comical sight—the old woman with
the man's hat on her cropped white head, leaning over the bright
mounds, her big backside in the air—but it wasn't comical, it was
something we could not name. We had to annoy her by whizzing a
pebble into her flowers or by yelling a dirty word, then dancing away
from her rage, reveling in our youth and mocking her age. Actually, I
think it was the flowers we wanted to destroy, but nobody had the nerve
to try it, not even Joey, who was usually fool enough to try anything.

"Y'all git some stones," commanded Joey now, and was met with
instant giggling obedience as everyone except me began to gather
pebbles from the dusty ground. "Come on, Lizabeth."

I just stood there peering through the bushes, torn between wanting to join the fun and feeling that it was all a bit silly.

"You scared, Lizabeth?"

I cursed and spat on the ground—my favorite gesture of phony bravado. "Y'all children get the stones, I'll show you how to use 'em."

I said before that we children were not consciously aware of how thick were the bars of our cage. I wonder now, though, whether we were not more aware of it than I thought. Perhaps we had some dim notion of what we were, and how little chance we had of being anything else. Otherwise, why would we have been so preoccupied with destruction? Anyway, the pebbles were collected quickly, and everybody looked at me to begin the fun.

"Come on, y'all."

We crept to the edge of the bushes that bordered the narrow road in front of Miss Lottie's place. She was working placidly, kneeling over the flowers, her dark hand plunged into the golden mound. Suddenly *zing*— an expertly aimed stone cut the head off one of the blossoms.

"Who out there?" Miss Lottie's backside came down and her head came up as her sharp eyes searched the bushes.

"You better git!"

We had crouched down out of sight in the bushes, where we stifled the giggles that insisted on coming. Miss Lottie gazed warily across the road for a moment, then cautiously returned to her weeding. *Zing*—Joey sent a pebble into the blooms, and another marigold was beheaded.

Miss Lottie was enraged now. She began struggling to her feet, leaning on a rickety cane and shouting. "Y'all git! Go on home!" Then the rest of the kids let loose with their pebbles, storming the flowers and laughing wildly and senselessly at Miss Lottie's impotent rage. She shook her stick at us and started shakily toward the road crying, "John Burke! John Burke, come help!"

Then I lost my head entirely, mad with the power of inciting such rage, and ran out of the bushes in the storm of pebbles, straight toward Miss Lottie chanting madly, "Old witch, fell in a ditch, picked up a penny and though she was rich!" The children screamed with delight, dropped their pebbles and joined the crazy dance, swarming around Miss Lottie like bees and chanting, "Old lady witch!" while she screamed curses at us. The madness lasted only a moment, for John Burke, startled at last, lurched out of his chair, and we dashed for the bushes just as Miss Lottie's cane went whizzing at my head.

I did not join the merriment when the kids gathered again under the oak in our bare yard. Suddenly I was ashamed, and I did not like being ashamed. The child in me sulked and said it was all in fun, but the woman in me flinched at the thought of the malicious attack that I had led. The mood lasted all afternoon. When we ate the beans and rice that was supper that night, I did not notice my father's silence, for he was always silent these days, nor did I notice my mother's absence, for she always worked until well into evening. Joey and I had a particularly bitter argument after supper; his exuberance got on my nerves. Finally I stretched out upon the pallet in the room we shared and fell into a fitful doze.

When I awoke, somewhere in the middle of the night, my mother had returned, and I vaguely listened to the conversation that was audible through the thin walls that separated our rooms. At first I heard no words, only voices. My mothers' voice was like a cool, dark room in summer—peaceful, soothing, quiet. I loved to listen to it; it made things seem all right somehow. But my father's voice cut through hers, shattering the peace.

"Twenty-two years, Maybelle, twenty-two years," he was saying, "and I got nothing for you, nothing, nothing."

"It's all right, honey, you'll get something. Everybody out of work now, you know that."

"It ain't right. Ain't no man ought to eat his woman's food year in and year out, and see his children running wild. Ain't nothing right about that."

"Honey, you took good care of us when you had it. Ain't nobody got nothing nowadays."

"I ain't talking about nobody else, I'm talking about *me*. God knows I try." My mother said something I could not hear, and my father cried out louder, "What must a man do, tell me that?"

"Look, we ain't starving. I git paid every week, and Mrs. Ellis is real nice about giving me things. She gonna let me have Mr. Ellis's old coat for you this winter—"

"Damn Mr. Ellis's coat! And damn his money! You think I want white folks' leavings? Damn. Maybelle"—and suddenly he sobbed, loudly and painfully, and cried helplessly and hopelessly in the dark night. I had never heard a man cry before. I did not know men ever cried. I covered my ears with my hands but could not cut off the sound of my father's harsh, painful, despairing sobs. My father was a strong man who could whisk a child upon his shoulders and go singing through the house. My father whittled toys for us and laughed so loud that the great oak seemed to laugh with him, and taught us how to fish and hunt rabbits. How could it be that my father was crying? But the sobs went on, unstifled, finally quieting until I could hear my mother's voice, deep and rich, humming softly as she used to hum to a frightened child.

The world had lost its boundary lines. My mother, who was small and soft, was now the strength of the family; my father, who was the rock on which the family had been built, was sobbing like the tiniest child. Everything was suddenly out of tune, like a broken accordion. Where did I fit into this crazy picture? I do not now remember my thoughts, only a feeling of great bewilderment and fear.

Long after the sobbing and the humming had stopped, I lay on the pallet, still as stone with my hands over my ears, wishing that I too could cry and be comforted. The night was silent now except for the sound of the crickets and of Joey's soft breathing. But the room was too crowded with fear to allow me to sleep, and finally, feeling the terrible aloneness of 4 A.M., I decided to awaken Joey.

"Ouch! What's the matter with you? What you want?" he demanded disagreeably when I had pinched and slapped him awake.

"Come on, wake up."

"What for? Go 'way."

I was lost for a reasonable reply. I could not say, "I'm scared and I don't want to be alone," so I merely said, "I'm going out. If you want to come, come on."

The promise of adventure awoke him. "Going out now? Where at, Lizabeth? What you going to do?"

I was pulling my dress over my head. Until now I had not thought of going out. "Just come on," I replied tersely.

I was out the window and halfway down the road before Joey caught up with me.

"Wait, Lizabeth, where you going?"

I was running as if the Furies[2] were after me, as perhaps they were—running silently and furiously until I came to where I had half-known I was headed: to Miss Lottie's yard.

---

2. **Furies:** Three spirits of revenge in Greek and Roman myth.

The half-dawn light was more eerie than complete darkness, and in it the old house was like the ruin that my world had become—foul and crumbling, a grotesque caricature. It looked haunted, but I was not afraid because I was haunted too.

"Lizabeth, you lost your mind?" panted Joey.

I had indeed lost my mind, for all the smoldering emotions of that summer swelled in me and burst—the great need for my mother who was never there, the hopelessness of our poverty and degradation, the bewilderment of being neither child nor woman and yet both at once, the fear unleashed by my father's tears. And these feelings combined in one great impulse toward destruction.

"Lizabeth!"

I leaped furiously into the mounds of marigolds and pulled madly, trampling and pulling and destroying the perfect yellow blooms. The fresh smell of early morning and of dew-soaked marigolds spurred me on as I went tearing and mangling and sobbing while Joey tugged my dress or my waist crying, "Lizabeth, stop, please stop!"

And then I was sitting in the ruined little garden among the uprooted and ruined flowers, crying and crying, and it was too late to undo what I had done. Joey was sitting beside me, silent and frightened, not knowing what to say. Then, "Lizabeth, look."

I opened my swollen eyes and saw in front of me a pair or large calloused feet; my gaze lifted to the swollen legs, the age-distorted body clad in a tight cotton night dress, and then the shadowed Indian face surrounded by stubby white hair. And there was no rage in the face now, now that the garden was destroyed and there was nothing any longer to be protected.

"M-miss Lottie!" I scrambled to my feet and just stood there and stared at her, and that was the moment when childhood faded and womanhood began. That violent, crazy act was the last act of childhood. For as I gazed at the immobile face with the sad, weary eyes, I gazed upon a kind of reality which is hidden to childhood. The witch was no longer a witch but only a broken old woman who had dared to create beauty in the midst of ugliness and sterility. She had been born in squalor and lived in it all her life. Now at the end of that life she had nothing except a falling-down hut, a wrecked body, and John Burke, the mindless son of her passion. Whatever verve there was left in her, whatever was of love and beauty and joy that had not been squeezed out by life, had been there in the marigolds she had so tenderly cared for.

Of course I could not express the things that I knew about Miss Lottie as I stood there awkward and ashamed. The years have put words to the things I knew in that moment, and as I look back upon it, I know that the moment marked the end of innocence. Innocence involves an unseeing acceptance of things at face value, an ignorance of the area below the surface. In that humiliating moment I looked beyond myself and into the depths of another person. This was the beginning of compassion, and one cannot have both compassion and innocence.

The years have taken me worlds away from that time and that place, from the dust and squalor of our lives and from the bright thing that I destroyed in a blind childish striking out. Miss Lottie died long ago and many years have passed since I last saw her hut, completely barren at last, for despite my wild contrition she never planted marigolds again. Yet, there are times when the image of those passionate yellow mounds returns with a painful poignancy. For one does not have to be ignorant and poor to find that his life is barren as the dusty yards of our town. And I too have planted marigolds.

Responding to the Story

1. Why do you think the narrator "leaped furiously into the mounds of marigolds and pulled madly, trampling and pulling and destroying the perfect yellow blooms"? How did you feel when you read these words and others describing that scene?
2. Why does the narrator describe "that violent, crazy act" as "the moment when childhood faded and womanhood began"?
3. Do you believe that whole phases of lives can change in moments, or are changes gradual? Explain.
4. "Memory is an abstract painting—it does not present things as they are but rather as they *feel*." Tell a story of a vivid incident that you recall because of how it felt, even if you can't recall exactly every detail of how it was.

Exploring the Author's Craft

One cannot read this story without feeling as if one has been in this poor, fading town. How does the author achieve this? Look over the story and list all the physical aspects of the town that Eugenia Collier describes. Note how repetition of details helps reinforce the reader's impressing of the setting. How important is setting in this story?

Writer's Workshop

Capture in words a place you know as vividly as Eugenia Collier knew her setting. Take your time and include all the details and references to the various senses that characterize this place.

Eudora Welty

Born in 1909 in Jackson, Mississippi, Eudora Welty began her working life as a publicity agent for the State Office of the Works Progress Administration (WPA) in 1933. She attended Mississippi State College for women from 1925 to 1927 and received her B.A. degree in 1929 from the University of Wisconsin. She also attended Columbia University.

Welty is known primarily as a short story writer and novelist. Her first collection of stories, *A Curtain of Green*, was published in 1941. This was followed by *The Wide Net* (1943), *The Golden Apples* (1949), and *The Bride of Innisfallen* (1955). The title story of *A Curtain of Green* won The O. Henry Memorial Award. Her novels include *Delta Wedding* (1946), *The Ponder Heart* (1954), *Losing Battles* (1970), and *The Optimist's Daughter* (1972), which won a Pulitzer Prize.

Though Welty's stories and novels are set in the South, they depict a wide spectrum of individuals, often portrayed humorously, who struggle to accommodate their lives and beliefs to a world that often seems puzzling and indifferent.

One Writer's Beginnings (1984) is an autobiographical work that describes incidents in Welty's life that influenced her writing. She received the National Medal of Arts in 1986 and an award from the National Endowment for the Arts in 1989. Welty is also a gifted photographer whose works have been exhibited.

"I'm a Campfire Girl. . . . I have to pay a visit to some old lady."

A Visit of Charity

It was mid-morning—a very cold, bright day. Holding a potted plant before her, a girl of fourteen jumped off the bus in front of the Old Ladies' Home, on the outskirts of town. She wore a red coat, and her straight yellow hair was hanging down loose from the pointed white cap all the little girls were wearing that year. She stopped for a moment beside one of the prickly dark shrubs with which the city had beautified the Home, and then proceeded slowly toward the building, which was of whitewashed brick and reflected the winter sunlight like a block of ice. As she walked vaguely up the steps she shifted the small pot from hand to hand; then she had to set it down and remove her mittens before she could open the heavy door.

"I'm a Campfire Girl. . . . I have to pay a visit to some old lady," she told the nurse at the desk. This was a woman in a white uniform who looked as if she were cold; she had close-cut hair which stood up on the very top of her head exactly like a sea wave. Marian, the little girl, did not tell her that this visit would give her a minimum of only three points in her score.

"Acquainted with any of our residents?" asked the nurse. She lifted one eyebrow and spoke like a man.

"With any old ladies? No—but—that is, any of them will do," Marian stammered. With her free hand she pushed her hair behind her ears, as she did when it was time to study Science.

The nurse shrugged and rose. "You have a nice *multiflora cineraria*[1] there," she remarked as she walked ahead down the hall of closed doors to pick out an old lady.

There was loose, bulging linoleum on the floor. Marian felt as if she were walking on the waves, but the nurse paid no attention to it. There was a smell in the hall like the interior of a clock. Everything was silent until, behind one of the doors, an old lady of some kind cleared her throat like a sheep bleating. This decided the nurse. Stopping in her tracks, she first extended her arm, bent her elbow, and leaned forward from the hips—all to examine the watch strapped to her wrist; then she gave a loud double-rap on the door.

---

1. *multiflora cineraria:* plant with clusters of white, red, or purple flowers and heart-shaped leaves.

"There are two in each room," the nurse remarked over her shoulder.

"Two what?" asked Marian without thinking. The sound like a sheep's bleating almost made her turn around and run back.

One old woman was pulling the door open in short, gradual jerks, and when she saw the nurse a strange smile forced her old face dangerously awry. Marian, suddenly propelled by the strong, impatient arm of the nurse, saw next the side-face of another old woman, even older, who was lying flat in bed with a cap on and a counterpane[2] drawn up to her chin.

"Visitor," said the nurse, and after one more shove she was off up the hall.

Marian stood tongue-tied; both hands held the potted plant. the old woman, still with that terrible, square smile (which was a smile of welcome) stamped on her bony face, was waiting. . . . Perhaps she said something. The old woman in the bed said nothing at all, and she did not look around.

Suddenly Marian saw a hand, quick as a bird claw, reach up in the air and pluck the white cap off her head. At the same time, another claw to match drew her all the way into the room, and the next moment the door closed behind her.

"My, my, my," said the old lady at her side.

Marian stood enclosed by a bed, a washstand and a chair; the tiny room had altogether too much furniture. Everything smelled wet—even the bare floor. She held onto the back of the chair, which was wicker and felt soft and damp. Her heart beat more and more slowly, her hands got colder and colder, and she could not hear whether the old women were saying anything or not. She could not see them very clearly. How dark it was! The window shade was down, and the only door was shut. Marian looked at the ceiling. . . . It was like being caught in a robbers' cave, just before one was murdered.

"Did you come to be our little girl for a while?" the first robber asked.

Then something was snatched from Marian's hand—the little potted plant.

"Flowers!" screamed the old woman. She stood holding the pot in an undecided way. "Pretty flowers," she added.

---

2. **counterpane:** bedspread.

Then the old woman in bed cleared her throat and spoke. "They are not pretty," she said, still without looking around, but very distinctly.

Marian suddenly pitched against the chair and sat down in it.

"Pretty flowers," the first old woman insisted. "Pretty—pretty . . ."

Marian wished she had the little pot back for just a moment—she had forgotten to look at the plant herself before giving it away. What did it look like?

"Stinkweeds," said the other old woman sharply. She had a bunchy white forehead and red eyes like a sheep. Now she turned them toward Marian. the fogginess seemed to rise in her throat again, and she bleated, "Who—are—you?"

To her surprise, Marian could not remember her name. "I'm a Campfire Girl," she said finally.

"Watch out for the germs," said the old woman like a sheep, not addressing anyone.

"One came out last month to see us," said the first old woman.

A sheep or a germ? wondered Marian dreamily, holding onto the chair.

"Did not!" cried the other old woman.

"Did so! Read to us out of the Bible, and we enjoyed it!" screamed the first.

"Who enjoyed it!" said the woman in bed. Her mouth was unexpectedly small and sorrowful, like a pet's.

"We enjoyed it," insisted the other. "You enjoyed it—I enjoyed it."

"We all enjoyed it," said Marian, without realizing that she had said a word.

The first old woman had just finished putting the potted plant high, high on the top of the wardrobe, where it could hardly be seen from below. Marian wondered how she had ever succeeded in placing it there, how she could ever have reached so high.

"You mustn't pay any attention to old Addie," she now said to the little girl. "She's ailing today."

"Will you shut your mouth?" said the woman in bed. "I am not."

"You're a story."

"I can't stay but a minute—really, I can't," said Marian suddenly. She looked down at the wet floor and thought that if she were sick in here they would have to let her go.

With much to-do the first old woman sat down in a rocking chair—still another piece of furniture!—and began to rock. With the fingers of one hand she touched a very dirty cameo pin on her chest. "What do you do at school?" she asked.

"I don't know . . ." said Marian. She tried to think but she could not.

"Oh, but the flowers are beautiful," the old woman whispered. She seemed to rock faster and faster; Marian did not see how anyone could rock so fast.

"Ugly," said the woman in bed.

"If we bring flowers—" Marian began, and then fell silent. She had almost said that if Campfire Girls brought flowers to the Old Ladies' Home, the visit would count one extra point, and if they took a Bible with them on the bus and read it to the old ladies, it counted double. But the old woman had not listened, anyway; she was rocking and watching the other one, who watched back from the bed.

"Poor Addie is ailing. She has to take medicine—see?" she said, pointing a horny finger at a row of bottles on the table, and rocking so high that her black comfort shoes lifted off the floor like a little child's.

"I am no more sick than you are," said the woman in bed.

"Oh, yes you are!"

"I just got more sense than you have, that's all," said the other old woman, nodding her head.

"That's only the contrary way she talks when *you all* come," said the first old lady with sudden intimacy. She stopped the rocker with a neat pat of her feet and leaned toward Marian. Her hand reached over—it felt like a petunia leaf, clinging and just a little sticky.

"Will you hush! Will you hush!" cried the other one.

Marian leaned back rigidly in her chair.

"When I was a little girl like you, I went to school and all," said the old woman in the same intimate, menacing voice. "Not here—another town. . . ."

"Hush!" said the sick woman. "You never went to school. You never came and you never went. You never were anything—only here. You never were born! You don't know anything. Your head is empty, your heart and hands and your old black purse are all empty, even that little old box that you brought with you you brought empty—you showed it to me. And yet you talk, talk, talk, talk, talk all the time until I think I'm losing my mind! Who are you? You're a stranger—a perfect stranger! Don't you know you're a stranger? Is it possible that they have actually done a thing like this to anyone—sent them in a stranger to talk, and rock, and tell away her whole long rigmarole? Do they seriously suppose that I'll be able to keep it up, day in, day out, night in, night out, living in the same room with a terrible old woman—forever?"

Marian saw the old woman's eyes grow bright and turn toward her. The old woman was looking at her with despair and calculation in her face. Her small lips suddenly dropped apart, and exposed a half circle of false teeth with tan gums.

"Come here, I want to tell you something," she whispered. "Come here!"

Marian was trembling, and her heart nearly stopped beating altogether for a moment.

"Now, now, Addie," said the first woman. "That's not polite. Do you know what's really the matter with old Addie today?" She, too, looked at Marian; one of her eyelids drooped low.

"The matter?" the child repeated stupidly. "What's the matter with her?"

"Why, she's mad because it's her birthday!" said the first old woman, beginning to rock again and giving a little crow as though she had answered her own riddle.

"It is not, it is not!" screamed the old woman in bed. "It is not my birthday, no one knows when that is but myself, and will you please be quiet and say nothing more, or I'll go straight out of my mind!" She turned her eyes toward Marian again, and presently she said in the soft, foggy voice, "When the worst comes to the worst, I ring this bell, and the nurse comes." One of her hands was drawn out from under the patched counterpane—a thin little hand with enormous black freckles. With a finger which would not hold still she pointed to a little bell on the table among the bottles.

"How old are you?" Marian breathed. Now she could see the old woman in bed very closely and plainly, and very abruptly, from all sides, as in dreams. She wondered about her—she wondered for a moment as though there was nothing else in the world to wonder about. It was the first time such a thing had happened to Marian.

"I won't tell!"

The old face on the pillow, where Marian was bending over it, slowly gathered and collapsed. Soft whimpers came out of the small open mouth. It was a sheep that she sounded like—a little lamb. Marian's face drew very close, the yellow hair hung forward.

"She's crying!" She turned a bright, burning face up to the first old woman.

"That's Addie for you," the old woman said spitefully.

Marian jumped up and moved toward the door. For the second time, the claw almost touched her hair, but it was not quick enough. The little girl put her cap on.

"Well, it was a real visit," said the old woman, following Marian through the doorway and all the way out into the hall. Then from behind she suddenly clutched the child with her sharp little fingers. In an affected, high-pitched whine she cried, "Oh, little girl, have you a penny to spare for a poor old woman that 's not got anything of her own? We don't have a thing in the world—not a penny for candy—not a thing! Little girl, just a nickel—a penny—"

Marian pulled violently against the old hands for a moment before she was free. Then she ran down the hall, without looking behind her and without looking at the nurse, who was reading *Field and Stream* at her desk. The nurse, after another triple motion to consult her wrist watch, asked automatically the question put to visitors in all institutions: "Won't you stay and have dinner with *us?*"

Marian never replied. She pushed the heavy door open into the cold air and ran down the steps.

Under the prickly shrub she stooped and quickly, without being seen, retrieved a red apple she had hidden there.

Her yellow hair under the white cap, her scarlet coat, her bare knees all flashed in the sunlight as she ran to meet the big bus rocketing through the street.

"Wait for me!" she shouted. As though at an imperial command, the bus ground to a stop.

She jumped on and took a big bite out of the apple.

Responding to the Story

1. "'How old are you?' Marian breathed. Now she could see the old woman in bed very closely and plainly, and very abruptly, from all sides, as in dreams. She wondered about her—she wondered for a moment as though there was nothing else in the world to wonder about. It was the first time such a thing had happened to Marian." What exactly has happened to Marian? Does it relate to the idea of "coming of age"? Explain.
2. Before Marian has spoken more than three full sentences the writer has conveyed certain information about her. What has been conveyed?
3. Why do you suppose the author ends the story as she does?

Exploring the Author's Craft

"A Visit of Charity" is told from the third-person point of view. Unlike many of the stories in this book, the narrator is not a character in the story but stands at some distance from the events. Sometimes a third-person narrator writes from an omniscient point of view and knows the thoughts and feelings of all the characters, but in this story the narrator tells the story from a limited point of view. Although we know what other people say, we have no insight into their thoughts; the point of view is limited to what Marian thinks and feels and observes. Although the point of view is limited to what Marian reacts to, the reader tends to understand more than Marian does.

1. What does the hallway of the Home feel and smell like to Marian?
2. What does the detail of the nurse's reading *Field and Stream* convey to the reader? Does Marian do more than notice this detail?
3. What is the author's purpose in having the two old women in constant disagreement with each other? What might the reader understand about them that Marian fails to grasp?

Writer's Workshop

Write a journal entry as Marian might have written it after her visit to the Old Ladies' Home.

Sylvia Plath

Sylvia Plath is known primarily as a poet, with most of her work published after her death by suicide in 1963. She was born in Boston in 1932, and after the death of her father in 1940, the family moved to Wellesley. The following short story was written when Plath was a teenager and was published in *Seventeen* just before she entered Smith College in 1950. After a suicide attempt in 1953, Plath returned to Smith and graduated summa cum laude in 1955. Her academic excellence enabled her to win a Fulbright scholarship for study at Cambridge in England. There she met English poet Ted Hughes, and they were married in 1956. She taught English at Smith during the 1957–58 year, but in 1959, she and her husband returned to England and lived in London and Devon. They had two children and were separated in 1962.

Plath's first book of poems, *The Colossus*, was published in 1960. Other poetry collections were *Ariel* (1965), *Crossing the Water* (1971), and *Winter Trees* (1972). Her only novel, *The Bell Jar*, appeared in 1963 under the pseudonym Victoria Lucas but was later republished under her own name. *Letters Home* edited by her mother appeared in 1975, and *Collected Poems*, edited by Ted Hughes, was published in 1981. In 1998 a new collection of Hughes's poems, *Birthday Letters*, dealt with his relationship with Plath. "Initiation" comes from *Johnny Panic and the Bible of Dreams* (1979), a collection of Plath's short stories and other prose.

What was the point of taking all these orders?

Initiation

The basement room was dark and warm, like the inside of a sealed jar, Millicent thought, her eyes getting used to the strange dimness. The silence was soft with cobwebs, and from the small, rectangular window set high in the stone wall there sifted a faint bluish light that must be coming from the fall October moon. She could see now that what she was sitting on was a woodpile next to the furnace.

Millicent brushed back a strand of hair. It was stiff and sticky from the egg that they had broken on her head as she knelt blindfolded at the sorority altar a short while before. There had been a silence, a slight crunching sound, and then she had felt the cold, slimy egg-white flattening and spreading on her head and sliding down her neck. She had heard someone smothering a laugh. It was all part of the ceremony.

Then the girls had led her here, blindfolded still, through the corridors of Betsy Johnson's house and shut her in the cellar. It would be an hour before they came to get her, but then Rat Court would be all over and she would say what she had to say and go home.

For tonight was the grand finale, the trial by fire. There really was no doubt now that she would get in. She could not think of anyone who had ever been invited into the high school sorority and failed to get through initiation time. But even so, her case would be quite different. She would see to that. She could not exactly say what had decided her revolt, but it definitely had something to do with Tracy and something to do with the heather birds.

What girl at Lansing High would not want to be in her place now? Millicent thought, amused. What girl would not want to be one of the elect,[1] no matter if it did mean five days of initiation before and after school, ending in the climax of Rat Court on Friday night when they made the new girls members? Even Tracy had been wistful when she heard that Millicent had been one of the five girls to receive an invitation.

"It won't be any different with us, Tracy," Millicent had told her. "We'll still go around together like we always have, and next year you'll surely get in."

---

1. **the elect:** people who belong to an exclusive group.

"I know, but even so," Tracy had said quietly, "you'll change, whether you think you will or not. Nothing ever stays the same."

And nothing does, Millicent had thought. How horrible it would be if one never changed . . . if she were condemned to be the plain, shy Millicent of a few years back for the rest of her life. Fortunately there was always the changing, the growing, the going on.

It would come to Tracy, too. She would tell Tracy the silly things the girls had said, and Tracy would change also, entering eventually into the magic circle. She would grow to know the special ritual as Millicent had started to last week.

"First of all," Betsy Johnson, the vivacious blonde secretary of the sorority, had told the five new candidates over sandwiches in the school cafeteria last Monday, "first of all, each of you has a big sister. She's the one who bosses you around, and you just do what she tells you."

"Remember the part about talking back and smiling," Louise Fullerton had put in, laughing. She was another celebrity in high school, pretty and dark and vice-president of the student council. "You can't say anything unless your big sister asks you something or tells you to talk to someone. And you can't smile, no matter how you're dying to." The girls had laughed a little nervously, and then the bell had rung for the beginning of afternoon classes.

It would be rather fun for a change, Millicent mused, getting her books out of her locker in the hall, rather exciting to be part of a closely knit group, the exclusive set at Lansing High. Of course, it wasn't a school organization. In fact, the principal, Mr. Cranton, wanted to do away with initiation week altogether, because he thought it was undemocratic and disturbed the routine of school work. but there wasn't really anything he could do about it. Sure, the girls had to come to school for five days without any lipstick on and without curling their hair, and of course everybody noticed them, but what could the teachers do?

Millicent sat down at her desk in the big study hall. Tomorrow she would come to school, proudly, laughingly, without lipstick, with her born hair straight and shoulder length, and then everybody would know, even the boys would know, that she was one of the elect. Teachers would smile helplessly, thinking perhaps: So now they've picked Millicent Arnold. I never would have guessed it.

A year or two ago, not many people would have guessed it. Millicent had waited a long time for acceptance, longer than most. It was as if she had been sitting for years in a pavilion outside a dance floor, looking in through the windows at the golden interior, with the lights clear and the air like honey, wistfully watching the couples waltzing to the never-ending music, laughing in pairs and groups together, no one alone.

But now at last, amid a week of fanfare and merriment, she would answer her invitation to enter the ballroom through the main entrance marked "Initiation." She would gather up her velvet skirts, her silken train, or whatever the disinherited princesses wore in the story books, and come into her rightful kingdom. . . . The bell rang to end study hall.

"Millicent, wait up!" It was Louise Fullerton behind her, Louise who had always before been very nice, very polite, friendlier than the rest, even long go, before the invitation had come.

"Listen," Louise walked down the hall with her to Latin, their next class, "are you busy right after school today? Because I'd like to talk to you about tomorrow."

"Sure. I've got lots of time."

"Well, meet me in the hall after homeroom then, and we'll go down to the drugstore or something."

Walking beside Louise on the way to the drugstore, Millicent felt a surge of pride. For all anyone could see, she and Louise were the best of friends.

"You know, I was so glad when they voted you in," Louise said.

Millicent smiled. "I was really thrilled to get the invitation," she said frankly, "but kind of sorry that Tracy didn't get in too."

Tracy, she thought. If there is such a thing as a best friend, Tracy had been just that this last year.

"Yes, Tracy," Louise was saying, "she's a nice girl, and they put her up on the slate, but . . . well, she had three blackballs against her."

"Blackballs? What are they?"

"Well, we're not supposed to tell anybody outside the club, but seeing as you'll be in at the end of the week I don't suppose it hurts." They were at the drugstore now.

"You see," Louise began explaining in a low voice after they were seated in the privacy of the booth, "once a year the sorority puts up all the likely girls that are suggested for membership. . . ."

Millicent sipped her cold, sweet drink slowly, saving the ice cream to spoon up last. She listened carefully to Louise who was going on, ". . . and then there's a big meeting, and all the girls' names are read off and each girl is discussed."

"Oh?" Millicent asked mechanically, her voice sounding strange.

"Oh, I know what you're thinking," Louise laughed. "But it's really not as bad as all that. They keep it down to a minimum of catting.[2] They just talk over each girl and why or why not they think she'd be good for the club. And then they vote. Three blackballs eliminate a girl."

"Do you mind if I ask you what happened to Tracy?" Millicent said.

Louise laughed a little uneasily. "Well, you know how girls are. They notice little things. I mean, some of them thought Tracy was just a bit *too* different. Maybe you could suggest a few things to her."

"Like what?"

"Oh, like maybe not wearing knee socks to school, or carrying that old bookbag. I know it doesn't sound like much, but well, it's things like that which set someone apart. I mean, you know that no girl at Lansing would be seen dead wearing knee socks, no matter how cold it gets, and it's kiddish and kind of green[3] to carry a bookbag."

"I guess so," Millicent said.

"About tomorrow," Louise went on. "You've drawn Beverly Mitchell for a big sister. I wanted to warn you that she's the toughest, but if you get through all right it'll be all the more credit for you."

"Thanks, Lou," Millicent said gratefully, thinking, this is beginning to sound serious. Worse than a loyalty test, this grilling over the coals. What's it supposed to prove anyway? That I can take orders without flinching? Or does it just make them feel good to see us run around at their beck and call?

"All you have to do really," Louise said, spooning up the last of her sundae, "is be very meek and obedient when you're with Bev and do just what she tells you. Don't laugh or talk back or try to be funny, or she'll just make it harder for you, and believe me, she's a great one for doing that. Be at her house at seven-thirty."

And she was. She rang the bell and sat down on the steps to wait for Bev. After a few minutes the front door opened and Bev was standing there, her face serious.

"Get up, gopher," Bev ordered.

There was something about her tone that annoyed Millicent. It was almost malicious. And there was an unpleasant anonymity about the

---

2. **catting:** making mean or spiteful remarks.
3. **green:** naive, unsophisticated.

label "gopher," even if that was what they always called the girls being initiated. It was degrading, like being given a number. It was a denial of individuality.

Rebellion flooded through her.

"I said get up. Are you deaf?"

Millicent got up, standing there.

"Into the house, gopher. There's a bed to be made and a room to be cleaned at the top of the stairs."

Millicent went up the stairs mutely. She found Bev's room and started making the bed. Smiling to herself, she was thinking: How absurdly funny, me taking orders from this girl like a servant.

Bev was suddenly there in the doorway. "Wipe that smile off your face," she commanded.

There seemed something about this relationship that was not all fun. In Bev's eyes, Millicent was sure of it, there was a hard, bright spark of exultation.

On the way to school, Millicent had to walk behind Bev at a distance of ten paces, carrying her books. They came up to the drugstore where there already was a crowd of boys and girls from Lansing High waiting for the show.

The other girls being initiated were there, so Millicent felt relieved. It would not be so bad now, being part of the group.

"What'll we have them do?" Betsy Johnson asked Bev. That morning Betsy had made her "gopher" carry an old colored parasol through the square and sing "I'm Always Chasing Rainbows."

"I know," Herb Dalton, the good-looking basketball captain, said.

A remarkable change came over Bev. She was all at once very soft and coquettish.

"You can't tell them what to do," Bev said sweetly. "Men have nothing to say about this little deal."

"All right, all right," Herb laughed, stepping back and pretending to fend off a blow.

"It's getting late." Louise had come up. "Almost eight-thirty. We'd better get them marching on to school."

The "gophers" had to do a Charleston[4] step all the way to school, and each one had her own song to sing, trying to drown out the other four.

---

4. **Charleston:** lively dance popular in the 1920s.

During school, of course, you couldn't fool around, but even then, there was a rule that you mustn't talk to boys outside of class or at lunchtime . . . or any time at all after school. So the sorority girls would get the most popular boys to go up to the "gophers" and ask them out, or try to start them talking, and sometimes a "gopher" was taken by surprise and began to say something before she could catch herself. And then the boy reported her and she got a black mark.

Herb Dalton approached Millicent as she was getting an ice cream at the lunch counter that noon. She saw him coming before he spoke to her, and looked down quickly, thinking: He is too princely, too dark and smiling. And I am much too vulnerable. Why must he be the one I have to be careful of?

I won't say anything, she thought, I'll just smile very sweetly.

She smiled up at Herb very sweetly and mutely. His return grin was rather miraculous. It was surely more than was called for in the line of duty.

"I know you can't talk to me," he said, very low. "But you're doing fine, the girls say. I even like your hair straight and all."

Bev was coming toward them, then, her red mouth set in a bright, calculating smile. She ignored Millicent and sailed up to Herb.

"Why waste your time with gophers?" she caroled gaily. "Their tongues are tied, but completely."

Herb managed a parting shot. "But that one keeps *such* an attractive silence."

Millicent smiled as she ate her sundae at the counter with Tracy. Generally, the girls who were outsiders now, as Millicent had been, scoffed at the initiation antics as childish and absurd to hide their secret envy. But Tracy was understanding, as ever.

"Tonight's the worst, I guess, Tracy," Millicent told her. 'I hear that the girls are taking us on a bus over to Lewiston and going to have us performing in the square."

"Just keep a poker face outside," Tracy advised. "But keep laughing like mad inside."

Millicent and Bev took a bus ahead of the rest of the girls; they had to stand up on the way to Lewiston Square. Bev seemed very cross about something. Finally she said, "You were talking with Herb Dalton at lunch today."

"No," said Millicent honestly.

"Well, I *saw* you smile at him. That's practically as bad as talking. Remember not to do it again."

Millicent kept silent.

"It's fifteen minutes before the bus gets into town," Bev was saying then. "I want you to go up and down the bus asking people what they eat for breakfast. Remember, you can' tell them you're being initiated."

Millicent looked down the aisle of the crowded bus and felt suddenly quite sick. She thought: How will I ever do it, going up to all those stony-faced people who are staring coldly out of the window. . . .

"You heard me, gopher."

"Excuse me, madam," Millicent said politely to the lady in the first seat of the bus, "but I'm taking a survey. Could you please tell me what you eat for breakfast?"

"Why . . . er . . . just orange juice, toast, and coffee," she said.

"Thank you very much." Millicent went on to the next person, a young business man. He ate eggs sunny side up, toast and coffee.

By the time Millicent got to the back of the bus, most of the people were smiling at her. They obviously know, she thought, that I'm being initiated into something.

Finally, there was only one man left in the corner of the back seat. He was small and jolly, with a ruddy, wrinkled face that spread into a beaming smile as Millicent approached. In his brown suit with the forest-green tie he looked something like a gnome or a cheerful leprechaun.

"Excuse me, sir," Millicent smiled, "but I'm taking a survey. What do you eat for breakfast?"

"Heather birds' eyebrows on toast," the little man rattled off.

"*What?*" Millicent exclaimed.

"Heather birds' eyebrows," the little man explained. "Heather birds live on the mythological moors and fly about all day long, singing wild and sweet in the sun. They're bright purple and have *very* tasty eyebrows."

Millicent broke out into spontaneous laughter. Why, this was wonderful, the way she felt a sudden comradeship with a stranger.

"Are you mythological, too?"

"Not exactly," he replied, "but I certainly hope to be someday. Being mythological does wonders for one's ego."

The bus was swinging into the station now; Millicent hated to leave the little man. She wanted to ask him more about the birds.

And from that time on, initiations didn't bother Millicent at all. She went gaily about Lewiston Square from store to store asking for broken crackers and mangoes, and she just laughed inside when people stared and then brightened, answering her crazy questions as if she were quite serious and really a person of consequence. So many people were shut up tight inside themselves like boxes, yet they would open up, unfolding quite wonderfully, if only you were interested in them. And really, you didn't have to belong to a club to feel related to other human beings.

One afternoon Millicent had started talking with Liane Morris, another of the girls being initiated, about what it would be like when they were finally in the sorority.

"Oh, I know pretty much what it'll be like," Liane had said. "My sister belonged before she graduated from high school two years ago."

"Well, just what *do* they do as a club?" Millicent wanted to know.

"Why, they have a meeting once a week . . . each girl takes turns entertaining at her house. . . ."

"You mean it's just a sort of exclusive social group. . . ."

"I guess so . . . though that's a funny way of putting it. But it sure gives a girl prestige value. My sister started going steady with the captain of the football team after she got in. Not bad, I say."

No, it wasn't bad, Millicent had thought, lying in bed on the morning of Rat Court and listening to the sparrows chirping in the gutters. She thought of Herb. Would he ever have been so friendly if she were without the sorority label? Would he ask her out (if he ever did) just for herself, no strings attached.

Then there was another thing that bothered her. Leaving Tracy on the outskirts. Because that is the way it would be; Millicent had seen it happen before.

Outside, the sparrows were still chirping, and as she lay in bed Millicent visualized them, pale gray-brown birds in a flock, one like the other, all exactly alike.

And then, for some reason, Millicent thought of the heather birds. Swooping carefree over the moors, they would go singing and crying out across the great spaces of air, dipping and darting, strong and proud in their freedom and their sometime loneliness. It was then that she made her decision.

Seated now on the woodpile in Betsy Johnson's cellar, Millicent knew that she had come triumphant through the trial of fire, the searing period of the ego which could end in two kinds of victory for her. The easiest of which would be her coronation as a princess, labeling her conclusively as one of the select flock.

The other victory would be much harder, but she knew that it was what she wanted. It was not that she was being noble or anything. It was just that she had learned there were other ways of getting into the great hall, blazing with lights, of people and of life.

It would be hard to explain to the girls tonight, of course, but she could tell Louise later just how it was. How she had proved something to herself by going through everything, even Rat Court, and then deciding not to join the sorority after all. And how she could still be friends with everybody. Sisters with everybody. Tracy, too.

The door behind her opened and a ray of light sliced across the soft gloom of the basement room.

"Hey, Millicent, come on out now. this is it." There were some of the girls outside.

"I'm coming," she said, getting up and moving out of the soft darkness into the glare of light, thinking: This is it, all right. The worst part, the hardest part, the part of initiation that I figured out myself.

But just then, from somewhere far off, Millicent was sure of it, there came a melodic fluting, quite wild and sweet, and she knew that it must be the song of the heather birds as they went wheeling and gliding against wide blue horizons through vast spaces of air, their wings flashing quick and purple in the bright sun.

Within Millicent another melody soared, strong and exuberant, a triumphant answer to the music of the darting heather birds that sang so clear and lilting over the far lands. And she knew that her own private initiation had just begun.

Responding to the Story

1. Why was the "part of initiation that I figured out myself" the "worst part, the hardest part" for Millicent?
2. How do you interpret the story's last sentence?
3. Do you agree with Millicent's decision not to join the sorority? Explain your response.

Exploring the Author's Craft

A *flashback* is an interruption in a chronological narrative. A flashback shows something that happened before that point in the story, and it provides background information on characters or events that helps explain a character's motivations and reactions. A flashback is not just reminiscence but an actual shift in time to show past events.

1. Where does the flashback in "Initiation" begin and end?
2. What does the flashback in this story accomplish?

Writer's Workshop

1. Create a one- or two-paragraph response in narrative form from the following people after they learn of Millicent's decision. Write from the first-person point of view.
    a. Beverly Mitchell
    b. sorority secretary Betsy Johnson
    c. Herb Dalton
    d. Millicent's friend Tracy
2. Author Sylvia Plath used two similes in this story to reflect Millicent's emotions: "The basement room was dark and warm, like the inside of a sealed jar . . ." and "It was as if she had been sitting for years in a pavilion outside a dance floor, looking in through the windows at the golden interior, with the lights clear and the air like honey, wistfully watching the couples waltzing to the never-ending music, laughing in pairs and groups together, no one alone."

    Choose a moment in the story—or maybe one that you envision just after Millicent reveals her decision not to join the sorority—and express it in terms of an appropriate simile. Use the third-person point of view.

Tim Wynne-Jones

Tim Wynne-Jones was born in England in 1948 but was educated and makes his home in Canada. Besides short stories, he has written novels and a play and even the words and music for an opera. He has worked as a designer and book editor, and also writes music for his rock band, The Suspects. The story "Dawn" appeared in Wynne-Jones's *The Book of Changes* (1994). An earlier collection of stories, *Some of the Kinder Planets*, was awarded the 1993 Governor General's Award for Children's Literature in Canada.

Barnsey had a little trouble with Dawn's look—the nine earrings, the nose ring, the orange and purple Mohawk . . .

Dawn

Barnsey met Dawn on the night bus to North Bay. His mother put him on at Ottawa, just after supper. His parents owned a store and the Christmas season was frantic, so for the third year in a row, Barnsey was going up to Grandma Barrymore's and his parents would follow Christmas day. He had cousins in North Bay, so it was fine with Barnsey, as long as he didn't have to sit beside someone weird the whole way.

"What if I have to sit beside someone weird the whole way?" he asked his mother in the bus terminal. She cast him a warning look. A let's-not-make-a-scene look. Barnsey figured she was in a hurry to get back to the store.

"You are thirteen, Matthew," she said. There was an edge in her voice that hadn't been there before. "Has anything bad happened to you yet?"

Barnsey was picking out a couple of magazines for the trip: *Guitar World* and *Sports Illustrated*. "I didn't say anything *bad* was going to happen. If anything *bad* happens, I make a racket and the bus driver deals with it. I know all that. I'm just talking about someone weird."

"For instance?" said his mother.

"Someone who smells. Someone really, really fat who spills over onto my seat. Someone who wants to talk about her liver operation."

His mother paid for the magazines and threw in a Kit Kat, too. Barnsey didn't remind her that she'd already bought him a Kit Kat, and let him buy a Coke, chips and some gum. And this was apart from the healthy stuff she had already packed at home. She was usually pretty strict about junk food.

"I just asked," said Barnsey.

"Come on," said his mother, giving his shoulder a bit of a squeeze. "Or the only *weird* person you're going to be sitting beside is your mother on the way back to the store."

Barnsey didn't bother to ask if that was an option. His parents put a lot of stock in planning. They didn't put much stock in spontaneity.

"What if I end up in Thunder Bay by mistake?"

His mother put her arm around him. He was almost as tall as she was now. "Matthew," she said in her let's-be-rational voice. "That would require quite a mistake on your part. But, if it were to happen, you have a good head on your shoulders *and* your own bank card."

His mother almost looked as if she was going to say something about how they had always encouraged him to be independent, but luckily she noticed it was boarding time.

They were at Bay 6, and his mother suddenly gave him a very uncharacteristic hug. A bear hug. They weren't a hugging kind of a family. She looked him in the eyes.

"Matthew," she said. "It's not so long. Remember that."

"I know," said Barnsey. But he wasn't sure if his mother meant the trip or the time before he'd see her again. He couldn't tell.

They moved through the line toward the driver, who was taking tickets at the door of the bus.

"Don't do the thing with the money," Barnsey whispered to his mother.

"Why not?" she said. Barnsey didn't answer. "It's just good business. And besides, young man, I'll do what I please."

And she did. As Barnsey gave the driver his ticket, Barnsey's mother ripped a twenty-dollar bill in half ceremoniously in front of the driver's face. She gave half the bill to Barnsey, who shoved it quickly in his pocket.

"Here, my good man," said his mother to the bus driver in her store voice. "My son will give you the other half upon arrival in North Bay. Merry Christmas."

The driver thanked her. But he gave Barnsey a secret kind of cockeyed look, as if to say, Does she pull this kind of stunt all the time?

Then Barnsey was on board the bus, and there was Dawn.

There was no other seat. His mother had once told him that if there weren't any seats left, the bus company would have to get a bus just for him. That was the way they did business. So Barnsey shuffled up and down the bus a couple of times even after he'd put his bag up top, looking—hoping—that someone would take the seat beside Dawn so he could triumphantly demand a bus of his own. But there were no other seats and no other passengers.

He suddenly wanted very much to go back out to his mother, even though she would say he was being irrational. But then when he caught a glimpse of her through the window, she looked almost as miserable as he felt. He remembered the bear hug with a shiver. It shook his resolve. Timidly he turned to Dawn.

"Is this seat taken?" he asked.

The girl took off her Walkman earphones and stared at the seat a bit, as if looking for someone. She took a long time.

"Doesn't look like it."

Barnsey sat down and made himself comfortable. He got out his own Walkman and arranged his tapes on his lap and thought about the order in which he was going to eat all the junk he had or whether he'd eat a bit of each thing—the chocolate bars, the chips, the Coke—in some kind of order so they all came out even. At home his mother had packed a loganberry soda and some trail mix. He'd keep those for last. Strictly emergency stuff.

Then the bus driver came on board and they were off.

"There's talk of big snow up the valley a way, so I'm gonna light a nice cozy fire," he said. People chuckled. There was already a cozy kind of nighttime we're-stuck-in-this-together mood on the bus. Nobody was drunk or too loud. And the girl beside Barnsey seemed to be completely engrossed in whatever was coming through her earphones.

It was only the way she looked that he had any problem with. The nine earrings, the nose rings and the Mohawk in particular—orange along the scalp and purple along the crest as if her skull was a planet and the sun was coming up on the horizon of her head. She was about twenty and dressed all in black, with clunky black Doc Martens.[1] But as long as she was just going to listen to her music, then Barnsey would listen to his and everything would be fine.

And it was for the first hour or so. By then the bus had truly slipped into a comfortable humming silence. It was about nine, and some people were sleeping. Others were talking softly as if they didn't want to wake a baby in the next room. That's when the mix-up occurred.

There isn't much room in a bus seat. And there wasn't much room on Barnsey's lap. Somehow a couple of his tapes slid off him into the space between him and Dawn, the girl with the horizon on her head, though he didn't know her name yet. The weird thing was, the same thing had happened to her tapes. And the weirdest thing of all was that they both found out at just about the same time.

Barnsey shoved the new Xiphoid Process tape into his machine and punched it on. While he was waiting for the music to start, he dug the cassette out from his backpack and looked again at the hologram cover. The band was standing under lowering skies all around an eerie-looking gravestone. Then if you tipped the cover just right, the guys all seemed to pull back, and there was a hideous ghoul all covered with dirt and worms standing right in the middle of them where the grave marker had been. It was great.

Barnsey pulled a bag of chips from the backpack at his feet, squeezed it so that the pressure in the bag made it pop open and crunched on a couple of chips as quietly as he could. He was busy enjoying the way the first sour cream and onion chip tastes and it took him a minute to notice he wasn't hearing anything.

He turned the volume up a bit. Nothing. Then he realized there *was* something. A tinkling noise and a bit of a whooshing noise, and a bit of what sounded like rain and some dripping and more tinkling.

Barnsey banged his Walkman. He thought the batteries were dying. Then Dawn changed tapes as well and suddenly yelled, as if she'd just

---

1. **Doc Martens:** heavy, high-top, lace-up boots.

touched a hot frying pan. Some people looked around angrily. The look on their faces made Barnsey think they had just been waiting for a chance to glare at her. One lady glanced at him, too, in a pitying kind of way, as if to say, Poor young thing. Having to sit beside a banshee like that.

Meanwhile, both of them opened up their Walkmans like Christmas presents. They held their tapes up to the little lights above them to check the titles.

"'Rain Forest with Temple Bells'?" Barnsey read out loud.

"'Scream for Your Supper!'" Dawn read out loud.

Barnsey apologized, nervously. Dawn just laughed. They made the switch, but before Barnsey could even say thank you, the girl suddenly took his tape back.

"Tell you what," she said. "You listen to that fer 'alf a mo, and I'll give this a try. 'Kay?"

She had a thick accent, British.

"Okay," said Barnsey, "but I think yours is broken or something."

She took her tape back and tried it. She smiled, and her smile was good. It kind of stretched across her face and curled up at the ends.

"Naa," she said. "Ya just 'av ta listen, mate. Closely, like."

So Barnsey listened closely. He turned it up. There was a rain forest. There were ravens croaking and other birds twittering away. And there were bells. He thought someone was playing them, but after a while he realized that it was just the rain playing them, the wind. He kept waiting for the music to start. He didn't know what the music would be. Any moment a drum would kick in, he thought, then a synthesizer all warbly and a guitar keening high and distorted and a thumping bass and, last of all, a voice. Maybe singing about trees. About saving them.

But no drum kicked in. Maybe the tape *was* broken?

It took him a minute to realize Dawn was tapping him on the shoulder. She had his Xiphoid Process tape in her hand and a cranky look on her face.

"This is killer-diller," she said.

"You like X.P.?" he asked.

"It's rubbish."

Barnsey laughed. *Rubbish.* What a great word. He pulled out Rain Forest with Temple Bells.

"What ya think?" she asked.

"It's rubbish."

Then they both started to giggle. And now people stared at them as if they were in cahoots and going to ruin the whole trip for everyone. Dawn hit him on the arm to shush him up.

He showed her the hologram cover of the X.P. tape.

"You think it's their mum?" she asked.

"Maybe," he said. He wished he could think of something to say. He just flipped the picture a few times. She leaned toward him. Her hand out.

"Dawn," she whispered.

It took him a minute to realize she was introducing herself. "Barnsey," he whispered back, as if it was a code. He shook her hand.

He offered her some chips. She took the whole bag and made a big deal of holding it up to the light so she could read the ingredients. She shuddered.

"It's a bleedin' chemical plant in 'ere," she said.

"Rubbish," said Barnsey. Then he dug out the trail mix and offered it to Dawn, and they both settled down to listen to their own tapes. Barnsey turned X.P. down to 2 because there was no way Dawn would be able to hear her forest with Spice-box wailing on the guitar and Mickey Slick pounding on the drums. After a couple of cuts he switched it off altogether.

He found himself thinking of the time he had traveled with his father out to British Columbia, where he was from, to Denman Island. He remembered the forest there, like nothing he'd ever seen in southern Ontario. Vast and high. It had been a lovely summer day with the light sifting down through the trees. But, he thought, if it rained there, it would sound like Dawn's tape.

He didn't put a tape in his cassette. He left the earphones on and listened to the hum of the bus instead.

"It's not so long."

It was the bus driver. Barnsey woke up with his mouth feeling like the inside of a bread box.

There was a stirring all around. People waking, stretching, chattering sleepily and my-my-ing as they looked out the windows. The bus was stopped.

"Will ya lookit that," said Dawn. Her nose was pressed up against the window. Outside was a nothingness of white.

They had pulled off the highway into a football field–sized parking lot. Another bus was parked up ahead. Through the swirling blizzard they could see lots of trucks and cars in the lot. It wasn't the stop Barnsey remembered from previous trips.

Barnsey could see the driver standing outside without his jacket, his shoulders hunched against the driving snow. He was talking to another bus driver, nodding his head a lot and stamping his feet to keep warm. Then he hopped back on the bus and closed the door behind him.

"Seems like we've got ourselves a little unscheduled stop," he said. "The road's bunged up clear through to Mattawa."

Someone asked him a question. Somebody interrupted with another question. The driver did a lot of answering and nodding and shaking his head and reassuring. Barnsey just looked over Dawn's shoulder at the outside, shivering a bit from sleepiness and the sight of all that whirling snow. Dawn smelled nice. Not exotic like the perfume his mother wore, but kind of bracing and clean.

"This here place doesn't have a name," said the driver. People laughed. He was making it all sound like fun. "But the barn there with all the blinking lights is called the Cattle Yard, and the owner says y'all er welcome to come on down and warm yerself up a spell."

Passengers immediately started to get up and stretch and fish around for handbags and sweaters and things. There was an air of excitement on the bus. The Cattle Yard was a big roadhouse painted fire-engine red and lit up with spotlights. It was no ordinary way station.

Still sleepy, Barnsey made no effort to move as people started to file past him, pulling on their coats. Dawn still had her nose pressed up against the glass.

"D'ya know where I spent last Christmas?" she said. Barnsey thought for a moment, as it maybe she'd told him and he'd forgotten.

"In Bethlehem," she said.

"*The* Bethlehem?"

"That's right," she said. "In a bar."

Barnsey looked at Dawn. She was smiling but not like she was fooling. "There are bars in Bethlehem?"

She laughed. "Brilliant bars. Smashing litt'l town is Bethlehem."

Barnsey tried to imagine it.

Then the bus driver was beside him. "Here, you might need this," he said. And with a flick of his fingers he produced the half-a-twenty

Barnsey's mother had given him. Barnsey was about to explain that it was meant to be a tip, but the driver waved his hand in protest. "Just don't get yourself all liquored up, son," he said, and then, laughing and clapping Barnsey on the back, he headed out of the bus.

"Wha's that then?" asked Dawn, looking at the half-a-twenty-dollar bill. Barnsey pulled the other half out of his pants pocket and held them side by side.

"Hungry?" he said.

And she was hungry. He hadn't realized how skinny she was, but she stored away a grilled cheese sandwich in no time and two pieces of apple pie with ice cream. She ordered hot water and fished a tea bag from deep in her ratty black leather jacket.

"Ginseng,[2] mate," she said. "Nothing illegal."

But Barnsey had only been noticing how stained the tea bag was and the little tab at the end of the string which had strange characters written on it.

It was all so strange. Strange for Barnsey to walk into a place with her, as if they were on a date—a thirteen-year-old and a twenty-year-old. He wondered if people thought she was his sister. He couldn't imagine his parents putting up with the way Dawn looked. She sure turned heads at the Cattle Yard. He wasn't sure if he minded or not. In his burgundy L. L. Bean coat, he didn't exactly look like he belonged in the place, either.

It was a huge smoke-filled bar with moose antlers on the knotty pine walls and two or three big TVs around the room tuned into the Nashville Network. There was a Leafs game[3] on the TV over the bar. Just about everyone was wearing a trucker's hat, and nobody looked like they were leaving until maybe Christmas.

The bus passengers were herded down to one end where a section had been closed off but was now reopened. The bus drivers smoked and made phone calls and made jokes to their passengers about not getting on the wrong bus when they left and ending up in Timbuktu. Through the window and the blizzard of snow Barnsey watched another bus roll in.

---

2. **ginseng:** a plant, grown in China and North America, with a sweet-smelling root often used for medicinal purposes.

3. **a Leafs game:** a hockey game featuring the Toronto Maple Leafs.

"I saw three ships cum sailin' in," sang Dawn. She was picking at Barnsey's leftover french fires—*chips,* she called them—trying to find ones that didn't have any burger juice on them. She was a vegetarian.

"Bloody heathen," she'd called him when he'd ordered a bacon burger and fries. He loved that.

"I've gotta go find the loo," she said.

"Bloody heathen," he said.

She flicked him on the nose with a chip as she clomped by in her Doc Martens. He wondered it it was possible to walk quietly in them.

"Rubbish," he said. He watched her walk through the bar toward the rest rooms. Somebody must have said something to her because she suddenly stopped and turned back to a table where five guys in trucking caps were sitting. They looked like all together they probably weighed a ton, but that didn't seem to bother Dawn. She leaned up close to one of them, her fists curled menacingly, and snarled something right at his face.

Barnsey watched in horror, imagining a scene from some movie where the whole place would erupt into a beer-slinging, window-smashing brawl. Instead, the guy whose face she was talking at suddenly roared with laughter and slapped the tabletop. The other four guys laughed, too. One of them ended up spilling half a mug of beer all over his friends. Then Dawn shook hands with her tormentors and sauntered off to the loo, as she called it.

Barnsey felt like he would burst with admiration. He picked up her teacup and smelled the ginseng. It smelled deadly. The writing on the little tab was Indian, he guessed. From India.

He looked around. On the big TV a country songstress with big country hair and dressed in a beautiful country-blue dress was draping silver tinsel on a Christmas tree while she sang about somebody being home for Christmas. Then the image would cut to that somebody in a pickup fighting his way through a blizzard. Same boat we're in, thought Barnsey. Then the image would cut back to the Christmas tree and then to a flashback of the couple walking up a country road with a bouncy dog, having an argument in the rain and so on. Then back to the guy in the truck, the girl by the tree. It was a whole little minimovie.

Barnsey found himself trying to imagine X.P. dressing that same tinsely Christmas tree in that nice living room. But of course the guy in the truck trying to get home for Christmas would be the grim reaper[4] or something, with worms crawling out of its eyes.

Then Dawn came back.

"What did you say to that guy?" Barnsey asked.

She smiled mysteriously. "I told 'im that if 'e'd said what 'e said to me in Afghanistan, 'e d 'ave to marry me on the spot."

It was around eleven before word came through that it was safe to leave. The drivers got everybody sorted out and back on board. Everyone at the Cattle Yard yelled Merry Christmas and held up their beer glasses in a toast. The guy who had been rude to Dawn stood and bowed as she passed by, and she curtsied. Then she made as if she was going to bite off his nose, which made his ton of friends roar again, their fat guts shaking with laughter.

By then Barnsey knew that Dawn had just got back from Nepal, where she'd been traveling with "'er mate" ever since she left Israel, where she'd been working on a kibbutz[5] after arriving there from Bloody Cairo, where she'd had all her kit stolen. Before that she'd been in Ghana and before that art school. Barnsey didn't know what a kit was, or a kibbutz. He wasn't sure where Nepal was, either, or what or who 'er mate might be. But he didn't ask. She'd called him mate, too.

On the bus the excitement of the unscheduled stop soon died down. The roads were only passable so it was slow going. It was kind of nice that the three buses were traveling together. In a convoy, the driver had called it. It sounded reassuring. Soon people were falling asleep, snoring. But not Barnsey. He sat thinking. Trying to imagine working on a flower farm in Israel, the heat, the fragrance of it. Trying to imagine Bethelem.

"Was it cold?"

"Freezin' at night," she said.

"See any stables?"

She laughed. "No, but I did see a good-sized shed behind a McDonald's."

---

4. **grim reaper:** a figure, usually a clothed skeleton with a scythe in one hand, that represents death.

5. **kibbutz:** a community farm owned, lived on, and run by a group of families or individuals.

Barnsey laughed. He tried to imagine the holy family pulling into Bethlehem today and huddling down in a shed out back of a McDonald's. Maybe Joseph would have a Big Mac. But Mary? Probably a vegetarian, he decided.

Quietness again.

"What kind of a store is it your people 'ave, master Barnsey?"

"A gift store," he said.

"Ah, well," said Dawn. "I can imagine a gift store would be busy at Christmas."

Finally, Barnsey dozed off. And the next thing he knew, the bus was slowing down and driving through the deserted streets of North Bay. It was past 2:00 A.M.

"That'll be 'er," said Dawn as they pulled into the bus terminal. Somehow she had recognized his grandma Barrymore in the little knot of worried folks waiting.

Barnsey just sat drowsily for a minute while people stirred around him. He felt like he weighed a ton.

"Get on with ya," said Dawn in a cheery voice. And she made a big joke of shoving him and roughhousing him out of his seat as if he was Dumbo the elephant. Then she gathered up all his wrappers and cans and threw them at him, saying, " 'Ere—lookit this! Yer not leavin' this for me, I 'ope." Barnsey found himself, weak with laughter, herded down the aisle. At the door he said good-bye and hoped that her trip to Vancouver would be nothing but rubbish the whole way. Grandma Barrymore was standing at the foot of the bus stairs. Much to her surprise, Dawn grabbed Barnsey by the head and scrubbed it hard with her knuckle.

"In Afghanistan, you'd have to marry me for that," said Barnsey.

"Toodle-oo, mate," said Dawn, blowing him a kiss. She blew one at Grandma Barrymore, too.

Dawn would arrive in Vancouver on Christmas Eve. Barnsey thought of her often over the next couple of days. He'd check his watch and imagine her arriving in Winnipeg, although all he knew of Winnipeg was the Blue Bombers football stadium that he'd seen on TV. And then Regina and Calgary. He imagined the three buses like wise men still traveling across the country in a convoy. But as much as Barnsey thought about Dawn, he gave up trying to talk to anyone about her. Grandma had seen her but only long enough to get the wrong impression. And when Barnsey tried to tell his cousins about her, it came out like a cartoon, with her wacky hair and her fat black boots. He couldn't get Dawn across to them—the *life* of her—only the image of her, so he stopped trying.

There was a lot to do, anyway. His cousins had arranged a skating party and Grandma wanted him to go shopping with her and help with some chores around the house. He enjoyed all the attention she showered on him. She spoiled him rotten just the way she'd spoiled his father rotten, she liked to say. But he'd never noticed it quite so much as this year. Anything he looked at, she asked him if he wanted it. It was spooky.

Then it was Christmas morning. It was a four-hour drive from Ottawa. His parents would arrive by 1:00 P.M. and that's when the celebration would start. When he saw his father's Mustang coming up the driveway at 10:30 A.M., Barnsey knew something was wrong.

He didn't go to the door. He watched from the window. They should have come in the big car. But there wasn't any they. Just his dad.

"Matthew, go help your dad with his parcels," said Grandma.

"No," said Barnsey. He was remembering the last time he had looked at his mother in the bus terminal, through the window. The look on her face. "It won't be so long," she had said.

It wasn't that his mother was sick or there was some problem at the store; they would have phoned. Barnsey's mind grew icy sharp. Everything was suddenly clear to him. He could see a trail of incidents leading to this if he thought about it. You just had to tilt life a bit, and there was a whole other picture.

His parents weren't very talkative. They didn't chatter; they didn't argue. And yet in the moments while his father unpacked the trunk of his salt-stained Mustang and made his way back and forth up the path Barnsey had shoveled so clean just the night before, Barnsey could hear in his head all the signs and hints stretching back through the months— how far, he wasn't sure. Right up to now, the past few days, with Grandma so attentive. Spoiling him rotten.

Then his father was in the living room, still in his coat, waiting for Barnsey to say something. His face didn't look good, but to Barnsey he didn't look anywhere near bad enough, all things considered. Grandma Barrymore was standing behind him with her hand on her son's shoulder. She looked very sad. They waited. Barnsey looked out the window. Old-fashioned lace curtains hung across the living-room window. They were always there, even when the drapes were open.

Barnsey stood between the lace and the cold glass. He turned and looked at his grandma through the veil of the curtain.

"I wish you'd told me," he said.

"She didn't know, Matthew," said his lather. "Not for sure."

The ball was back in his court. That was the way his parents were with him. Lots of room. His father would not press him. He could wait forever and his father would never start saying stuff like "I'm sorry, honey," or "It's all for the better," or "Your mother still loves you, Matthew." Barnsey could wait forever and he wouldn't see his father cry. He would have done his crying already, if he had any crying to do. His parents didn't hold much with spontaneity.

He glanced at his father in his black coat and white silk scarf. He wanted him to do something.

Barnsey stared out the window.

"When did you get the ski rack?" he said.

"When I needed something to carry skis."

There was a pair of skis on the top of the car. Rossignols.

"They're yours," said his father. "I couldn't exactly wrap them."

Barnsey had been wanting downhill skis. And one of the large boxes piled in the hall was probably a good pair of ski boots. His parents would have read consumer reports about this. Even while they were breaking up.

"Your mother is hoping maybe you'll go on a skiing trip with her later in the holidays. Maybe Vermont."

"That would be nice," said Barnsey. Then he left the window and went to his room. His father didn't follow. It was his way of showing respect. He didn't say that; he didn't have to. He was there for him. He didn't say that, either, but it was something Barnsey had heard often. "We're here for you, chum."

Barnsey stayed in his room a long time, long enough to hear both sides of the new X.P. tape he hadn't had time to listen to on the bus. He flipped the cassette cover again and again. The ghoul glowed and vanished. Glowed and vanished.

Then his mother phoned. They had probably worked all this out, too.

"Must have been a terrible shock . . .

"Decided it was best this way . . .

"We couldn't dissolve the partnership in time for the shopping season. . . .

"Couldn't see us play-acting our way through Christmas . . ."

Barnsey listened. Said the right things.

"Do you think we could head down to Mount Washington for a long weekend?" said his mother. "Give those new skis a workout?"

"They aren't new," said Barnsey.

"They sure are," said his mother. "They're the best."

"There's a lot of snow between here and Ottawa," said Barnsey. It took his mother a minute to realize it was a joke. A lame kind of joke.

Then, with plans tentatively set and the call over and his mother's voice gone, Barnsey joined his father and his father's mother in the living room. They both gave him hugs.

"You okay?" his father asked.

"Yes."

"You want to talk now? Or later?"

"Later," he said.

"I think we all need a sherry," said Grandma. She poured Barnsey a glass. He liked the idea better than the sherry.

They ate lunch and then, since it was Christmas, they sat in the living room opening presents. Barnsey kept glancing at his father, expecting to see a little telltale tear or something. But all he ever glimpsed were the concerned looks his father was giving him.

He took his father's place as the hander-outer. When he came to his own present for his mother, he said, "Where should I put this?" His father piled the package on a chair in the hall.

Barnsey wasn't looking forward to Christmas dinner at his aunt's. His father had already taken that into consideration and would stay with him at Grandma's, if he liked. They'd make something special, just the two of them. But when he phoned to explain things, his sister wouldn't hear of them not coming, and his cousins got on the phone and begged Barnsey to come and try out their new computer game and in the end he went. Nobody talked about his mother not being there, at least not while Barnsey was around. Everyone was really considerate.

In bed he lay thinking about what kind of a place his mother would live in. She was the one leaving the relationship, so she was the one leaving the house. Barnsey wondered whether there would be a room for him or whether she'd just make up a couch when he came to visit. Then he wondered if his father would stay in Ottawa or move back to the west coast. He tried to think what else could possibly go wrong. He didn't want any more surprises.

"I just wish someone had told me," he said.

"We'll turn it around, Matthew," his father had said when he came to say good-night. "We'll make this into a beginning."

Was that from some kind of a book? How could he say that? Couldn't he tell the difference between a beginning and an ending?

There wasn't another man in his mother's life. His father hadn't found another woman.

"At least it isn't messy," his father said. He needn't have bothered. Nothing they ever did was messy.

In his sleep, Barnsey escaped. He found himself back on the bus.

"Rubbish," Dawn kept saying, and she pounded her fist into her palm every time she said it. Then the man in the seat ahead of them turned around, and it was the guy who had been in the country video heading home in his pickup through a blizzard to his tinsel-happy lady.

"Rubbish," he said. And then all of Xiphoid Process, who were *also* on the bus, turned around in their seats, pounding their fists and saying, "Rubbish. Rubbish. Rubbish." Soon the bus driver joined in and the whole bus sang a "Hallelujah Chorus" of "Rubbish, rubbish, rubbish."

Barnsey woke up, his head spinning. All he could think about was rubbish. He thought about the talk he had to have with his father that day. His father wouldn't insist, but he would be expecting it. He would say all the right things and, before Barnsey knew it, *he* would be saying all the right things, too. They'd talk it out. Get things out in the open. It would all make perfect sense.

Rubbish.

So he left.

He didn't pack a bag, only stuffed a couple of extra things in his backpack. He wasn't sure what a ticket to Vancouver cost, but it didn't matter. He had his bank card. He had no idea what he was going to do and he didn't care. He would not run away like his mother, carefully planning it all out first. How far did that get you?

And so, by nine o'clock on Boxing Day[6] morning, he was at the bus terminal, a ticket in his pocket, sitting, waiting. He had his Walkman

---

6. **Boxing Day:** the first weekday after Christmas, a legal holiday in Canada and Great Britain.

with him and he rooted around in his backpack for a tape other than X.P. He didn't think he could take that right now.

He had five or six tapes in the bottom of his bag. He hadn't emptied it since the trip. He pulled them out one by one: Alice in Chains, Guns 'n' Roses, Nirvana, Rain Forest with Temple Bells——

Rain Forest with Temple Bells?

Barnsey stared at the tape. He must have packed it up in the dark of the bus without noticing. Then he saw a piece of paper sticking out of the edge of the cassette. He opened the cassette and took out a folded-up note written in pencil.

> *dear barnsey this is for the meal and for the fun and for when the rubbish gets to be too much but you're snoring while i write this so maybe i'll shove the note in your gob!!![7] no i won't i'll hide it and it'll be your xmas present from dawn xox*

Barnsey found himself shaking. He read the note again and again. He smelled it—trying to catch her scent—and held it and then folded it up carefully and put it back in the cassette. He took out the tape and put it on. He closed his eyes and let the rain on the bells and the ravens and the smaller birds and the ferns and the trees and the wind fill his ears.

How crazy it had been to wait for the music to start. You had to supply your own. Make it out of what was there. Because there was more than the rain forest. Beyond his earphones there were people talking, departure announcements, a man waxing the floor—they were all part of the music.

Then suddenly there was a voice much closer.

"Matthew," said the voice, and Matthew became part of the music. "Matthew." Barnsey opened his eyes and his father was sitting there beside him. He touched his son's knee so tentatively, it was as if he was afraid the boy might break, like some fragile ornament from the gift store. Barnsey wondered if he would break, but he wouldn't. He was going to Vancouver to find Dawn. He stared at his father, who could not know this.

---

7. *gob:* British slang for "mouth."

His father was in his black coat and white scarf, but his hair was a complete mess. Barnsey had never seen his father out of the house unshaven and looking such a mess. His eyes were the worst mess of all.

"You look scared," said Barnsey. His father nodded. He didn't speak. He was waiting, giving Barnsey space. Then Barnsey looked closer into those wrecked eyes and suddenly it occurred to him that his father wasn't giving him space. He just didn't have a clue what to say or do. He was a million miles from the safe world of the gift store. He looked as if all his careful plans had fallen through.

Barnsey wanted to shake him, to knuckle his head, to throw stuff at him, laughing and shoving. To wake him up.

"Here," he said. He took off his earphones and put them on his father.

"What is it?" his father asked. "Is it broken?"

"No," said Barnsey. "Listen closely."

He watched his father listening. Barnsey listened, too. He didn't need the earphones to hear it.

Responding to the Story

1. Which character is more appealing to you, Dawn or Barnsey? Give several specific reasons for your opinion.
2. At the story's end, why does Barnsey give his father the earphones?
3. Do you see any significance to Dawn's name? How might the name work symbolically in the story from Barnsey's point of view?

Exploring the Author's Craft

1. *Contrast* is a very effective technique in writing. Besides their age and appearance, what are some of the specific differences between Dawn and Barnsey? Why did the two characters have to be different for this story to work effectively?
2. Tim Wynne-Jones includes a number of similes in this story. Pick three and explain why they work for you.

Writer's Workshop

Create a scene about two contrasting characters who start interacting with each other. Make the scene long enough to show their differences in speech and ideas as well as appearance.

Alternate Media Response

In a video of four or five minutes, capture the bus ride that Barnsey and Dawn took. Be sure that the video shows both the different appearances of each character as well as their different ways of speaking.

Susan Engberg

Susan Engberg was born in Dubuque, Iowa, in 1940. She married architect Charles Engberg in 1963. They have two children and live in Milwaukee.

She graduated from Lawrence University in Appleton, Wisconsin, and did graduate study at the University of Iowa from 1972 to 1974. She worked as a fiction reader for the *Iowa Review* and was a teacher at the Iowa Writer's Workshop.

In 1983 Engberg received a fiction award from the Society of Midland Authors and the Banta Award from the Wisconsin Library Association. In 1987 she received a Creative Writing Fellowship from the National Endowment for the Arts.

Engberg has had short stories included in *Prize Stories: the O. Henry Awards* in 1969, 1977, and 1978 and in *Pushcart VI: Best of the Small Presses,* 1982. Her three collections of stories are *Pastorale* (1982), *A Stay by the River* (1985), and *Sarah's Laughter and Other Stories* (1991). Reviewing Engberg's first collection, Russell Banks observed, "[These] stories are so good they could change your life."

"She caused trouble no mattter where she was . . . "

On the Late Bus

Other people always stirred things up. Here was a fat man asking in a wheezy voice if the seat was taken, sweetheart, when Alison had barely gotten the sound of her stepmother's *Sorry it didn't work out* simmered down in her head, and so she had to cram her duffle under her feet on the filthy bus floor and allow this monstrous body to stuff itself down next to her, so close, just inches away. There was something wrong with the way buses were made. His breaths eddied around her. She heard him sucking, on a hard candy maybe. She was empty herself, no food. Going far? he wanted to know. What was *far*? not speaking, she tilted her face toward the window and pressed her knees together, angled away from him. At least she had the window.

She was fifteen years old and nobody's sweetheart. The window was what she'd had for the last hour, and she'd used it to put golden aspens and red maples and dark green pines in the place of the people in her head, the ones who stirred things up the most—a father and stepmother in the place she was going from and mother and her boyfriend in the place she was going toward. Sorry it didn't work out, said the woman in one place. Who do you think you are! said her mother, the one who was supposed to know who her own daughter was, in the other place. Don't listen too much to your mother, said her father, she's what you might call disturbed. Cool it, said her mother's boyfriend. The evening light in the aspens was like a cloud of gold. Last night in bed—actually, a mattress on the floor of her father's small house—she had heard geese flying high overhead, the same direction her bus was going now, south, but for her that didn't make much difference because she was still riding straight into winter. The geese had sounded like geese and also like someone rubbing on the window glass, far away.

The man had stopped sucking and was now peeling off the top of a package of gum. His arm poked out in front of her, too close, as he offered her a piece. She shook her head, no. She felt light-headed with hunger. Don't talk much, do you? said the man. He was unspeakable. She ducked her face. Fat people were disgusting to start with, and then when they did and said disgusting things, it could make you gag to be around them. She should vomit in his lap—that would cause a stir. She could be just as good a troublemaker as anyone else.

But the trouble was, she didn't have anything to throw up. She had refused her stepmother's cold cereal this morning and her sandwiches this noon—she wasn't going to take any more food from a woman who didn't even want her around. Finicky, she had been called, so all right finicky was what she was really, really going to be. Her stepmother had two new children, one a baby guzzling breast milk. Every time Alison turned around out came the bare breast again and there was another baldheaded half-brother getting exactly what he wanted and slurping while he was about it, too. The expression on her father's face as he watched was so silly it made Alison want to put a cooking pot or a grocery bag down over his head. The other kid always wanted her to get down on the floor and play with him, and the first few visits she had, until she finally figured out that this was just what her father and her stepmother wanted, to get her down on the floor and out of the way, and so this time she stayed stubbornly on their level, at the table, on the couch, her arms folded over her chest. Anyway, it was impossible for her to play like a kid, getting interested in whether or not the blocks were going to fall over, making the sounds of a truck—there was no way she was ever going to have that again.

What she did have was her eyes, good eyes, better than twenty-twenty, the doctor said. She wished she could go back to that doctor once a week and have him look at her and tell her about her eyes. Right now she could see so far into the trees that she could probably be a wild animal if she needed to. She could get off the bus and streak into the woods as her eyes were doing and never have to go back to one house or the other. Wild animal mothers sometimes took care of human babies. But she was too old for that. Anyway, what wild animal mother would want a child like her, an upright stick of a girl with ringworm on her left thigh and a coil of black feeling in her heart? She'd have to learn to *be* the wild animal, tough and wily, all on her own. Trouble was, in the woods she'd run out of that vile ointment she had to rub on the raised, scaly circle of the worm and then pretty soon her whole body would become one gigantic parasite. She'd be eaten up. Then she'd start infecting the whole forest. The other animals would run her out.

She caused trouble no matter where she was, even when she was absolutely still, her arms over her chest, just existing. Every time she came into a room where there were other people, in one house or the other, she could tell that she was stirring thing up. No one knew what to do with her, even when she was doing nothing but breathing. One day her mother had fallen and torn a tendon in her ankle while Alison was walking right beside her, and just before her mother fell Alison had seen the split in the sidewalk—the concrete square was like a hardened country, she had thought swiftly, with something wrong in its middle—probably in time to warn her mother, clicking along beside her in her stupid high heels, and probably her mother knew that—that her daughter was to blame for the cast and the crutches and the difficulties every day in getting to work and making her way home and trying to stand up to cook dinner. Alison tried to help, but her mother didn't like her messing up the kitchen. Then, when she wandered into the living room to sit with her mother's boyfriend, her mother shouted at her for watching television when there was so much to be done. She was sent up to her father's so that at least the house would be quiet for the weekend.

At her father's she caused more trouble than she ever had before. Anyone could see that with the new baby there wasn't room for her now. This time they had put down a mattress for her behind a tacked-up sheet at the end of the bedroom hallway, under a tiny window. Well, at least she had had the window and heard the far-away, matter-of-fact music of the geese and seen the full moon, with its gigantic eyes looking back at her. *Sorry it didn't work out.* What did *it* mean? There was something wrong with the way sentences were put together.

It's going to get dark now, said the fat man, leaning toward her slightly and peering out the glass. Gets dark early now.

Oh boy, what a genius this guy was, a regular Sherlock Holmes. That's what her stepfather had called her the other day when she had said that college would probably cost too much. You're a regular Sherlock Holmes, Alison.

You goin' home or goin' away from home? asked the fat man.

Neither one, she couldn't stop herself from saying. Oh god, you open your mouth once and then there's no telling what will rush back to you.

Neither one? he said, breathing hard. Now that's a situation peculiar like mine. Me, I'm goin' from one daughter to t'other. Neither one wants their old pa. I bet you wouldn't do that to your old pa, would you? You're a nice, smooth-like girl. My girls, they've got pricklers all over them. He shook his head sadly. He sounded as if he talked to himself a lot.

What a creep! She wished she could give him her ringworm, that itchy, creeping circle that made her feel so dirty. She'd have to slide down her jeans and press her palm on the discolored patch and then find someplace to transfer it to him when he wasn't paying attention. She'd show him how smooth she was!

Her teachers used to think she was a good girl, before she started crossing her arms and not saying anything. She knew most of the answers, but what good did it do any more to let people hear her? Besides, knowing an answer and keeping it to herself gave her a kind of invisible arrow that she could send out through her eyes toward the teacher, or anybody else she needed power against. The secret to being able to send the arrow, she was discovering, was not saying anything. She cast a sideways glance at the fat man, just with her eyes, and saw that his chin was lowered to his chest. Mr. No-neck. She'd save her arrow for when she really needed it.

Outside there were fewer pine trees, more coppery oaks, dying colors. And there were more signs of people and the messes they made. When she got back to the city, she'd be drinking softened water again and sleeping in the room right next to the giant legs of the electrical transformer tower. The water up north at her father's tasted like rocks. Her mother's boyfriend called the ice cubes in his whiskey glass rocks. He'd probably be the one to meet her bus, practically at midnight, and he'd be mad because her father hadn't come out of the woods with his chain saw in time to get her on the early bus. Her mother would be at home with her foot up, or maybe already asleep. The cast went nearly to her knee, and her toes sticking out of it were discolored.

The fall, the bad injury, the cast, the days and nights even more messed up than before—everything had happened so fast. One minute Alison had been walking beside her mother, being scolded and criticized by her and at the same time sort of daydreaming about the broken sidewalk just ahead, and the next minute her mother was down on the ground, crying, Oh, my foot, my foot, and then every minute in their lives got more difficult. Like that, just like that mothers and fathers divorced—one day in the same house, the next day not. Earthquake, crack down the middle, fast.

And fast was how her best friend Lois had died last year, inside her white cast, from a greenstick fracture. Well, of course it hurts, you've broken it, just let it heal now, her parents kept saying, but Lois couldn't stop talking about how much her arm hurt. They took her back to the hospital too late. Alison had sat stiffly on the couch at her own house and heard her mother saying the words *gangrene* and *shock*. In the coffin at the funeral home Lois's honey-colored hair had been clipped back neatly with two barrettes, just the way she had always worn it to school. Don't get hysterical now, her mother had whispered behind her, but Alison wasn't about to let anything out on her own lips. It was only in her room, with the door locked, that she would take out Lois's picture, prop it on the stem of her desk light, and let her own face crack open as she looked and looked at the smooth hair, the serene heavy brows, the sweet mouth that were now flat underground, facing up beneath the lid of the coffin. Fast, unfair—what could possibly be said? Lois was the last person she had laughed with, the real kind of laughter.

The trouble was with the people who were supposed to be parents. There was something so wrong about the parents that you couldn't even talk about it. Fast was how they wanted you out of their house, before their lives were worn out, before they had to admit the mistake they had made in having you. She had one other friend, Joann, who had been given exactly three more years to live at home. Graduation, and she had to be out the door, out, and that meant no more money, no food, no bed, no nothing, so she was supposed to start thinking now about what she could do ahead. Her mother had a new baby, too, and a new husband. Joann told Alison that having a high-school-age daughter around must remind her mother of how old she was. I could really give her gray hair if I wanted to, said Joann, but she's not worth it, I'm saving my energy.

The fat man was right: it was getting nearly dark. She should say to him, Hey, genius, look at that, you were right, it got dark. Pretty soon there wouldn't be much at all to see out the window. A wild animal at night, unless it was the night kind, crawled into its home with a full belly and went to sleep until daylight. Human beings didn't live like that. They traveled all night if they wanted to. They played around with what was normal. They turned everything inside out and upside down, they broke things in half, in thousands of pieces.

Close beside her the fat man took out a soiled handkerchief and blew his nose, loud enough to blow up the bus. Honk, blast. Alison closed her eyes. She felt faint with disgust, or was it just hunger? Her mouth tasted awful. She had never gone a whole day without a single thing to eat. Suddenly she thought, I don't know anything about life, I don't know any of the answers.

Are you one tired girl? The man's voice made her open her eyes. He didn't even wait for an answer—he had caught on to her fast—he just kept on talking. I'll tell you, I'm one tired old man. I don't have much left, and that's the truth. I don't know how it got to be this way, but it sure has.

There was that *it* again! Words sounded so queer to her tonight. Everything seemed put together in the strangest way, without enough reason. Maybe that's what happened to your head when you didn't eat. She thought about her duffle bag under the seat, no food in it, just her flannel pajamas and some extra jeans and her American history book. She saw that the fat man's hands were shaking a little as he clumsily folded his handkerchief and stuffed it back in the jacket of his cheap-looking suit coat. But he couldn't be shaking from hunger—oh no, he was too fat to be hungry.

Most people around the world didn't have much, she knew that now. But for as long as she could remember her father had talked about wanting to be rich, the head of a big family—a sprawl of horses, dogs, buildings, pastures, children. Even these days he had schemes for getting the life he wanted, and he usually talked about someone or other who was going to help him. What he actually had now was a small house near a small woodlot, a chain saw, a stack of firewood, a job in a cannery, and a different family. If her father had been the one to offer her the sandwich at lunch, she might have taken it. But he hadn't even been in the house most of the day—he had been out in the lot making his saw scream through wood.

There was an acid-tasting heat in her throat. She wasn't going to cry! Not in this repulsive place!

I'd say we're going to have ourselves another moon tonight, like last night, said the man.

Well, what did he expect! That's what she could say to him—Hey, genius, what did you expect, it's like twenty-four hours later than the moon last night.

Then he leaned slightly toward her to peer out the window, and she was forced to see the side of his creased face, his jowls, his whiskers, his nose hair, his sad, red-rimmed, drooping eyes. He was a lot older than she had thought at first. Yes sir, it can be real pretty when it comes up like that, he said, wheezing, pursing his lips. For a while I thought maybe those clouds would keep it from us.

That's what he had meant, clouds. She hadn't understood him. She was sorry that she hadn't understood him. She looked as he pointed. The orange moon had just cleared the horizon. She didn't think she had ever seen it so close and so big. Last night she had had the moon whole, and tonight right here she had it again, even better. And so had this old man beside her, the one whose daughters didn't like him anymore. What could he have done to them? she wondered. Would she ever be like that some day—not wanting her father to visit? And where was this place she was going to live in, when she was old enough to have a father visiting her? And what was the way she was going to live, how was she going to be?

This tells me it's time to eat, said the man. He brought to his lap the vinyl bag that had been wedged between his feet. Mind if I do? he asked as he flipped on the little light over their seats. Now what do we have here? Well, ha, I ought to know, I packed it myself. Peanut butter and more peanut butter. Belle—she's the one daughter—didn't have much else to pick from. I would've liked a turkey sandwich, I could get my teeth into that. Now, what do you like little miss? Are you going to help me eat these peanut butter sandwiches? I've got four. I thought, well, even if that's all she's got, I'd better take plenty. I learned a long time ago not to pass up a meal.

He lowered the bag to the floor, balancing the wrapped pile of sandwiches on his lap. Now, he said, do you want number one, two, three, or four?

None, she was going to say, I'm finicky, see. I don't eat much, though she would restrain herself from adding that she was especially finicky about whom she took food *from*, but at that very moment she was aghast to see her own hand snaking out like an animals' to grasp the top square package. Thank you, her voice said. It was what he had said about getting his teeth into a turkey sandwich that had gotten her own mouth so crazy for anything to put in it, she didn't care what kind of bread, or what was between it. And her stomach had grown hands that were grabbing and clawing for something to fill them.

That's better, said the man. It wouldn't do any good to have me sitting here eating in front of you. Though I've done that plenty, I'll have to say. Oh, he sighed as he bit into his own bread. It's not too bad. It'll do. You can turn that light off now, honey. You don't have to see to fill your mouth with what you've already got in your hands. Isn't that so? Oh, lordy, I always feel better when I'm eating.

She turned out the light and unwrapped her own sandwich. There was moonlight on her hands. She bit in. She had the moon to look at while she chewed, the watchful moon. Last night, tonight, this feeling of being seen was something new. She had a new secret, the strength of the moon, looking at her.

I'm not what you might think I am, said the old grandfather beside her. I've just been through some hard times. She turned and nodded at him.

This business about trouble, she thought. Everybody caused trouble or had troubles. And everyone lived off other people, in one way or another. She went back to chewing and staring at the cavernous eyes of the moon. There was something she was trying to get right in her head, a thought that had just appeared out of nowhere at the moment she had first bitten into the sandwich, something else about trouble, people stirring things up. Here it came again, from she didn't know where: if people could turn on the trouble, they could make other things happen, too, besides trouble. Was that what she had thought? Was that what could be called an idea of her own?

Responding to the Story

1. Explain how the life situation of the girl in this story has contributed to her mood. Be specific.
2. Although the girl resents the man who is with her on the bus, how are their life situations similar?
3. Is the ending of the story optimistic or pessimistic? Explain.
4. Why do you think the author ends the story stressing the girl's having "an idea of her own"? Explain your answer.

Exploring the Author's Craft

Writers sometimes use something concrete as a symbol of some abstract quality or idea. How does the moon function as a symbol here? Trace its use in the story.

Writer's Workshop

"Other people always stirred things up." In this story we learn about a number of people, all of whom have "stirred things up" in the girl's life. In a short sketch of about 750 words, create a character and show his or her life being influenced by one person who "stirs things up." Show incidents that reveal the stirring up; don't just summarize someone's actions.

Jamaica Kincaid

Jamaica Kincaid was born on the Caribbean island of Antigua in 1949. She immigrated to the United States. when she was 17. In 1976 Kincaid became a staff writer for *The New Yorker* . She married Allen Shawn, and they have a daughter. The family now lives in Vermont.

Kincaid won the Morton Dauwen Zabel Award from the American Academy and Institute of Arts and Letters for her story collection *At the Bottom of the River*, published in 1983. *Annie John*, also a collection of stories, was published in 1985. Both works deal with life on Antigua. Her other works include the novels *Lucy* (1990) and *The Autobiography of My Mother* (1994); as well as two works of nonfiction, *A Small Place* (1988), which deals with the colonial history of Antigua and its aftermath, and *My Brother* (1997).

Everyone must finally leave home.

A Walk to the Jetty

My name is Annie John." These were the first words that came into my mind as I woke up on the morning of the last day I spent in Antigua,[1] and they stayed there, lined up one behind the other, marching up and down, for I don't know how long. At noon on that day, a ship on which I was to be a passenger would sail to Barbados,[2] and there I would board another ship, which would sail to England, where I

---

1. **Antigua:** an island in the West Indies, a chain of islands between Florida and South America.
2. **Barbados:** island in the West Indies.

would study to become a nurse. My name was the last thing I saw the night before, just as I was falling asleep; it was written in big, black letters all over my trunk, sometimes followed by my address in Antigua, sometimes followed by my address as it would be in England. I did not want to go to England, I did not want to be a nurse, but I would have chosen going off to live in a cavern and keeping house for seven unruly men rather than go on with my life as it stood. I never wanted to lie in this bed again, my legs hanging out way past the foot of it, tossing and turning on my mattress, with its cotton stuffing all lumped just where it wasn't a good place to be lumped. I never wanted to lie in my bed again and hear Mr. Ephraim driving his sheep to pasture—a signal to my mother that she should get up to prepare my father's and my bath and breakfast. I never wanted to lie in bed and hear her get dressed, washing her face, brushing her teeth, and gargling. I especially never wanted to lie in my bed and hear my mother gargling again.

Lying there in the half-dark of my room, I could see my shelf, with my books—some of them prizes I had won in school, some of them gifts from my mother—and with photographs of people I was supposed to love forever no matter what, and with my old thermos, which was given to me for my eighth birthday, and some shells I had gathered at different times I spent at the sea. In one corner stood my washstand and its beautiful basin of white enamel with blooming red hibiscus painted at the bottom and an urn that matched. In another corner were my old school shoes and my Sunday shoes. In still another corner, a bureau held my old clothes. I knew everything in this room, inside out and outside in. I had lived in this room for thirteen of my seventeen years. I could see in my mind's eye even the day my father was adding it onto the rest of the house. Everywhere I looked stood something that had meant a lot to me, that had given me pleasure at some point, or could remind me of a time that was a happy time. But as I was lying there my heart could have burst open with joy at the thought of never having to see any of it again.

If someone had asked me for a little summing up of my life at that moment as I lay in bed, I would have said, "My name is Annie John. I was born on the fifteenth of September, seventeen years ago, at Holberton Hospital, at five o'clock in the morning. At the time I was born, the moon was going down at one end of the sky and the sun was coming up at the other. My mother's name is Annie also. My father's name is Alexander, and he is thirty-five years older than my mother.

Two of his children are four and six years older than she is. Looking at how sickly he has become and looking at the way my mother now has to run up and down for him, gathering the herbs and barks that he boils in water, which he drinks instead of the medicine the doctor has ordered for him, I plan not only never to marry an old man but certainly never to marry at all. The house we live in my father built with his own hands. The bed I am lying in my father built with his own hands. If I get up and sit on a chair, it is a chair my father built with his own hands. When my mother uses a large wooden spoon to stir the porridge we sometimes eat as part of our breakfast it will be a spoon that my father has carved with his own hands. The sheets on my bed my mother made with her own hands. The curtains hanging at my window my mother made with her own hands. The nightie I am wearing, with scalloped neck and hem and sleeves, my mother made with her own hands. When I look at things in a certain way, I suppose I should say that the two of them made me with their own hands. For most of my life, when the three of us went anywhere together I stood between the two of them or sat between the two of them. But then I got too big, and there I was, shoulder to shoulder with them more or less, and it became not very comfortable to walk down the street together. And so now there they are together and here I am apart. I don't see them now the way I used to, and I don't love them now the way I used to. The bitter thing about it is that they are just the same and it is I who have changed, so all the things I used to be and all the things I used to feel are as false as the teeth in my father's head. Why, I wonder, didn't I see the hypocrite in my mother when, over the years, she said that she loved me and could hardly live without me, while at the same time proposing and arranging separation after separation, including this one, which, unbeknownst to her, *I* have arranged to be permanent? So now I, too, have hypocrisy, and breasts (small ones), and hair growing in the appropriate places, and sharp eyes, and I have made a vow never to be fooled again."

Lying in my bed for the last time, I thought, This is what I add up to. At that, I felt as if someone had placed me in a hole and was forcing me first down and then up against the pressure of gravity. I shook myself and prepared to get up. I said to myself, "I am getting up out of this bed for the last time." Everything I would do that morning until I got on the ship that would take me to England I would be doing for the last time, for I had made up my mind that, come what may, the road for me now went only in one direction: away from my home, away from my mother, away from my father, away from the everlasting blue sky, away from the everlasting hot sun, away from people who said to me, "This happened during the time your mother was carrying you." If I had been asked to put into words why I felt this way, if I had been given years to reflect and come up with the words of why I felt this way, I would not have been able to come up with so much as the letter "A." I only knew that I felt the way I did, and that this feeling was the strongest thing in my life.

The Anglican church bell struck seven. My father had already bathed and dressed and was in his workshop puttering around. As if the day of my leaving were something to celebrate, they were treating it as a holiday, and nothing in the usual way would take place. My father would not go to work at all. When I got up, my mother greeted me with a big, bright "Good morning"—so big and bright that I shrank before it. I bathed quickly in some warm bark water that my mother had prepared for me. I put on my underclothes—all of them white and all of them smelling funny. Along with my earrings, my neck chain, and my bracelets, all made of gold from British Guiana,[3] my underclothes had been sent to my mother's obeah woman,[4] and whatever she had done to my jewelry and underclothes would help protect me from evil spirits and every kind of misfortune. The things I never wanted to see or hear or do again now made up at least three weeks' worth of grocery lists. I placed a mark against obeah women, jewelry, and white underclothes. Over my underclothes, I put on an around-the-yard dress of my mother's. The clothes I would wear for my voyage were a dark-blue pleated skirt and a blue-and-white checked blouse (the blue in the blouse matched exactly the blue of my skirt) with a large sailor collar and with a tie made from the same material as the skirt—a blouse that came down a long way past my waist, over my skirt. They were lying on a chair, freshly ironed by my mother. Putting on my clothes was the last thing I would do just before leaving the house. Miss Cornelia came and pressed my hair and then shaped it into what felt like a hundred corkscrews, all lying flat against my head so that my hat would fit properly.

---

3. **British Guiana:** now Guyana, a country on the northeast coast of South America.
4. **obeah woman:** woman who practices sorcery and magic.

At breakfast, I was seated in my usual spot, with my mother at one end of the table, my father at the other, and me in the middle, so that as they talked to me or to each other I would shift my head to the left or to the right and get a good look at them. We were having a Sunday breakfast, a breakfast as if we had just come back from Sunday-morning services: salt fish and antroba and souse and hard-boiled eggs, and even special Sunday bread from Mr. Daniel, our baker. On Sundays, we ate this big breakfast at eleven o'clock and then we didn't eat again until four o'clock, when we had our big Sunday dinner. It was the best breakfast we ate, and the only breakfast better than that was the one we ate on Christmas morning. My parents were in a festive mood, saying what a wonderful time I would have in my new life, what a wonderful opportunity this was for me, and what a lucky person I was. They were eating away as they talked, my father's false teeth making that clop-clop sound like a horse on a walk as he talked, my mother's mouth going up and down like a donkey's as she chewed each mouthful thirty-two times. (I had long ago counted, because it was something she made me do also, and I was trying to see if this was just one of her rules that applied only to me.) I was looking at them with a smile on my face but disgust in my heart when my mother said, "Of course, you are a young lady now, and we won't be surprised if in due time you write to say that one day soon you are to be married."

Without thinking, I said, with bad feeling that I didn't hide well, "How absurd!"

My parents immediately stopped eating and looked at me as if they had not seen me before. My father was the first to go back to his food. My mother continued to look. I don't know what went through her mind, but I could see her using her tongue to dislodge food stuck in the far corners of her mouth.

Many of my mother's friends now came to say goodbye to me, and to wish me God's blessings. I thanked them and showed the proper amount of joy at the glorious things they pointed out to me that my future held and showed the proper amount of sorrow at how much my parents and everyone else who loved me would miss me. My body ached a little at all this false going back and forth, at all this taking in of people gazing at me with heads tilted, love and pity on their smiling faces. I could have left without saying any goodbyes to them and I wouldn't have missed it. There was only one person I felt I should say goodbye to, and that was my former friend Gwen. We had long ago drifted apart, and when I saw her now my heart nearly split in two with embarrassment at the feelings I used to have for her and things I had shared with her. She had now degenerated into complete silliness, hardly able to complete a sentence without putting in a few giggles. Along with the giggles, she had developed some other schoolgirl traits that she did not have when she was actually a schoolgirl, so beneath her were such things then. When we were saying our goodbyes, it was all I could do not to say cruelly, "Why are you behaving like such a monkey?" Instead, I put everything on a friendly plain, wishing her well and the best in the future. It was then that she told me that she was more or less engaged to a boy she had known while growing up early on in Nevis,[5] and that soon, in a year or so, they would be married. My reply to her was "Good luck," and she thought I meant her well, so she grabbed me and said, "Thank you. I knew you would be happy about it." But to me it was as if she had shown me a high point from which she was going to jump and hoped to land in one piece on her feet. We parted, and when I turned away I didn't look back.

My mother had arranged with a stevedore to take my trunk to the jetty ahead of me. At ten o'clock on the dot, I was dressed, and we set off for the jetty. An hour after that, I would board a launch that would take me out to sea, where I then would board the ship. Starting out, as if for old time's sake and without giving it a though, we lined up in the old way: I walking between my mother and my father. I loomed way above my father and could see the top of his head. We must have made a strange sight: a grown girl all dressed up in the middle of a morning, in the middle of the week, walking in step in the middle between her two parents, for people we didn't know stared at us. It was all of half an hour's walk from our house to the jetty, but I was passing through most of the years of my life. We passed by the house where Miss Dulcie, the seamstress that I had been apprenticed to for a time, lived, and just as I was passing by, a wave of bad feeling for her came over me, because I suddenly remembered that in the months I spent with her all she had me to do was sweep the floor, which was always full of threads and pins

---

5. **Nevis:** island in the British west Indies in the Leeward Islands.

and needles, and I never seemed to sweep it clean enough to please her. Then she would send me to the store to buy buttons or thread, though I was only allowed to do this if I was given a sample of the button or thread, and then she would find fault even though they were an exact match of the samples she had given me. And all the while she said to me, "A girl like you will never learn to sew properly, you know." At the time, I don't suppose I minded it, because it was customary to treat the first-year apprentice with such scorn, but now I placed on the dustheap of my life Miss Dulcie and everything that I had had to do with her.

We were soon on the road that I had taken to school, to church, to Sunday school, to choir practice, to Brownie meetings, to Girl Guide meetings, to meet a friend. I was five years old when I first walked on this road unaccompanied by someone to hold my hand. My mother had placed three pennies in my little basket, which was a duplicate of her bigger basket, and sent me to the chemist's shop to buy a penny worth of senna leaves, a pennyworth of eucalyptus leaves, and a pennyworth of camphor. She then instructed me on what side of the road to walk, where to make a turn, where to cross, how to look carefully before I crossed, and if I met anyone that I knew to politely pass greetings and keep on my way. I was wearing a freshly ironed yellow dress that had printed on it scenes of acrobats flying through the air and swinging on a trapeze. I had just had a bath, and after it, instead of powdering me with my baby-smelling talcum powder, my mother had, as a special favor, let me use her own talcum powder, which smelled quite perfumy and came in a can that had painted on it people going out to dinner in nineteenth-century London and was called Mazie. How it pleased me to walk out the door and bend my head down to sniff at myself and see that I smelled just like my mother. I went to the chemist's shop, and he had to come from behind the counter and bend down to hear what it was that I wanted to buy, my voice was so little and timid then. I went back just the way I had come, and when I walked into the yard and presented my basket with its three packages to my mother, her eyes filled with tears and she swooped me up and held me high in the air and said that I was wonderful and good and that there would never be any body better. If I had just conquered Persia, she couldn't have been more proud of me.

We passed by our church—the church in which I had been christened and received and had sung in the junior choir. We passed by a house in which a girl I used to like and was sure I couldn't live without had lived. Once, when she had mumps, I went to visit her against my mother's wishes, and we sat on her bed and ate the cure of roasted, buttered sweet potatoes that had been placed on her swollen jaws, held there by a piece of white cloth. I don't know how, but my mother found out about it, and I don't know how, but she put an end to our friendship. Shortly after, the girl moved with her family across the sea to somewhere else. We passed the doll store, where I would go with my mother when I was little and point out the doll I wanted that year for Christmas. We passed the store where I bought the much-fought-over shoes I wore to church to be received in. We passed the bank. On my sixth birthday, I was given, among other things, the present of a sixpence.[6] My mother and I then went to this bank, and with the sixpence I opened my own savings account. I was given a little gray book with my name in big letters on it, and in the balance column it said "6d." Every Saturday morning after that, I was given a sixpence—later a shilling,[7] and later a two-and-sixpence piece—and I would take it to the bank for deposit. I had never been allowed to withdraw even a farthing from my bank account until just a few weeks before I was to leave; then the whole account was closed out, and I received from the bank the sum of six pounds ten shillings and two and a half pence.

We passed the office of the doctor who told my mother three times that I did not need glasses, that if my eyes were feeling weak a glass of carrot juice a day would make them strong again. This happened when I was eight. And so every day at recess I would run to my school gate and meet my mother, who was waiting for me with a glass of juice from carrots she had just grated and then squeezed, and I would drink it and then run back to meet my chums. I knew there was nothing at all wrong with my eyes, but I had recently read a story in *The Schoolgirl's Own Annual* in which the heroine, a girl a few years older than I was then, cut such a figure to my mind with the way she was always adjusting her small, round, horn-rimmed glasses that I felt I must have a pair exactly like them. When it became clear that I didn't need glasses, I began to

---

6. **sixpence:** former British unit of money. The symbol for pence is "d."
7. **shilling:** former British unit of money equal to twelve pence. The farthing, mentioned later, is equal to one-fourth of a penny. A pound is a unit of money in several countries.

complain about the glare of the sun being too much for my eyes, and I walked around with my hands shielding them—especially in my mother's presence. My mother then bought for me a pair of sunglasses with the exact horn-rimmed frames I wanted, and how I enjoyed the gestures of blowing on the lenses, wiping them with the hem of my uniform, adjusting the glasses when they slipped down my nose, and just removing them from their case and putting them on. In three weeks, I grew tired of them and they found a nice resting place in a drawer, along with some other things that at one time or another I couldn't live without.

We passed the store that sold only grooming aids, all imported from England. This store had in it a large porcelain dog—white, with black spots all over and a red ribbon of satin tied around its neck. The dog sat in front of a white porcelain bowl that was always filled with fresh water, and it sat in such a way that it looked as if it had just taken a long drink. When I was a small child, I would ask my mother, if ever we were near this store, to please take me to see the dog, and I would stand in front of it, bent over slightly, my hands resting on my knees, and stare at it and stare at it. I thought this dog more beautiful and more real than any actual dog I had ever seen or any actual dog I would ever see. I must have outgrown my interest in the dog, for when it disappeared I never asked what became of it. We passed the library, and if there was anything on this walk that I might have wept over leaving, this most surely would have been the thing. My mother had been a member of the library long before I was born. And since she took me everywhere with her when I was quite little, when she went to the library she took me along there, too. I would sit in her lap very quietly as she read books that she did not want to take home with her. I could not read the words yet, but just the way they looked on the page was interesting to me. Once, a book she was reading had a large picture of a man in it, and when I asked her who he was she told me that he was Louis Pasteur and that the book was about his life. It stuck in my mind, because she said it was because of him that she boiled my milk to purify it before I was allowed to drink it, that it was his idea, and that that was why the process was called pasteurization. One of the things I had put away in my mother's old trunk in which she kept all my childhood things was my library card. At that moment, I owed sevenpence in overdue fines.

As I passed by all these places, it was as if I were in a dream, for I didn't notice the people coming and going in and out of them, I didn't

feel my feet touch ground, I didn't even feel my own body—I just saw
these places as if they were hanging in the air, not having top or bottom,
and as if I had gone in and out of them all in the same moment. The sun
was bright; the sky was blue and just above my head. We then arrived at
the jetty.

My heart now beat fast, and no matter how hard I tried, I couldn't keep
my mouth from falling open and my nostrils from spreading to the ends
of my face. My old fear of slipping between the boards of the jetty and
falling into the dark-green water where the dark-green eels lived came
over me. When my father's stomach started to go bad, the doctor had
recommended a walk every evening right after he ate his dinner.
Sometimes he would take me with him. When he took me with him,
we usually went to the jetty, and there he would sit and talk to the
night watchman about cricket or some other thing that didn't interest
me, because it was not personal; they didn't talk about their wives, or
their children, or their parents, or about any of their likes and dislikes.
They talked about things in such a strange way, and I didn't see what
they found funny, but sometimes they made each other laugh so much
that their guffaws would bound out to sea and send back an echo. I was
always sorry when we got to the jetty and saw that the night watchman
on duty was the one he enjoyed speaking to; it was like being locked up
in a book filled with numbers and diagrams and what-ifs. For the thing
about not being able to understand and enjoy what they were saying
was I had nothing to take my mind off my fear of slipping in between
the boards of the jetty.
   Now, too, I had nothing to take my mind off what was happening to
me. My mother and my father—I was leaving them forever. My home
on an island—I was leaving it forever. What to make of everything? I felt
a familiar hollow space inside. I felt I was being held down against my
will. I felt I was burning up from head to toe. I felt that someone was
tearing me up into little pieces and soon I would be able to see all the
little pieces as they floated out into nothing in the deep blue sea. I
didn't know whether to laugh or cry. I could see that it would be better
not to think too clearly about any one thing. The launch was being
made ready to take me, along with some other passengers, out to the
ship that was anchored in the sea. My father paid our fares, and we
joined a line of people waiting to board. My mother checked my bag to

make sure that I had my passport, the money she had given me, and a sheet of paper placed between some pages in my Bible on which were written the names of the relatives—people I had not known existed—with whom I would live in England. Across from the jetty was a wharf, and some stevedores were loading and unloading barges. I don't know why seeing that struck me so, but suddenly a wave of strong feeling came over me, and my heart swelled with a great gladness as the words "I shall never see this again" spilled out inside me. But then, just as quickly, my heart shriveled up and the words "I shall never see this again" stabbed at me. I don't know what stopped me from falling in a heap at my parents' feet.

When we were all on board, the launch headed out to sea. Away from the jetty, the water became the customary blue, and the launch left a wide path in it that looked like a road. I passed by sounds and smells that were so familiar that I had long ago stopped paying any attention to them. But now here they were, and the ever-present "I shall never see this again" bobbed up and down inside me. There was the sound of the seagull diving down into the water and coming up with something silverish in its mouth. There was the smell of the sea and the sight of small pieces of rubbish floating around in it. There were boats filled with fishermen coming in early. There was the sound of their voices as they shouted greetings to each other. There was the hot sun, there was the blue sea, there was the blue sky. Not very far away, there was the white sand of the shore, with the run-down houses all crowded in next to each other, for in some places only poor people lived near the shore. I was seated in the launch between my parents, and when I realized that I was gripping their hands tightly I glanced quickly to see if they were looking at me with scorn, for I felt sure that they must have known of my never-see-this-again feelings. But instead my father kissed me on the forehead and my mother kissed me on the mouth, and they both gave over their hands to me, so that I could grip them as much as I wanted. I was on the verge of feeling that it had all been a mistake, but I remembered that I wasn't a child anymore, and that now when I made up my mind about something I had to see it through. At that moment, we came to the ship, and that was that.

The good-byes had to be quick, the captain said. My mother introduced herself to him and then introduced me. She told him to keep an eye on me, for I had never gone this far away from home on my own.

She gave him a letter to pass on to the captain of the next ship that I would board in Barbados. They walked me to my cabin, a small space that I would share with someone else—a woman I did not know. I had never before slept in a room with someone I did not know. My father kissed me goodbye and told me to be good and to write home often. After he said this, he looked at me, then looked at the floor and swung his left foot, then looked at me again. I could see that he wanted to say something else, something that he had never said to me before, but then he just turned and walked away. My mother said, "Well," and then she threw her arms around me. Big tears streamed down her face, and it must have been that—for I could not bear to see my mother cry—which started me crying, too. She then tightened her arms around me and held me to her close, so that I felt that I couldn't breathe. With that, my tears dried up and I was suddenly on my guard. "What does she want now?" I said to myself. Still holding me close to her, she said, in a voice that raked across my skin, "It doesn't matter what you do or where you go, I'll always be your mother and this will always be your home."

I dragged myself away from her and backed off a little, and then I shook myself, as if to wake myself out of a stupor. We looked at each other for a long time with smiles on our faces, but I know the opposite of that was in my heart. As if responding to some invisible cue, we both said, at the very same moment, "Well." Then my mother turned around and walked out the cabin door. I stood there for I don't know how long, and then I remembered that it was customary to stand on deck and wave to your relatives who were returning to shore. From the deck, I could not see my father, but I could see my mother facing the ship, her eyes searching to pick me out. I removed from my bag a red cotton handkerchief that she had earlier given me for this purpose, and I waved it wildly in the air. Recognizing me immediately, she waved just as wildly, and we continued to do this until she became just a dot in the matchbox-size launch swallowed up in the big blue sea.

I went back to my cabin and lay down on my berth. Everything trembled as if it had a spring at its very center. I could hear the small waves lap-lapping around the ship. They made an unexpected sound, as if a vessel filled with liquid had been placed on its side and now was slowly emptying out.

Responding to the Story

It is difficult to read Jamaica Kincaid's story without thinking of separations in one's own life. "I shall never see this again," she thinks, both joyfully and sadly. Describe the recollections you had reading this story or just the feelings the story brought you. If you want to put the feelings in a poem or, perhaps, a drawing, go ahead.

Exploring the Author's Craft

Sometimes being a good writer is just having the willingness and patience to recall and write everything down in a clear manner. And sometimes being a good writer is just being honest; it's a great start, in any case.

Without looking at "A Walk to the Jetty" again, write two or three paragraphs spelling out the sense impressions, the details, the ideas, and the varied feelings that stood out to you from this piece. The more you can recall from the writing, the more of a tribute it is to the author's craft.

Writer's Workshop

The narrator of this story describes her room, the only room she had ever lived in, in exquisite detail. "Everywhere I looked stood something that had meant a lot to me, that had given me pleasure at some point, or could remind me of a time that was a happy time," she writes. And she names specific things. She goes on to say that she was also glad she was leaving this place, but let's leave that aside for a moment.

Name the specifics—and describe them—of a place you know intimately. It may be your own room, or another room in your home.

Alternate Media Response

This story should have evoked many feelings. It's a tribute to the author that one might never have seen any place like Antigua, in the West Indies, but one can still "feel" this story. Here's your chance to show that feeling in your own art form—a drawing, a dance, a drama, a short film. Let yourself go.

Making Connections in
PART FOUR

Complete one or more of the following assignments as your teacher directs.

1. Being out in the world involves contacts with persons beyond one's familiar circle of family and friends. These contacts may be exhilarating, puzzling, frightening, or painful, but always challenging. What challenges do Marian in "A Visit of Charity" and the narrator in "Initiation" meet and how well do they meet them, in your opinion?

2. Both "Dawn" and "On the Late Bus" involve strangers meeting on a bus. Write an essay that points out the similarieties and differences between the two stories.

3. In your opinion, is the mood of "On the Late Bus" like or unlike that of "A Walk to the Jetty"? Try to think of a single word that could describe the mood of each story? Do you come up with a different word for each one?

4. The stories in *Coming of Age, Volume One* deal with a variety of topics and themes involving youth and adolescence. Write several paragraphs explaining how three of the stories in this collection could appropriately appear in another part of the book than they do.

Acknowledgments

PART 1

3 "The First Day, pgs. 33-8 from *Lost in the City* by Edward P. Jones. Copyright © 1992 by Edward P. Jones. By permission of William Morrow & Company, Inc. **9** "The Secret Lion" is reprinted from *The Iguana Killer: Twelve Stories of the Heart*, Copyright 1984 by Alberto Alvaro Rios. Reprinted by permission of Confluence Press at Lewis-Clark State College, Lewiston, Idaho. **16** "Eleven" from *Woman Hollering Creek*. Copyright © 1991 by Sandra Cisneros. Published by Vintage Books, a division of Random House, Inc., New York, and originally in hardcover by Random House, Inc. Reprinted by permission of Susan Bergholz Literary Services, New York. All rights reserved. **21** "Raymond's Run" from *Gorilla, My Love* by Toni Cade Bambara. Copyright © 1971 by Toni Cade Bambara. Reprinted by permission of Random House, Inc. **31** "Two Kinds." Reprinted by permission of G. P. Putnam's Sons from "Two Kinds" from *The Joy Luck Club* by Amy Tan. Copyright © 1989 by Amy Tan. **45** "Bad Influence" from *An Island Like You* by Judith Ortiz Cofer. Copyright © 1995 by Judith Ortiz Cofer. Reprinted by permission of Orchard Books, New York. **66** "Louisa, Please Come Home", copyright © 1960 by Shirley Jackson, from *Come Along with Me* by Shirley Jackson. Used by permission of Viking Penguin, a division of Penguin Putnam, Inc. **84** "The Man in the Casket" by Beth Cassavell. Copyright 1990 by Beth Cassavell. Reprinted by permission of author.

PART 2

92 "They Are My Friends" from *Cat's Eye* by Margaret Atwood. Copyright © 1988 by O. W. Toad, Ltd. Used by permission of Doubleday, a division of Bantam Doubleday Dell Publishing Group, Inc., and McClelland & Stewart, Inc. *The Canadian Publishers*. **98** "Sucker" from *The Mortgaged Heart* by Carson McCullers. Copyright 1940, 1941, 1942, 1945, 1949, 1953, © 1956, 1959, 1963, 1967, 1971 by Floria V. Lasky, Executrix of the Estate of Carson McCullers. Reprinted by permission of Houghton Mifflin Co. All rights reserved. **109** "Guess What? I Almost Kissed My Father Goodnight!" by Robert Cormier from *Eight Plus One* © 1980 by Robert Cormier. Published by Pantheon Books, reprinted by permission of Random House, Inc. **122** "Why Can't They Tell You Why?" from *Color of Darkness* by James Purdy, copyright © 1957 by James Purdy, published by New Directions Publishing Corporation. Reprinted by permission of author. **130** "Shaving" from *Collected Stories* by Leslie Norris, copyright © 1996 by Seren (Poetry Wales Press). **138** "My Mother and Father", from *The Leaving and Other Stories* by Budge Wilson. Copyright © 1990 by Budge Wilson, compilation. Used by permission of Philomel Books, a division of Penguin Putnam Inc. **153** "Asphalt" by Frederick Pollack. From *Literary Cavalcade*, May 1963. Copyright © 1963 by Scholastic Inc. Reprinted by permission of Scholastic Inc.

PART 3

164 "Broken Chain" from *Baseball in April and Other Stories*, copyright © 1990 by Gary Soto, reprinted by permission of Harcourt Brace & Company. **174** "The Osage Orange Tree" by William Stafford. Originally published in *The Oregon Centennial Anthology* 1959. Reprinted by permission of the Estate of William Stafford. **182** "The Bass, The River, and

Sheila Mant" from *The Man Who Loved Levittown*, by W. D. Wetherell, © 1985. Reprinted by permission of the University of Pittsburgh Press. **191** "I Go Along" by Richard Peck, copyright © 1989 by Richard Peck from *Connections: Short Stories* by Donald R. Gallo, Editor. Used by permission of Delacorte Press, a division of Bantam Doubleday Dell Publishing Group, Inc. **199** "The Endless Streetcar Ride into the Night, and the Tinfoil Noose" from *In God We Trust, All Others Pay Cash* by Jean Shepherd. Copyright © 1966 by Jean Shepard. Used by permission of Doubleday, a division of Bantam Doubleday Dell Publishing Group, Inc. **206** "And Summer is Gone" by Susie Kretschmer. Reprinted by permission of author. **212** "Sophistication" by Sherwood Anderson, from *Winesburg, Ohio* by Sherwood Anderson, introduction by Malcolm Cowley. Copyright © 1919 by B. W. Huebsch; Copyright 1947 by Eleanor Copenhaver Anderson. Used by permission of Viking Penguin, a division of Penguin Putnam, Inc.

PART 4

224 "Adjö Means Good-Bye" by Carrie A. Young. Originally published in *The Angry Black*, © 1962 Lancer Books. **230** "Veil of Water" by Amy Boesky. Reprinted by permission of author. **236** "Marigolds" by Eugenia Collier. Originally published in the *Negro Digest*, November 1969. Reprinted by permission of the author. **247** "A Visit of Charity" from *A Curtain of Green and Other Stories*, copyright © 1941 and renewed 1969 by Eudora Welty, reprinted by permission of Harcourt Brace & Company. **256** "Initiation" from *Johnny Panic and the Bible of Dreams* by Sylvia Plath. Copyright © 1962 by Sylvia Plath. Copyright 1979 by Ted Hughes. Published by Faber and Faber Ltd., London. Reprinted by permission of the publisher. **267** "Dawn" from *The Book of Changes* by Tim Wynne-Jones. Copyright © 1994 by Tim Wynne-Jones. Reprinted by permission of Orchard Books, New York. **285** "On the Late Bus" from *Sarah's Laughter and Other Stories* by Susan Engberg. Copyright ©1991 by Sarah Engberg. Reprinted by permission of Alfred A. Knopf, Inc. **294** "A Walk to the Jetty" from *Annie John* by Jamaica Kincaid. Copyright © 1985 by Jamaica Kincaid. Reprinted by permission of Farrar, Straus & Giroux, Inc.

Index of Authors and Titles